IT'S NOT TOO LATE...

A journey into health, healing and love of God our Father

DANIEL CONNORS

RIVERSTONE GROUP
PUBLISHING

This book is dedicated to:

Those yearning to know God;
To those whose hearts have been broken;
And to my family, friends
And family of believers.

To contact the author email inquires to: i.n.t.l.canisiusquad1986@gmail.com

Published by:
Riverstone Group, LLC, Jasper, Georgia
d.b.a. Riverstone Group Publishing

Softcover ISBN: 979-8-9857349-0-4

Scripture quotations from:
Holy Bible, New International Version®, NIV® Copyright ©1973, 1978, 1984, 2011 by Biblica, Inc.® Used by permission. All rights reserved worldwide.

King James Version: Public Domain

New King James Version®. Copyright © 1982 by Thomas Nelson. Used by permission. All rights reserved.

"I want to thank Ernest Pullen and Riverstone Group Publishing, including my editor Carolyn Cunningham, for their assistance, professionalism and their friendship. I was at times challenged, taken down off my 'soap box,' and reminded of the message I was to bring forward. Ernest Pullen is a man after God's heart, and I trust him. This experience, in total, has been daunting, but Ernest has made this process easier for this new, budding author. We are brothers in Christ, and I am grateful to God for sending this gentleman into my life. He is yet another, unexpected guardrail from my Father."
– Daniel

CONTENTS

It's not too late...

I turned 50 years old recently and felt it was time to write the book that was placed on my heart. First and foremost and with all sincerity, I want you, Reader, to know that I claim to be no one special. I am an ordinary man with an ordinary life. I am not unique. However, I have had some unique experiences that I would like to share.

1) In the summer of 1985, I had markings on my body similar to stigmata.

2) I saw and interacted with the Holy Trinity while in an intoxicated marijuana-induced state in the fall of 1986.

3) In 1990, while taking a year off from college, I spoke to and saw Jesus while dreaming.

4) In the winter of 2015, I was in God's presence, His Son, the Holy Spirit and a beast I would call the fallen angel.

Why did I have visions of God? Why these experiences? I don't know. *I imagine there are many others out there with whom God is communicating in similar ways.* I am prepared for skeptics, and I will walk in faith. In telling my story and the experiences of my life, it is my hope that God will use me to do His will and not mine. I pray that the Lord leads me as I recount these experiences and that any message heard by you, Reader, falls on fertile ground. Amen.

As I edit this book and return to writing after a brief lapse, I am in awe of His power and the "God-incidences" (coincidences) that surround us — if, that is, we have eyes to see and ears to hear. I have just watched the movie "I Can Only Imagine" (a beautiful movie about the redemptive power of the Gospel, about Christ and about human growth). In the movie, the phrases "I imagine" and "I can only imagine" are written time and time again throughout the main character's journal. The main character is overcome with the phrase "I can only imagine." From the phrase "I can only imagine," the main character goes on to write a beautiful hit song that becomes a number-one hit Christian song. In my first paragraph, I wrote, "I imagine there are many others out there with whom God is communicating in similar ways." Yes, "I imagine" is just a phrase; and yes, I am "looking into it" or perhaps overanalyzing it. However, that is often how God works. It is a coincidence or, as I like to say, a "God-incidence."

God communicates with us in small ways (most of the time). It is our job to try and listen. As I sat back down to write after a two-week lapse and read "I imagine" in the above paragraph after watching the movie, it gave me an "aha" type of experience. It was a "yes moment" and an encouragement for me to continue to write. I have inserted this paragraph to illustrate and validate a point that God walks with us in our everyday life through the Holy Spirit.

I believe God desires to talk with and communicate with us every day. God is with us all the time through His Holy Spirit, but it is up to us to tune in. Sometimes in very rare circumstances, God knocks someone off their horse, shines a light in their face and tells him to follow, as in the New Testament Apostle Paul.

The point of this book is to shine light in a dark age and let you, Reader, know that God is with us through the Holy Spirit. He is here. I believe He hurts when you hurt — as evidenced when Jesus' friend Lazarus died. Jesus wept when His good friend Lazarus died. "When Jesus therefore saw her weeping, and the Jews also weeping which came with her, he groaned in the spirit, and was troubled. And said, Where have ye laid him? They said unto him, Lord, come and see. Jesus wept" (John 11:33-35, KJV).

Our God feels our pain and hears your prayers. Your prayers do not land on deaf ears or fall into the vastness of space. Rather, God hears you and will answer you. Listen…

Discernment is the key to understanding God's will in our lives. "My sheep hear my voice, and I know them, and they follow me" (John 10:27, KJV). Hearing God's voice – and not listening to our voice or the enemy's voice – is critical. An old Jesuit professor of mine, Father Kelly said, "Discernment is listening to the signs of the times. Be aware of what is going on around you." In other words, reflecting on the daily events of one's life, analyzing our interactions at the end of our day, bouncing ideas and thoughts off trusted friends, loved ones and "people of God" are all part of the discernment process. God is good and, through Him, flows the spring of everlasting water. Does your discernment pass the sniff test? Does it "smell good"? God wants the best for all His people. Good parents want only the best for their children, and this holds true for our Father God as well.

What my journey has led me to are biblical truths. The Bible is an amazing instrument to teach us about God. There are skeptics and critics who, when reading this book, will scoff. There always have been and there always will be doubters. Even when the Messiah, the Christ, the fulfillment of Jewish prophecy walked, talked, performed miracles and preached on this earth, people discounted Him. Then they discounted and murdered Him. I find that very interesting, and it breaks my heart.

It's not too late…. I echo these words from God and state them now in this book. What's not too late? It's not too late to say you're sorry to a friend or family member, to forgive, to love, to follow His Way, to change your broken ways, to heal, to seek God and to become the person God intended you to be. And for me, "it's not too late" to sound the gong and announce the return of The Lord. **Jesus is coming, and He is coming very soon. I have been told to write this book and send this message.** "Told" – not like one hears words spoken but "told" in a spiritual sense. Even if my assertion, "Jesus is coming very soon," is off by hundreds of years, you, Reader, will see Him soon. If you are 50 years of age, you will have an average of 30 years left. If you're 40, maybe 40 years left? Maybe … and so on and so on.

Life is too short! You will meet Him soon – one way or another. At this point in my life, 20 years seems like a heartbeat.

This book hopefully, through my story, will allow you to experience the same peace and understanding that I now feel.

I hope to walk with you in these next several pages and explain where I found life. I will show you my reality of death and try to warn you of the shortcomings of poor life choices. As my Father (God) once told me, "It's not too late."

To write this book is mind blowing, and I feel more than inadequate. I have started and stopped several times.

"Dulce Vikram."

On May 31, 2020, I sat in my kitchen journaling and praying. I wrote, "If You, Lord, desire for me to write the book that You have placed on my heart, I will." (It has been nearly a year since I last wrote.) I continued, "Who am I? I am a sinner. I have faltered and have failed on numerous occasions in my life, but I get up. I just listened to the news, and it is not good. A pandemic looms large throughout the world. Father, please send Your Son. 100% I am in. If You want me to write, I will. Father, forgive me; but can You give me a sign that this is how You want me to proceed?"

At this point, a phrase came to my mind, "Dulce Vikram." I said it out loud, "Dulce Vikram?" The phrase rang out over and over in my mind. So I googled this phrase and found a poem written by Vikram Babu. The Google search had hit on "dulce" and "vikram." The article was a critique of a poem written by Vikram Babu.[1] Within this article was the phrase "What are you waiting for?" Part of the article states, "We rendered Vikram Babu's ending question: '¿A que esperais sentados?' by means of a common idiomatic near-expletive, **'What are you waiting for?'** (Beatrix Gates/ Electa Arenal, May 2008), That expression spoke into my soul. "What are you waiting for?" Moments prior to this Google search, I had asked the Lord for a sign. So today I sit here and write! What was I waiting for? A sign. To place this book "out there" for the general public and make myself vulnerable are daunting. But I will walk by faith and not by sight.

Today, 2/18/21, I will receive a vaccination against the COVID-19 virus; and I am very grateful to God for His strength and for granting intelligence to scientists to find a vaccine. Today I journaled the following in my journal prior to reading Acts 22 in the Bible:

"I ask Your help, my Lord and my God, in the logistics and implementation of *It's Not Too Late....* Also Lord, please help me with the content of this book. I will let it pour out of me, and then You and I can edit it."

I then proceeded to read Acts 22, and the words spoke into my heart. Today I read the words intended for me so that I may write to you, Reader.

"Then he said: 'The God of our ancestors has chosen you to know his will and to see the Righteous One and to hear words from his mouth. You will be his witness to all people of what you have seen and heard. **And now what are you waiting for?** Get up, be baptized and wash your sins away, calling on his name'" (Acts 22: 14-16, NIV).

Is it purely coincidence? I had never heard of Vikram Babu before and asked God for a sign. The Google search led me to finding the phrase, "What are you waiting for?" The words within Acts in the Bible leapt off the page before me. Today, Reader, was a good day; for our Lord has shown me that I am on the way....

Paul often refers to following our Lord and Savior Jesus as The Way. Before Christianity was known as "Christianity," the early followers and nonbelievers referred to following Christ as The Way. There is a Way in which we, as a people, are called to live in accordance with living a life pleasing to God.

"However, I admit that I worship the God of our ancestors as a follower of the Way, which they call a sect" (Acts 24:14a, NIV).

I, too, am trying the best I can to follow the Way in which my Father has called me to live. I stumble and fall, but I get up. I dust myself off and ask my Lord and my God for forgiveness.

Please know that the following passages are an illustration of the life I have lived thus far, and it is also an apology. I am truly sorry to those who I have hurt along my way. To those who I did not act as the arms, hands and the feet of Jesus, I am sorry. I am a sinner who has been saved. Thanks be to God, I was saved not because of any actions of my own but the actions of my Savior, Jesus. "Amazing grace, how sweet the sound that saved a wretch like me. I once was lost, but now am found, was blind, but now I see" (lyrics to *Amazing Grace* [2] by Pastor John Newton).

I was baptized in 2015 by my pastor and friend, Pastor Randy. He is a man of God – humble, intelligent and a friend of Jesus. I was baptized as an infant within the Roman Catholic Church, but I chose to be baptized again as an adult to show an outward expression of my inward reality. As infants, we are pure and innocent; but as an adult, I know that my life has been hardly innocent. Thus, for me, baptism as an adult made more sense.

I started my journey in earnest in 2012 when my wife and daughters gave me a personalized Bible for Christmas. They had my name engraved in a leather-covered Bible, and the three of my family signed their names inside. This act of giving spoke deep into my soul; and I knew for certain I was on the Way, traveling back on the road that God was calling me.

However, I have been on the journey since early childhood; but I have only been walking in faith since approximately 2011. Prior to that, I had been walking in the ways of this world and was not leading a life I was proud of. Now I can say I am living as God intended me to live. When I fall, I get up, brush myself off and ask my Lord for forgiveness. I know that no one is perfect – except for my Friend, Lord and Savior, Jesus. Therefore, I do not hold myself to that standard but try and live as He has called me to live. Jesus asks us to be humble, to pray, to seek after God, to forgive, to mind our tongue, to be gentle and, most importantly, to love.

I am an ordinary, middle-aged, middle-class man who has had a burning desire to write this book placed on my heart for the past 34 years. I am not extraordinary and proclaim no "special relationship" with my Father, but I do have a relationship with my Father God. I know that God is my Father, and that is comforting. I have a dad, Jim, who reared me as his son; but I have a Father, who saved me, who has redeemed my soul.

I believe there are, more than likely, other people reading this book who also have had unique experiences with our Father God. I do not know why I or we had these experiences with God, but I need to write them down. Like a marathoner who needs water while running the race, I need to share this story.

I write this book *for the brokenhearted and for those who place their hope in a person who broke their heart.* For when we place our hope in anyone but God, our hope can be broken. But when we place our faith and hope in God our Creator, we will never be let down.

"...but those who hope in the LORD will renew their strength. They will soar on wings like eagles; they will run and not grow weary, they will walk and not be faint" (Isaiah 40:31, NIV).

I write this book: *for anyone who is contemplating suicide.* The hope placed in suicide to end the suffering is not the way in which God calls us home. Life is good; and through this book, it is my prayer that you find peace. You, Reader, are not alone. There are a countless number of people who are struggling with all types of suffering and loss. When we realize we are not alone, it can give us strength. Many have similar thoughts as you. Most importantly, our Father hears you, is with you and loves you dearly.

"Have I not commanded you? Be strong and courageous. Do not be afraid; do not be discouraged, for the LORD your God will be with you wherever you go" (Joshua 1:9, NIV).

I write this book: ***for the person plagued with anxiety.*** I say, "It's not too late." It's not too late to rid yourself from the chain of anxiety and depression that binds you. For me, it was a long process and took many, many years to fully get a grasp on my anxiety and panic attacks. I had to bike across the United States twice and become a commercial fisherman in Kenai, Alaska to finally rid myself of debilitating panic attacks. Unfortunately, even to this day, if I'm tired – especially when I'm tired, anxiety can still show its face. Therefore, I keep my nose in His Good Book, and I "practice what I preach" in my book.

Jesus says, "Come to me, all you who are weary and burdened, and I will give you rest. Take my yoke upon you and learn from me, for I am gentle and humble in heart, and you will find rest for your souls. For my yoke is easy and my burden is light" (Matthew 11:28-30, NIV). Jesus is here for you, Reader, and is here to help you.

I also write this book: ***for you, Reader, who is on the fence spiritually — the agnostic and the atheist.*** I hope this book touches your heart, adds to your current faith and/or leads you to believe there is a God who wants the best for you. One day in this lifetime or the next, you will meet Him face to face. This I know to be true. Faith is synonymous with trusting — as a child takes his or her first steps.

Reader, I am an average Joe, a struggling writer trying to express to you the glory of God. However, I know my Father wants to hear from you. Why not ask Him to show you His Way? Ask Him in faith — with an open heart — to show His love for you. Be open and I truly believe that you, Reader, will find Him. Take a step....

"You will seek me and find me when you seek me with all your heart" (Jeremiah 29:13, NIV).

If I never tried, I would have never walked as an infant, never run marathons as an adult, never bicycled across this country as an anxiety-ridden young man, never fished in Alaska and never healed my anxiety and panic attacks that plagued me. Everything that happened in my life that was positive can be found in trusting, acting in faith and moving forward in faith. All I can say at this point, doubting "Thomas," is place your hand in His wounds and look upon Him. Very abstract I know but, in the depth of your heart, is a very small voice calling. Listen.

Unfortunately, many of you have "been there" and "done that" already. You were reared in a household of believers, but now you rebel against a notion of a God. My question is why are you reading this book? The God of the universe, the Creator, Your Father, your good Daddy is calling your name....

I write also for you, Reader, who was never caught when they fell. For you were reared in a very difficult situation. Far too many people reading this book come from abusive homes. Our Father is a chain breaker. A good song regarding this notion is by Zach Williams, "Chain Breaker." Reader, God will walk with you into health and healing. Be open and be prepared to utilize resources around you. God will use all aspects of our lives to create the best and brightest people we were intended on becoming. However, we must do our part, and God will do His part.

I write this book: *for those struggling with any and all addictions.* There is hope! You have a way out of the darkness. "The light shines in the darkness, and the darkness has not overcome it" (John 1:5, NIV). That light is the light of God made manifest in His Son Jesus; but we must do our part, and God will do His part. Collaboratively, you can fight any addiction that binds you.

I write this book: *for you, devout Christian.* For there are false prophets among you. "Watch out for false prophets. They come to you in sheep's clothing, but inwardly they are ferocious wolves. By their fruit you will recognize them. Do people pick grapes from thornbushes, or figs from thistles?" (Matthew 7:15-16, NIV). Reader, question everything! Use the brain that God gave you! If what I am writing does not seem true to you, question it and reject it if you must. However, just so you know, I am bound by the truth. What I am writing is, for me, 100% accurate; and I am not intentionally writing anything that is not true.

Father, give the reader eyes to see and ears to hear the words written in this book. I pray that the reader is open to receive this message of hope, faith and love and that it leads them to You. I pray this prayer in Jesus' Holy Name. Amen.

CHAPTER 1

Ravaged by divorce

As I look back on my life, I see God's presence was always there, always with me, always guiding, protecting and placing people in my life, acting as guardrails.

In 1981, I was 13 years old, in eighth grade; and I was getting confirmed in the Roman Catholic Church. Confirmation is a rite of passage from childhood to adulthood in the Catholic Church. I took it seriously – as seriously as a 13-year-old can take it. I asked my grandmother to be my sponsor. As my sponsor, she would be responsible to stand next to me, with her hand on my shoulder, and support me in my faith as the Bishop welcomed and confirmed me into the Roman Catholic Church.

Grandma Connors was a strong Irish Catholic woman, who had a tough upbringing. She was educated to the sixth grade but read books all the time. She was a devout Roman Catholic, sweet but strong, loving but stern, an amazing cook and my Irish Catholic grandmother. She taught my brother, sisters and me pieces of the puzzle that our mom missed in our upbringing. She was motherly and, on more than one occasion, put me in my place. I love her, miss her; and little did I know at the time, she was one of the many people who God utilized to help form me into the man I am today. I thank You, Lord, for my grandmother, one of the many guardrails You placed in my life.

In eighth grade prior to confirmation, we were taught, we were told that we must confess our sins. My friends and I stood outside the confessional, joking before we went in to tell the priest our sins. "What are you going to tell him?" We all had some vague, minor infraction that we joked about and for which we would be absolved by the priest. In the Roman Catholic tradition, the priest individually listens to the sins of his congregation and issues you a "to do" list of prayers to recite to absolve you from sin.

Something stirred inside me as I waited in line. I entered the confessional and kneeled down in the darkness. A small 12"-by-12" window slid open, revealing the priest's face in profile and his hands clasped together in prayer. I told the priest everything in my past. I was sincerely sorry. I told the priest everything! If I was going to take the step of faith and be confirmed, I would clear my young conscience. It was the first step in an authentic relationship with my God. I told the priest about drinking alcohol with friends, smoking pot and losing my virginity.

As an eighth grader about to be confirmed, I carried shame and remorse around with me like a wet blanket. I knew that my behavior was not right. The priest absolved me from my sin. The priest was a holy man of God. He

Daniel and Grandma Connors 1981 before Confirmation

did not shame me or make me feel worthless for the weight of my sins. He was what priests should be – an instrument of God.

I came out of the confessional, wiping my eyes; and my friends looked at me like I had two heads. "What's wrong? What did you tell him?" "Nothing, it was nothing! Ok, I told him everything...." My friends were in shock. "You did what? You told him that?"

I had started my journey. Real repentance, real remorse and a forgiving, loving God. Through His grace, through the symbolic gesture of a caring priest, I was set free. I stumbled out of the confessional, wiping my eyes, but did not realize my journey had started. I was in search of God, and God was leaving me breadcrumbs that led The Way to Him.

Unfortunately, I overlooked the breadcrumbs and numbed my pain of adolescence with drinking and smoking pot, followed by carelessness and reckless ways. I was not ready to truly begin living as God intended. But our Father is a good Father, and He has never given up on me. Thanks be to God.

Seventh grade, 1980

One day, I got a phone call from a friend while I lay at home sick in my bed. My friend asked, "Did you hear what happened to Mike?" I replied, "No, what's up?" Mike was my best friend in middle school and got us into a lot of trouble. "Mike pulled a fire alarm and is suspended for one week." I laughed out loud on the phone when I heard that he had been suspended. The next day, I felt better and returned to school. At lunchtime, my friends showed me the fire alarm pull station that Mike pulled the previous day. I walked over and told everyone, "It won't work. Watch this." I pulled it. Approximately two seconds later, the fire alarm was sounding. We all ran, and I was terrified!

The previous week, Mike and I went around our entire school, pulling fire alarms. None of them were working; and that is why I was certain the fire alarm would not work when I boldly stated, "It won't work. Watch this." It worked, and it worked well. The school was evacuated, and the fire trucks came. I huddled among my friends — scared — and wondered who would "narc" on me.

The students and staff returned, and we went to our classes. I changed into my gym clothes and proceeded to do laps in the gym. About the second or third lap, I was grabbed by my gym teacher by my t-shirt and thrown into the locker room. I hit the lockers hard. As I was physically muscled through the locker room, I saw before me, seated in the gym office, a pair of shoes and two crossed legs. It was Mr. Johnson, the vice principal. I was in the habit of looking down when getting yelled at; and so I grew to know his feet, his shoes.

Mr. Johnson acted as an instrument of God, and he disciplined me. "Why? Why, Dan? Why did you pull it?" I did not deny it. I simply said, "I didn't think it would work." A week of suspension was like someone gave me a winning lottery ticket. At that time, my parents both worked, so I had the run of the house! My siblings were at school, and I was being punished? Looking back on it, I don't think it was much of a punishment. I celebrated at home by myself. I played loud music on the radio. I listened to "Space Cowboy" by Steve Miller Band, danced around our family room and watched the first shuttle launch in U.S. history. The week was fun, and I had not yet learned any life lessons.

It was not until I was in the police station the next week for giving a friend alcohol that I really got a rude awakening. My friend Mike had gotten alcohol; and by association, I was involved. A friend of ours drank to excess and almost drowned in a pond near our middle school. Although we were not there when this happened, we were part of the chain of events that almost ended in tragedy. This was the beginning of a life change for me. We were "read the riot act" and banned from hanging out together for a while.

Shortly after those two discipline experiences, I came to a decision in my life. I needed change and changed friends. I became a "jock." The next year, eighth grade, I joined the soccer team in the fall and lacrosse team in the spring. I excelled in lacrosse and found my niche. I found an outlet for my anger and frustrations and worked them out physically. Soccer was not my thing....

I played football during my freshman year of high school and started at defensive nose tackle and offensive guard. My life changed through sports. Or biblically, I look at it this way. In the gospel of Matthew 5:29a, NKJV, it reads, "If your right eye causes you to sin, pluck it out...." Seems harsh, huh? It is harsh, but Jesus spoke to us in parables. How about it spoken this way? "If those who are your friends are bringing you down the wrong road, change your friends. Pluck them out."

I thank God for people like Mr. Johnson who, on more than one occasion, yelled at me, spoke to me with honesty and conviction and treated me fairly. He was my guardrail in middle school, a very pivotal year for me. He epitomized the word *discipline*. He was the man who kept me from going over a cliff. Mr. Johnson "woke me up" from the bleak reality in which I was living. Thank you, Mr. Johnson, for disciplining me well. You epitomized what it means to be a leader, a good disciplinarian; and you were instrumental in my development. God used you in my life to bring much-needed change into my way of acting and behaving. Thank you again, Mr. Johnson.

As for the gym teacher who threw me against the lockers, he meant well. I understand him. He was frustrated with a young "punk" kid and let his temper get the best of him. However, teachers, please remember that children sometimes have a very rough life at home.

Oprah Winfrey once did a story on CBS-TV's *60 Minutes*[3] regarding ACE scores. The score ranged from 1 to 10. The higher the ACE score, the harder the life experience for that child. Oprah interviewed a program director and school administrator, who were implementing a new strategy in their school in Detroit. Essentially, instead of asking a troubled child, "What the heck is wrong with you?! Why did you do x, y, z?"; they reframe the question. The question now becomes: "What happened to you to make you behave the way you do? What is your story?" Now children report feeling heard, cared for and empathized with. The program is making a difference in the lives of abused children. Unfortunately, I can relate to this Oprah Winfrey *60 Minutes* special. As you will read, I was negatively affected by my upbringing and rebelled.

Teachers, help your students by being the eyes, ears, arms and feet of Jesus. You were given an honored position in society, so use your gift well. Your students are listening, and they will remember your values. In addition, our Father God is also watching as you teach, so treat your children well.

The scars of childhood could have derailed me. I thank God that He placed special people (guardrails) in my life who mentored, corrected and loved me. God was with me among the chaos, and He corrected and mentored me through others.

If we open our eyes, if we rise from our slumber, we will see God's hand directing traffic in our busy freeway of life. If we look even further, we will see the guardrails He laid along our road to keep us on the highway. Did you make a detour? Are you on the right road? If we look too hard with the microscope, the lens will crack the glass. We are to discern God's will in our lives, and that takes patience and practice. Hindsight is often much easier to see God's hand in our lives rather than foresight. There are lists of do's and don'ts in a good book I like to read. In this good book, God lays out the road map. If we follow it, we will stay on His roadway, a roadway to peace and joy. I once was lost, but now I am found – thanks be to God. I read His good book daily, and it keeps me on the right road and in the right mindset.

Mom

Mom was a true blessing in my life, and I love her with all my heart. As a 5-6-year-old child, I remember creating a piece of artwork that I made from a banana skin. I brought it to Mom and said, "This is a bird, Mom.

Do you like it?" She, in turn, said, "It's beautiful, Danny." I later brought this same skilled piece of artwork to Grandma Connors; but she told me, "Throw that banana peel away!" (I literally laugh out loud at this memory! I love it!) Here were two women who I loved dearly, and both had totally different reactions to the same piece of "artwork." I later learned that Grandma Connors was correct. My artwork was just a banana peel; but now looking through "parent eyes," I love Mom's ability to find beauty in simplicity and her way in which she made people feel special.

Our family was ravaged by divorce. A once-loving home environment became a nightmare, and my siblings and I rebelled.

Unfortunately, suicide and the hope placed in suicide by my mother was one of the hell environments in which my siblings and I grew up. My mother attempted suicide by slicing her wrists and taking pills. As a young teenager trying to process her decision, I was left short-circuited, and I did not cope well.

On our way to visit our mother in the psychiatric hospital after her attempted suicide, my older brother and I smoked pot in the car as we drove down to see her. We got stoned, and we tried to cope the best we

This is my wonderful, loving mom. She unfortunately was hurt tremendously by divorce.

could. My mom was living her hell here on earth. Her marriage dissolved with her husband, my dad. She eventually was released from the hospital and returned home. My mother unfortunately was not any healthier. She slept all day but woke up to make meals for us when we came home from school.

Reader, please do not get me wrong. My mother is a beautiful soul, but she was ravaged by divorce and depression. I now believe this is why the Bible instructs us on how to live. The Bible clearly states not to divorce and to live morally. These laws and rules were meant as aides to help society. God, in His infinite wisdom, wants the best for us. He gave us basic, loving, helpful instructions to follow. I am not implying that a person who is being physically abused should stay in a marriage that is life threatening. We, however, should try our hardest, seek good therapy when needed and bring our concerns in prayer to our Father God.

Mom taught us, her children, many valuable life lessons. Mom was a fantastic cook. She was empathetic, and she was the most caring person with the biggest heart I have ever known. My mother was a beautiful soul, and she was physically stunning. Beyond physical beauty, my mother possessed qualities that are hard to come by. She was an "empath." What I mean by that is she felt the pain of others deeply. She had a remarkable way in which to listen to others. When she was with you, you knew she was with you. She was not distracted. She listened intently and with conviction. This quality is a lot harder than it seems.

Unfortunately, my mother's brokenness and her depression manifested itself into a hoarding disorder. Out of an unconscious need to fill the void of divorce, she collected and collected. Unfortunately, what I have learned is that Mom hoarded to fill her broken heart. Her space that was broken was a bottomless pit, and no amount of collecting would ever fill the void.

As the saying goes, "Hurt people hurt others." I now know that my mom did not mean to hurt us by way of collecting. It was her way of coping. But her collecting affected us; and for years after college and into my adult life, I couldn't eat without a table in front of me. Dinner on the couch as a "recreational activity" was off limits. In other words, I was unable to sit anywhere else but at a table to eat meals. Mom did not mean to place this feeling of anxiety within me by way of her hoarding behavior. Mom was broken inside, and her pain filtered throughout our family.

What's your story? Where were you wounded? There is hope, and there is light in the darkness. That light is the light of Christ. In our weakness, Christ is God's strength.

"So do not fear, for I am with you; do not be dismayed, for I am
your God. I will strengthen you and help you; I will uphold you
with my righteous right hand" (Isaiah 41:10, NIV).

God wants the best for us and beckons us, calling us to love despite our wounds. God is love, and He wants us to act out of love - not out of our brokenness. Therefore, we must break chains that shackle us from childhood and perhaps debilitate us as adults. We are called to rid ourselves from our past and move forward with God. We are not meant to pass along generational dysfunction. There are approximately 40 Bible verses that describe breaking chains, breaking the yoke that binds us, cutting bars of iron and on and on.... God is calling you, Reader, here and now! Where in your life do you need to break the chains that bind you?

"Then they cried to the LORD in their trouble, and he saved them
from their distress. He brought them out of darkness, the utter
darkness, and broke away their chains" (Psalm 107:13-14, NIV).

For several years throughout high school, we had three seats in our family room in front of our TV, where we could sit and have our meals. Every other space throughout our house, except our bedrooms, was filled with clutter. Our kitchen table was buried with debris. You could not see the kitchen countertops that were covered with papers and various items. Our dining room table all but disappeared from "priceless" collectibles from garage sales. We had pathways approximately 18 inches wide that led from room to room.

I was broken and deeply affected by this dysfunction; but through therapy and counseling, I learned to strategize and cope. But, most importantly, discovering the love of God freed my soul and broke the chains that bound me. However, this newfound freedom was not to come for several decades from this period in my life.

CHAPTER 2

A message from God

It was the **summer of 1985.** I would be going into my senior year of high school in the fall, and it was now time to have fun. My friends and I decided to go camping near one of our houses in the woods. It was not a traditional campground – just some woods near our friend's house. We brought, of course, the usual camping equipment: food, campfire materials, tents, sleeping bags and, of course, alcohol. I say, "Of course, alcohol" because at that time in my life, that is how we operated. I think a good majority of us, including you, Reader, could all look back at the course of our lives and say, "I should have died that night." And as I look back, I do think, "I could have died a horrific death that night camping with friends."

I got drunk – as was my norm during that season in my life. I was numbing the pain of divorcing parents, of childhood abuse; and I was incapable of socially drinking. I drank to get drunk – fall down drunk. My friends placed me in bed a couple of yards from the campfire and gave me orders not to move from my sleeping bag. I had apparently been too loud and obnoxious for even my intoxicated high school friends to handle.

I decided to sneak out of my sleeping bag while they were not looking. I stuffed my sleeping bag with the clothes I was wearing and stripped naked. It appeared like I was still inside the sleeping bag. I hid in the woods and covered my body with mud from the riverbank. I had recently watched the movie *Rambo*, and in one scene, *Rambo* covers himself with mud and hides from his enemy. I was playing *Rambo*, but my friends did not know it yet.

I snuck up on my friends in the pitch dark, hiding behind trees as I inched closer and closer. The fire was bright, and their eyes were focused on the flames. I ran through the campsite butt naked and jumped through the fire. I screamed, and they all scrambled. In no short time, they found my sleeping bag empty, and they realized I was streaking through the campsite. They chased me with their flashlights in hand, and I ran and hid in the woods. I tried swimming in the stream, but it was too shallow. Some began to throw rocks at me; and at that moment, I got scared. It was a game. What if their aim was off? I hid and then snuck back into our campsite later that night. In the morning, I climbed a tree above the camp. It was probably 15 to 20 feet high. I thought it would be funny, so I did it. It was funny until I slipped out of the tree and landed on a tent post. Fortunately, the tent post snapped in half. The tent post left a deep scratch and bruised my ribs. It hurt something terrible. I would later break those same ribs playing lacrosse during my sophomore year of college. Unfortunately, in my high school senior yearbook, I decided to write a caption forever memorializing that camping experience. It reads, "Run naked through the woods. It's a pleasure, Rambo."

Later in that same week, after the camping experience, there was a pool party. My friend Keith had a pool. His parents weren't home, and he had a large party. I dove into my friend Keith's pool after he told us not to. The pool sides gently slope, and the bottom of the pool was covered with a cement-like substance. I hit my face on the sloping rough pool bottom. I was able to push off as I hit face first and severely scraped the palms of my hands and the top of my feet. I had deep raspberry patches the size of quarters on the palms of my hands and on the top portions of my feet to match my palms. My chin also was bruised and had an abrasion, and it looked like I had been in a fight. Of course, my friend Keith was angry with me. I was apologetic, but I also was grateful to be standing. I could have been paralyzed!

Unfortunately, that close call did not wake me from my carelessness and reckless ways. The next day I looked in the mirror in shock and disbelief. My ribs were scraped and bruised from the tent post incident; my palms and tops of my feet were marked with quarter-size abrasions from the rough pool surface. I looked as though I had been in a fight. The marks on my body reminded me of Christ's passion experience. I had heard of the term "stigmata" from my religious upbringing, and it looked like it. I felt scared. Initially, I thought that my God may be trying to get my attention. It scared me on a couple of different levels. I decided to discount the thought and "write it off."

Never in my wildest imagination would I think I would be marked with the sign of "stigmata." Was it stigmata? I don't know, but it was one of many signs in my life pointing and pulling me toward God. Stigmata or not, the wounds and markings on my body were an exit sign, saying, "Exit this present way you're living, and come follow Me."

I place the "stigmata" in quotes because I don't know if it was for certain. I can say for certain that I am grateful that I did not snap my neck that night at Keith's pool party; grateful that I did not skewer myself falling from the tree; that I am grateful for the precious life I have been given and that I did not die an early death. Amen.

The date was **April 1986**. We had a big game ahead of us "under the lights" versus rival West Genesee High School. I was a senior and the starting goalie for Fayetteville-Manlius High School. At that time in my life, lacrosse was my god. I had the mindset of a teenager. The world revolved around my lacrosse friends and me. So when I write that this game was the biggest night of my life, I am understating how important it was to me, to us. To our amazement, we were keeping up with our rival. West Genesee was the best lacrosse school in the state for many decades. As the game progressed, I made a couple of saves. At one point in the game, I was clearing the ball downfield after I made a save. The defenders did not pick me up. I ran down field, face-dodged a defender and shot the ball at the opposing goalie's net. I saw everything in slow motion. I saw where I wanted to shoot. I practiced all week for this moment.

Our coaches had scouted this team, and they knew their weakness. They advised me that I could have an opportunity to shoot "on net" during the game.

As I shot the ball from my goalie stick, the ball soared past the opposing goalie's hip and hit the back of the net. I scored! My team surrounded me; and with shock and disbelief in their eyes, we all began to believe we could win! I pumped my fist high in the air. I was on cloud 9. My dad was in the stands, and he was reported to have jumped three bleachers down as I scored the goal. I made the local news, was celebrated by my friends and family after the game; but we lost 7-8 in double overtime.

How could we have lost? This was not the way a storybook evening should end. It was a quiet bus ride back to our school. This loss was the beginning of birth pains and rumblings in my world. There was a "new world" fast approaching that I did not want to know anything about. I wanted to remain with my friends in that time and place. As chaotic as my family life was, I wanted time to stand still. Life was good, so I thought.

I thank God for sports at that time in my life. Sports gave me structure,

J-D vs. F-M 1986. Dan cleared the ball downfield.

allowed for friendships and kept me out of trouble. However, sports also can bring about some odd thinking and can be damaging to young minds if not carefully crafted.

During the off season of lacrosse, I also dabbled in football, wrestling and box lacrosse. I played freshman and J-V football. As a first-string (starter), I rotated through various positions throughout the season, including nose tackle, guard, linebacker and defensive end. I was medium-sized but strong and quick. Unfortunately, I had multiple concussions throughout my sports career. During my junior year, I made the varsity football team but sat on the bench – except for special teams (kick-off and punting teams). It was hard to get used to not being on the field and contributing more to the game. In hindsight, it probably was best that I didn't get much playing time because of the concussions I previously experienced.

My freshman football coach was also the wrestling coach, and he recruited me to try out for wrestling during my freshman year. It was the winter season. I was interested in keeping in shape and wanted to try it out. I tried it and hated it. It was hard, exhausting; and I didn't have the interest in staying on the team. Mr. Hennigan was a fatherlike figure, and I did not want to let him down. However, I quit; and to this day, it is something I regret. Quitting for no reason is wrong and has haunted me. To be fair to myself, I was a kid, and I was hurting. My best friend had moved to California; my parents were divorcing and my dad had moved out of our home. I was essentially raising myself. When my dad left, my mom fell further into depression. I too was depressed but did not have the words or understanding to articulate myself. My coach, Mr. Hennigan, was not pleased with my decision to quit; and he knew I was making a mistake.

During my junior year, I decided to right a wrong and went back out for wrestling. I was playing box lacrosse one night a week, and I also was wrestling. I wrestled 155 pounds and "held my own." I was determined to give this season my best shot. The coach was more than willing to bring me back on the team. Mr. Hennigan was a good man. He was fatherly, and he wanted the best for his athletes. Coach made me an impromptu captain for the J-V team during my first match. It was sort of humiliating to be wrestling on J-V as a junior, but the sting was less with the title of captain. The Varsity 155 lbs. spot could be won if I put in more time and effort. I could be a good wrestler. I knew I had the physical attributes. My first match was also my last match. The match went three periods, and we were equally suited. The score was approximately 12-13, but I ended up getting pinned. I was humiliated and literally sick to my stomach. I was so dizzy that I couldn't see straight. I was physically exhausted, and I went to the wrong "bench" after the match. My coach and teammates gathered me from the other side of the mat. I stumbled to the bathroom where I had diarrhea, and my head spun out of control. This was the most exhausted I had been up to that point in my life, a very low point for my ego. All I could think of was: "How do I get out of this situation?" I knew I couldn't quit again. I would not humiliate myself by quitting, and I would not disappoint my coach again.

I formulated a plan. I knew that, if I was injured, I would not have to wrestle. I could save face and not disappoint my coach. Being hurt was my way out. Now how do I get hurt? I decided to take a baseball bat and break my hand. When I went home, I placed my left hand on my bedpost because I am right-handed. This made sense to me at the time. With a broken left hand, I could still hold a pen and could still do schoolwork. I had it all planned out. I thought to myself, "I will not be a two-time quitter." I raised the bat high in the air and struck my hand hard. It hurt. I thought to myself, "Broken? No, I did not break it." I smacked it again and winced with pain. Again I thought, "Broken? Nope." I hit it again and again and again....

Eventually, my hand looked like a grapefruit. I went to school and had it wrapped with an ace bandage. I went to see Mr. Hennigan and told my coach, "Coach, some weights fell on my hand." I told him I would be unable to wrestle. He said, "No, I think you will be alright. Just take some time off from wrestling, but you can still run. I will see you at practice." My plan had failed. I wouldn't quit again! My hand was so swollen I couldn't fit it in my pants pocket, and I hurt myself for no reason.

I told my best friend Herb what I had done. His eyes became as large as saucers, and he shook his head in disbelief. I was even more embarrassed when a couple of friends heard of my adventure into self-harm. They couldn't believe I would hit myself with a bat! What they didn't know was that I was desperate and did not want to embarrass myself or let down the coach. However, now I looked even worse than a quitter.

I was a "bit short-sighted" because I wanted to continue to play box lacrosse. I managed to get my lacrosse glove over my swollen hand and was able to play in the night box game. As our indoor lacrosse game was coming to an end, I was able to manage the pain and knew I could wrestle as well.

We were playing the team from LaFayette High School, and they were good. Toward the end of the game, there was a break away, and I was one-on-one with an opposing attack man. He wound up and shot on net from about six feet away or top of the crease. It was overkill to "wind up" when you're that close. A simple placement shot could get the job done, but he let it fly. I put my stick up and held one hand out to create more surface area. It worked. The ball ricocheted off my left pinky, and into the net. They scored. I went up to the referee and said, "I think I broke my finger." Blood was dripping down my arm and onto the turf. The referee said and I quote, "There are 20 seconds left in the game. Get off the field, or get back in the cage." I got back in the cage. My friend's father, who was in the stands, drove me to the hospital after the game; and my mom met us there. My finger took the impact of a lacrosse ball traveling at approximately 100 miles an hour. The ball twisted my pinky finger around and bent the tip over at the first knuckle. The impact of the ball also pushed my nail through the skin and into the meat of the finger. Luckily, the doctor was able to save the nail. My finger was broken in a couple of places, but surgery was not needed. To this day, I cannot straighten my finger. I wore a splint and now had a semi-legitimate reason not to wrestle. I saved face and told my wrestling coach, "Sorry, but I can't wrestle with a broken finger." I had found an excuse but regretted my decision.

However, I continued to play box lacrosse the following week. I did not want any other goalie to take my spot. I put my lacrosse glove over the finger splint and then taped a racquetball can over my (gloved) pinky and ring finger as additional protection. It worked. I was able to finish the box lacrosse season and transition into the spring field lacrosse season.

To any athletes reading this, I say: Once you start something, don't quit. Literally to this day, I wish I had continued to wrestle. I hated it, but I hate telling this story more. Quitting like I did takes something out of you that is hard to replace. I can never get that back. My only hope is to pass the word and teach others the error in my thinking, the error of quitting. Hopefully, it goes without saying; but don't hit yourself with a bat! If I had waited just a little while longer, it would have all worked out.

Desperation is not a good feeling and a tough place to be in. As an adult I say, if you ever feel desperate and think irrational thoughts, pray. Call out to God. Literally, verbally, call out to God. He has answered many of my prayers, and He will answer your prayers as well. I wish I knew then what I know now, and I wish someone had told me this truth back then.

Your prayers may not be answered "quickly"; but know they are heard and will be answered. The prayers may not be answered as timely and in the way we want, but they will be answered. Also, seek advice from a trusted teacher, friend or confidant. They may, in fact, be the arms and ears who God is intending to use. Unfortunately, some acts of desperation cannot be taken back. What seems tragic and unmanageable can seem much smaller and less volatile as we move away from the subject in time or distance.

Unfortunately, I had a friend, Harrison, who committed suicide. As an adult, I worked as a firefighter, and it is where I met Harrison. Throughout my career, I have witnessed many attempted suicides and unfortunate deaths through suicide. This act of desperation can never be taken back;

and if you, Reader, may be thinking about the subject, please stop. Read the remainder of this book; reach out to friends, family and loved ones. We get one chance at this life, and God wants only the best for His children.

1986, midway through my senior year lacrosse season, we were playing Liverpool High School. Unfortunately, at one point in that game, my arm was injured – cut at the elbow by an opposing Liverpool player's stick. Fast forward to college for a minute. I was sharing my war stories and scars with some lacrosse friends, some college teammates; and as "small world" stories go, a Liverpool player was now a friend of mine at Canisius. Pat told me that the kid, the Liverpool lacrosse player who sliced me with his stick, did it on purpose – per Pat the Liverpool attackman (name of the lacrosse position he played) sharpened the end of his stick to hurt me, to hurt the F-M goalie. It was dumbfounding as a young man to hear Pat tell me that and a little scary that someone would do that intentionally. I did not go head hunting, and I did not retaliate. I thank God that He had begun a new work in my life. "But I tell you, love your enemies and pray for those who persecute you" (Matthew 5:44, NIV). I am glad that, as a young man, I did not pursue revenge. As the saying goes, "Before you embark on a journey of revenge, dig two graves." (attributed to Confucius)

As we jubilantly got on our bus after the Liverpool game, I was standing in the aisle and talking to my teammates on the bus. I cleaned off my elbow that was caked with mud from the game. As I brushed off what I thought was a piece of mud from my elbow, a large chunk of skin flopped over. You could see the bone as I brushed off my arm. My teammates gave some shouts of disgust and turned away. I was surprised that it did not hurt and received seven stitches later on at the doctor's office.

As a competitive player, I did not want to lose my starting spot and was determined to play in the next game – stitches and all. The next week, we played another rival, Jamesville Dewitt High School. My girlfriend, who was a cheerleader, went to J-D, which made me that much more despised by their team. Our schools were bitter rivals. As rivalries go, our school burned a large hole in their football field's 50-yard line, and they cut down our symbolic oak tree in front of our school. The oak tree is in our school song, "Guided by our old oak tree, symbol of our...."

My elbow throbbed, and I did not have the dexterity because of the bandage and extra elbow padding. Excuses, excuses ...unfortunately, we lost by one goal. We (F-M) were a good team, J-D was a great team; and they ended up at the state playoffs that season. I had a decent game; but I mistakenly told my lacrosse coach, "Coach, the fans got on me, and they got in my head." This was a mistake....

My lacrosse coach had a great idea (note my sarcasm). At practice the next day, he had my teammates stand on the end line behind my net, and he instructed them to yell derogatory names at me while he warmed me up and shot on goal. My coach had an excellent shot for an older coach. As I played catch with him from the goal, attempting to deflect and save his shots, my team yelled, "You suck! Siv in the cage (a very derogatory term for a goalie)! My sister can play better!" The insults and verbal attacks went on for about 10 minutes.

I get it. I get the fact that we cannot let someone get into our head to manipulate our actions. Whether in sports, while driving your car or in any part of life, we should be objective and be above insults. This may seem like an unachievable notion; but it is an important concept in mental health and in becoming a better person, a better you.

Unfortunately, for about a decade after my graduation from high school, I had recurring nightmares that would happen during times of stress and uncertainty. The dream was always about lacrosse and not being "good enough." I could hear their taunts and jeers as they called me names on the end line, as my coach warmed me up in the goal. The dream came in difficult seasons in my life, but it is no longer with me.

I write this more for you – coaches, teachers, parents, people of influence in children's lives – of what not to do. You have power and with power comes great responsibility. Teach and build up the children in your lives, empower them and do no harm. If in doubt, follow love! What would loving actions do in this situation? Fill in the variable, and fill in the equation. Coaches, teachers, parents, let love guide your actions for your children, your students, your players; and they will thrive.

If my coach had said, "Danny, next game — if the fans get on you, know that I believe in you. You're a good kid, and you're doing a good job in the net." Unfortunately, he was not perfect. I understand him, and I forgive him for being human. He was the epitome of a great coach, but he still had some things to learn. My coaches were just a product of their coaching experiences and their upbringing. In fact, my coach is a family friend, a good man; and he would never do anything intentionally to hurt me. My recommendation to coaches is to be "cool," be good and know that sports are just a game. Have fun with the game.

It was May 1986, and we were in the division semi-finals. playing Henninger H.S. They had beaten us by one goal two times that season. The reality of this being my last game with my friends, the last moment in the sun, the last of this worldview hit home like a sledgehammer.

On the bus ride to the game, I stood up from my seat and told my team, "I don't want this to be our last game!" I was emphatic and demonstrative, and my teammates all shouted in agreement. But did they understand this might be it? This could be our last game together! If we lost, that was it.... Our season, our season in the sun, would be over.

I had the best game of my high school career. I was angry and felt passionate that this would not be our last game in high school. I felt an abundance of energy. I felt quick, and I was physically and mentally prepared for this game. I didn't care about my coaches' opinions or their intimidation techniques that controlled me for the entire season. I was going to play my game the way I was going to play it, and we were going to win! Midway through the game, we were tied 2-2. The referee gave the ball to Henninger, the offense, behind our net. The ball was passed over my net; I stole it out of the air and ran downfield. I passed to my teammate and ran back to my goal. The fans went crazy. However, Henninger ran down the field again. The front of our goal was packed with players. I yelled to my defense, "Clear the crease! Clear them out!" I was being screened by the other team and couldn't see the ball. They shot; an opposing player jumped high into the air, and I felt the ball as it went through my legs into the net behind me. That moment in time was captured in *Lacrosse Magazine* for the lacrosse world to see. The picture was phenomenal! A Henninger player jumping into the air, me with my stick down looking for the ball and the ball going through my legs into the net. I was honored that my picture was in the magazine but humbled and embarrassed at the same time.

We lost 2-3 to Henninger High School for the third time that season by one goal. My world and one of the buildings in my world collapsed. I had a sudden realization that my immediate future would be significantly different, and it now loomed large in front of me. High school lacrosse was over!

I received "Honorable Mention" for my goalie abilities that season for our division. As my coach often reminded me, I was "adequate." It was his way to motivate me to improve my game. He would often refer to me as "adequate." Coaches, you hold a fragile human being in your hands – whether they let you know that or not. Children, at that age, are vulnerable. I know I thrive when people believe in me. Even to this day, I know that when I have the support and encouragement of those around me, I thrive.

From outside appearances in high school, I was living the teenage dream. I was on the varsity lacrosse team, dating the rival J-D High School cheerleader. I was popular, strong, athletic and good-looking (so I was told).

My friend and I sold kisses at our senior high school class fundraiser. We wore sunglasses, jeans and a jean jacket and had no shirts underneath. We stood on stage, and girls bid on us. The picture of our antics was placed in the following year's yearbook. Unfortunately, for my already inflated ego, we made several dollars for our senior class fundraiser.

Unfortunately, the girl who "won" the bidding wore braces. She kissed me so hard that her lips bled. I felt bad. I remember wishing that I could have given her a better kiss. I had a heart. I was a sensitive boy — wrapped in a jock's body — and had loads of unresolved family baggage. I had potential; and on occasion, my potential, my kindness showed through the clouds of egotism that pervaded my life.

Now, 32 years later, I can honestly say, "Thank God for His loving grace." I am a great dad and a devoted, loving husband. I love my wife with all my heart. I am good for her, and she is good for me. God, in His infinite wisdom, brought us together; and we fit. There is hope for jocks and egotistical maniacs of this world. For me to get to where I am has been daunting. I was disciplined by my Father God and rebuilt from the ground up. God has been here with me, molding me and shaping my life one brick, one piece of mortar at a time. Smoothing my rough surfaces with sometimes very coarse sandpaper. Sometimes shaping me with a mallet and chisel. God has built a new city within my soul.

It was July of 1986, and college was starting in early September. I literally woke from a dream one morning and knew I could not go to Potsdam State. It was not a lucid dream, and I do not remember it; but I awakened confident that I could not attend SUNY Potsdam and would now go to Canisius College. Everything was crashing down. The dream pulled me toward Canisius. I called the registrar's office at Canisius, informed the school that I wanted to go to their college and would attend the summer orientation.

I had applied to Canisius on a whim a couple of months before, and I got in. How I got in was unknown to me? Canisius College is known to be a good Jesuit school. I didn't know at that time what the word *Jesuit* meant, but I would soon become very familiar with this world.

Jesuit, as I learned, is an order of Roman Catholic priests founded by St. Ignatius of Loyola. Jesuit priests tend to be in academia, and they are involved with social justice issues. (They have an extensive history. There is an amazing movie I recommend called "The Mission" with Robert De Niro, regarding Jesuit missionaries.) Incidentally, our current Pope, Pope Francis, is a Jesuit.

My best friend from F-M, Herb, would be going to the University of Buffalo and would be just down the street. Life could be similar to what I had known. But it would never be the same, and I was just beginning to find that out.

Throughout the remainder of my summer before college, my friends and I were celebrating like rock stars. We were free and we were alive. That is until one day when I got a phone call from my friend Dave. I answered my phone, and Dave said, "Did you hear the news?" I replied, "What news?" Dave said, "Turn on channel 5." Pam's car was on the news. It was destroyed. No one could have survived the accident they showed on the news, and she didn't. Pam was not drinking, and the accident was just that – an accident. A collision with another vehicle, an accident and the subsequent death of a friend created another new worldview. *This should not be happening!* I thought to myself. I rode in that car numerous times going to and from our local ski center. Pam and I were ski instructors, and we taught tiny tots how to ski. She was a good friend, and she was accepted to go to Penn State. "My God, why? What is happening?"

Dan and Herb 1984 F-M High School

My world shook and the earth quaked as I stood in line at Pam's wake. We were friends and confidants. I felt more alone standing there with a group of friends than I had ever experienced. As I embraced her sister Wendy, my ski instructor boss, my heart broke for her family, and I felt pain as never before. I felt honored that Pam and I were friends. Pam and I were good friends — not best — but friends, good friends; and her death hurt. I cry as I write this, revisiting the tragedy and a beautiful life lost. The fragility of life slapped me hard, and I rebelled. The next day, I did not go to the funeral. I stayed home alone, rejected the funeral and felt very lonely. An old girlfriend stopped by. We talked and consoled each other, and we decided against the funeral. This is something I regret and now live with. I wish I had gone to the funeral for the sake of closure.

I found Pam's grave a couple of years ago. I was approximately 47 years old, and I had never visited Pam's gravesite. I went jogging through our hometown, and I went into the cemetery for the first time in almost 30 years. I found Pam's tombstone and said a prayer. I jogged to a flower shop about two miles away and sent my sister Kathy flowers. We were fighting; it was near her birthday, and the realization that life is too short is now all around me. Life is a snapshot that we look at and wonder, "Where did the time go?"

It was the fall semester of 1986. I was 18 years old and a freshman at Canisius College in Buffalo, New York. I had scored an 890 on my SATs, and I could barely read aloud in public. I was plagued with debilitating anxiety that made it very difficult for me to read in front of others. I could not formulate a written sentence. I thought at that time, *Why am I in college? How did I make it into college? Was the Army recruiter right? Maybe I should have gone into the military?* I was not ready for academia, or was I?

My dad took me to freshman orientation at Canisius College, the last orientation of the summer. Since it was the last orientation, I also would be dropped off at school at the same time, and it was the first time I had seen this school in person.

41

As I sat in the auditorium listening to Father Dempsey, a Jesuit priest and college president, I began to daydream how different my life would be here in Buffalo, New York instead of Potsdam, New York....

I was supposed to go to Potsdam State in Potsdam, New York. I was supposed to be the starting goalie on their lacrosse team. The Potsdam coach recruited me and a few of my buddies, Chris, Bobby and TC – all from F-M (Fayetteville Manlius High School).

We traveled to Potsdam as requested by the head coach. I drove my mom's 1983 Tourismo. I sped the entire way with my three friends in the car. We raced a couple of players from the rival West Genesee lacrosse team enroute to see the college. It is a wonder we did not all die that day since we were speeding at more than 100 miles an hour and cars that were "in our way" nearly caused us accidents. Such was the mindset of a teenager. "Cars in our way"… life revolved around us. I acted carelessly. It was reckless and fun; we were alive and living the dream.

(A little aside, fast forward here for perspective: I am now nicknamed "Safety Dan." I am a firefighter, a paramedic and a nurse. I pray that my daughters never act as foolishly as their daddy.)

We were privileged children and did not realize there was a world around us. We were teens; we were self-absorbed; and we ruled the world we lived in – so we thought. We arrived safely on Potsdam campus – thanks be to God. Our practice session in front of the coach was fun. We played at the school gymnasium. I had one of the best lacrosse days of my life. I stopped almost every ball shot at me and made an impression on the coach. He recruited me to play and fed me what I wanted to hear. "Dan, you're my number-one recruit. You will start next year." He fed my ego and I dove in. A starting freshman goalie was all I needed to hear. I felt elated. Division 3 did not give sports scholarships, and my grades were nothing to write home about.

I would now have to face my dad and tell him I did not get a scholarship. I promised him I would "go" Division 1 and get a scholarship.

I had no idea about the level of competition "out there." Never in my wildest dreams growing up did I think I would be the starting goalie for F-M. My inflated ego thought, if I could play and start for F-M, I could play lacrosse anywhere. At that time and to this day, Fayetteville-Manlius High School was one of the best lacrosse schools in New York state. I'm a little biased, but that statement is accurate. Unfortunately (or fortunately), I could not play lacrosse at any college. I was not recruited D-1, and I did not get a scholarship.

Awakened from my daydream at the Canisius auditorium, my dad turned to me in our seats at freshman orientation and said, "There must be a reason you're here." What did he mean? Was he right? Was there a reason I was here? I wondered where life was leading me. I felt the sincerity and almost "God-breathed" message from my dad, "There must be a reason you're here."

I can definitively say this ... if I had changed where I went to college, I would not be sitting here typing. I would not have eventually met the love of my life Veronica, and I would not have the two most wonderful children in the world. Yes, Reader, God used the circumstances and places I was in at the time to bring about a change of mind, heart and soul within me. My dad was right. There was a reason I attended Canisius College. "In their hearts humans plan their course, but the LORD establishes their steps" (Proverbs 16:9, NIV). Unbeknownst to me at that time, I was discerning the will of God in my life and following "the small voice" inside my heart. I had listened — as a young 18-year-old man — to a dream I had, and I followed. Something in that dream spoke to my mind and heart, and I obeyed. Reader, I am not saying we should listen to every dream that comes "during the night"; but this dream rang a loud gong within my heart and soul, and I knew I must follow. I "discerned" the decision before me and made a good choice.

It was fall 1986. I was a freshman in college, and my high school sweetheart broke up with me. Rather than rush home every weekend from

Buffalo, I was able to learn what it really meant to be a freshman in college. I made fast friends with my hallmates, and they learned that I liked to have a good time. We smoked pot in the closet and drank beer in our dorm room. This was high school on steroids. Canisius even had a lacrosse team. They were a club team, and I was a big fish in a small pond. I was nominated captain during my freshman year, and I started every game throughout my college lacrosse career. Life was good. I fed addictive behaviors, squeaked out a whopping 1.8 during my freshman year and ended up on academic probation.

I was a good Catholic "boy" and went to mass every Sunday evening on campus. It was a beautiful service that was held by candlelight. The songs and incense stirred my soul; and for brief moments, I experienced God calling me by name. It was not an audible noise or even an internal noise but a deep peace beyond understanding. After service, I would leave church and go back to studying, drinking or watching David Letterman on TV.

It was fall semester 1986, and I returned home for Thanksgiving break with my family. Holidays were very difficult and were a mere shadow of what we once lived as a family unit. My parents' legal separation affected every holiday, and turkey had lost its flavor. My mother's pain was too much for me to bear. Her hoarding behaviors had become worse since I left for college. Every discussion revolved around their marriage and ultimately ended with crying, anger — and all of us feeling sad for Mom.

My prayer at that time — and since I was about eight years of age — was to heal my family. As a child, I would often lay awake at night, listening to my parents fight and praying to God, "Father, please heal my family. Please, Lord, make my family whole again. I want to have a home like my friends. Please, Lord."

Sometimes I would lay awake as a young boy and think of my wife and where she might be in the world. *What does she look like? Where is she living? When will I meet her?* The thought of her brought me comfort. Little did I know — as a small child — that my wife had just been born in Athens,

Greece; and someday would make it (literally) to my doorstep.

My dad had been back and forth three different times in their marriage throughout my childhood. Dad would leave for six months to a year; they would make up; and he would return home for a year. Leave and return for a year. Leave and return for a year. Leave and return for a year. It was the pattern to which our family became accustomed, and I knew he would return again! It was awful listening to them discuss their adult issues with the mindset and ears of a child, but it was not as bad as the silence that followed when Dad left.

Each time he left, we were given the "It's not your fault" speech that some "pop psychologist" came up with. At least, that was the way my 10-12-15-year-old mindset at the time processed their speech. And now as a parent, I get what my parents were trying to tell us. They tried to let us know that they loved us, but they could not live with each other any longer. It was truly not our fault.

(Little Reader, it is not your fault that your parents are divorcing. Know this: God loves you. We all have a good, good Father in heaven, a good Daddy; and He will take care of you. Trust this message and read Psalm 91. Reach out to Him in prayer. He does hear you, and He is listening. Talk and explain your feelings, hurts and worries; and give them all to Him. He wants to hear from you, and He cares deeply.)

In the fall of 1986, after the tumultuous Thanksgiving break at my home in Fayetteville, New York, it felt good to be back in my dorm in Buffalo. Canisius was now becoming home, and my hallmates were becoming family. As I lay in my dorm room unable to sleep, I heard laughing and loud music coming from down the hall. Rather than pray before falling asleep, I went to see what the commotion was all about.

My friends Dan and Chuck were partying with some guys I had not met before. They invited me into their dorm room and passed me the bong. I hit that bong hard. I was used to smoking pot and needed a good stress release after a tough visit home. I started to feel high, but this was

45

not the high I was used to. *Was it laced? Did I smoke too much?* All I knew was I began to feel bumps all over my body. The bumps grew so large that I couldn't breathe! I sat there panic stricken, feeling out of control and like I was dying. *Can they see the bumps on my face? Should I run? What's going on? Help me!* An inner battle raged in my mind. I did not want my friends to know I was panicking. I did not understand what was happening to me. As I sat there in the dorm room, I could feel myself begin to float. I floated out of my body and looked down on the group of us. I saw me and my friends sitting there in the dorm room partying. I was floating above, hovering. In an instant, I returned into my body, got up and hurried out of my friend's dorm room. *Hang in there, Dan.* Internally, I was self-talking my way out of the room, *You can do this. Hold on.* I thanked my friends — so as not to bring suspicion or attention to myself — and politely left.

My friends sensed I was starting to lose it and said, "Where are you going Dan-o?" I tried not to let on; but my voice cracked, and I was hyperventilating. They giggled and said, "He's freaking out. You ok, man?" I went back to my dorm room but found an enormous football player with a red beard and some hard-core munchies in my room, eating my food. I played it cool and said, "Hey there, help yourself. Eat all you want." He was hungry, literally on steroids, and intoxicated. I wanted no part of a fight and was trying to manage this overwhelming, internal, panic-stricken, intoxicated emotion. He ate and ate and thanked me. He then said something that rocked me and left me wondering, *What in the world?* The football player said, "Hey, thanks for the food, Dan-o." I replied something to the effect of: "No problem, man. My pleasure." He said something that made me pause, "Hey Dan, maybe I will save your life sometime." He was huge, a good guy to have on your side in a fight and not someone I wanted to rumble with. His timing was impeccable; and I can say, for certain, I am glad I let him eat all my crackers and the vast majority of my care package. He left my room, but the panic was still there.

I decided to run to my best friend's university. I got some sweats on

46

and knew the cold air would do me good. Herb was at U.B. – only 10 miles away. In high school, Herb and I used to, on a whim, run seven miles as a way to keep in shape. Ten was a bit far, but I knew I could do it. I had to do it to live. I went downstairs prepared to run but quickly realized I needed medical help. I couldn't breathe. I decided to go to the school nurse. I ran across campus, but the RN was not there. A desk attendant was in the lobby and asked me, "Are you ok?" I replied, in the best nonanxious way I could, "Oh yah, I'm fine." I lied and walked out. I thought to myself, *I will go back to my dorm and call an ambulance.*

I began to walk through Canisius quad back to my dorm. I stopped by a large boulder that has since been removed. I returned years later to visit my alma mater; and unfortunately, the administration renovated the campus and removed the boulder and fireplace that once were in our quad.

As I stood motionless by the boulder on that cold November night, I looked up at the Buffalo night sky. I felt paralyzed with fear, awe and remorse. The clouds were soft pink and white, and they were motionless. There, in front of me in the clouds above, I saw God.

He had a large beard and long hair about shoulder length. There was a lamb's head to His right and a message in the clouds that read, IT'S NOT TOO LATE... to His left.

How do I express the majesty of that moment? That moment in time has shaped my life and changed the trajectory of my life journey. And it is the reason I write this book. For I was given a message that cold November evening.

I begged and pleaded with my Father God. "I will become a priest. I will be good from now on. I will do whatever You want. Let me live!" I promised and pleaded for my life.

I tried to go back upstairs to my dorm room multiple times. Each time I tried, I was stricken with fear and panic and couldn't breathe. I ran downstairs and back outside to the quad. I looked up once again at the clouds; and now within the cloud, I saw the women in my family crying.

The cloud changed from one person to the next to the next. The cloud changed from my mother crying to my sisters crying, grandmother, etc. I then had a realization, a thought, *I died.* It felt like purgatory.

In my Roman Catholic upbringing, I was taught that purgatory was a place one goes after they die but before they go to heaven. It is a place to atone for sins. I realized I must follow what my Father (God) told me, so I went to the front of the dorm and stood outside for what seemed to be an eternity.

I could not run to my friend's university because behind the cars in the parking lot were small demon-like figures waiting for me. If you've ever watched the movie "Ghost" with Demi Moore – as poor as the graphics are in the movie – the demons looked just like that.

The friends with whom I was partying earlier in the evening, Chuck and Dan, came downstairs — out to where I was standing and asked me, "You ready for the ride, Dan-o?" I told them, "I'm ready." It felt cryptic – like they were messengers of God and part of this whacked-out experience. *Am I ready for the ride? How did they know I needed a ride?* They drove me to the U.B. North campus. I had no idea where my friend's dorm was or what it looked like – other than Herb said it was the tallest building on campus. I was dropped off on the U.B campus; and I ran for miles, looking for my friend's dorm. I was panicked, intoxicated; and it was hard to breathe. I was literally and figuratively lost. I finally found his dorm. Herb was up and waiting for me. Apparently, I called him earlier in the night, telling him I was in trouble and on my way over to his dorm. He put me to bed in his dorm room; and in the morning, I told him my story.

This event began the dissolution of our friendship. I was crazy or so he thought. I was saying crazy things. I explained my experience from the previous night. Who in their right mind sees God and then believes they saw God? "It was drugs, right?" For me, it was real. Today, as I sit here and write, I believe the following Scripture passage to be true, "And we know

48

that in all things God works for the good of those who love him, who have been called according to his purpose" (Romans 8:28, NIV). God can and does work for the good in all things – even a drug-induced, intoxicated state of mind – for those who love Him and are called according to His purpose. I love Him, and I know that He is using my experiences for the good.

That fateful night in the Canisius quad, God switched on a light and figuratively said, "My Way or the highway. You live under My roof, and you will behave accordingly." I, of course, agreed but continued to rebel. I had one foot in and one foot out. I had reluctantly begun my journey. A journey that began years earlier, but I did not realize it at the time.

CHAPTER 3

God was calling me home

I came home on breaks throughout my first year of college. Each time I returned to my childhood home, I returned to a house filled with clutter and debris and unfortunately lived in a hoarder environment. When I was away at college, my life returned to normal. I could organize my dorm room and lived a carefree college existence. I was away from the misery and the continuous reminder of what my mom collected and brought into our home.

Please, Reader, do not get me wrong. I loved my mom and still do. God bless her soul! However, her hoarding behavior was impacting my emotional health. The only rooms not cluttered and filled with debris in our affluent, suburban 3,000-square-foot home were our bathrooms, children's bedrooms and three spots on the couch in front of the television. My sister and I shared a bathroom, and we kept our rooms and bathroom moderately clean for teenagers. However, the rest of the house was destroyed. There were pathways approximately 18 inches wide through our house. There was even clutter on our stove. Have you ever seen a documentary or reality show on hoarders? I have lived it, and it is not fun.

I will be perfectly transparent. I came home unannounced on a weekend break from Canisius. No one was home when I walked in. "Hello? Anybody home?" I looked around at the mess in our home. A home once filled with laughter and love was now filled with clutter and chaos. Debris was everywhere. Stacks of magazines, papers, boxes of "prize" garage sale items, flowers picked at the roadside that had the promise of becoming a bouquet, clothing strewn here and there, dirty dishes and filth everywhere. It was extremely hard to walk into this mess and not feel extremely saddened.

There were newspapers and unopened mail stacked high on the stove. A thought came across my mind to "turn the knob on the stove." The entire house would go up in an instant. I am so thankful I did not do this terrible act of violence. This act of arson would have changed my life. A message from the enemy filled my mind, "Turn on the burner."

Just as God wants us to hear His voice and do His will, there is an enemy wanting you to hear his voice, and he wants the worst for you. My life and my family's lives would have been tragically changed if I had followed through with that temptation.

I once heard a good quote from a Jesuit friend who said, "Never make decisions in times of desolation or consolation" (Fr. Don Maldari). In other words, do not make decisions when you're elated or depressed; but make good, sound decisions when you're at an even keel. I certainly was depressed. I came home to surprise my family. Each and every time I came home, I *hoped* the house would be as I remembered it as a child, but it would never again be the same. From my relatively clean college dorm room and fun life as a college kid, returning home to an endless abyss of belongings sapped life energy from me. My heart continued to break and hurt for my mother and younger sister who continued to live in this filth.

I had enough and decided to make some significant changes in my living condition. In 1987, upon returning home during my summer break, I told my mom I couldn't live like this anymore and couldn't live here in this home any longer. I told my mom, "I am moving in with dad." My mom was caught off guard and was very hurt. This was not my intention. She replied, "You're just like your father!" and proceeded to slap me across my face. The slap hurt a bit, but the real pain was felt by the anguish I caused my mother. She was self-destructing, and I felt myself being pulled down with her. Intuitively, I knew I had to move out of my home and live with my dad. At this time in my life, I had no instruction. I had no mentor. I had no one guiding me.

My dad was a bachelor and living life to its fullest. We, their children, tried to stay out of the mix of their arguments the best we could. However, we all naturally took the side of our mother, the weaker of the two parents. We loved them both very much.

My dad had a two-bedroom apartment in a nice, upper-scale apartment complex. It had a pool! It was clean; it had a fireplace; and there was no clutter. I felt elated. I felt free. My adolescence was restored, and I felt *hopeful.* That is until one night when my dad poked his head into my bedroom. I was just about to fall asleep. "Dan, you asked me to tell you when the legal separation is over. It's over. We are now divorced. Good night." My dad shut my bedroom door, and my world crumbled!

The hope in our family unification was an unconscious knowledge that they would reunite and our family would be a family again. The *hope* that I had carried around with me since my early childhood was now strangling me. I started to panic. I didn't know what was happening to me. Wave after wave of anxiety flooded through me, and I felt utterly and completely out of control. These feelings were totally foreign to me. I sat there in my new bedroom alone, abandoned; and I felt emotionally helpless.

This experience was the beginning of a debilitating week of anxiety and detachment. I didn't tell my dad what was happening because I could not articulate what I was experiencing. I did not have the vocabulary to understand the emotional response I was having. I was almost catatonic – without feeling or emotions.

During that time period, my dad and I had a cold sort of relationship, so my quiet behavior was not foreign to him. My quietness did not raise any flags, and I was able to go about my day and week without questions. During the week, we visited my grandmother, Gramma Connors. She was the best, and I miss her dearly. As we — my dad, grandmother and I — were sitting at her kitchen table, she turned to me and said, "Knock it off! Danny, you stop this nonsense right now." That woke me up, and she got my attention. For more than a week, I had walked around in a "tunnel," feeling anxiety that I had never known before and what psychologists would term disassociation. Grandma, however — in her loving, strong Irish manner — woke me up and snapped me back to reality. Thank You, God, and thank you, Gramma. Thank you, Gramma, for loving me! Thank you for modeling your faith for me to see throughout my childhood and adolescence. Thank you for being strong when I needed strength. Thank you, Gramma, and I will see you again someday. This I know for certain.

Unfortunately, the strong but loving rebuke from Gramma Connors did not end the panic attacks and anxiety that plagued me for years to follow. I will add here as a prelude, Reader, God has helped me overcome my anxiety, which I will describe further in this book. What seemed like an insurmountable mountain is now a rolling hill and can be managed.

> "'...if you have faith as small as a mustard seed, you can say to this mountain, "Move from here to there," and it will move. Nothing will be impossible for you'" (Matthew 17:20, NIV).

Later that week, my dad and I went to the movies. As we sat watching the movie, I had the sudden urge to run! I had to get out of the theater, but I didn't want to draw attention to myself or upset my dad. I excused myself and went to the bathroom. I went into a stall, sat down and recited the Hail Mary prayer that I learned as a youth. "Hail, Mary, full of grace, the Lord is with thee. Blessed art thou amongst women and blessed is the fruit of thy womb, Jesus. Holy Mary, Mother of God, pray for us sinners, now and at the hour of our death. Amen." I repeated that prayer over and over and over and over until I was finally able to go back into the movie theater.

I intuitively learned that prayer helped my emotional state and eased my anxiety. I had begun my journey to health, but it was only through God's loving grace that I was able to deal with this problem and learn to live in a healthy state of mind.

What I learned through this anxiety experience was that when we place our *hope* in the wrong place – in politics, in people, places, things or in parents reuniting – we can be let down. However, when we place our hope in our Father, we will always be secure. *Hope* in the wrong place can be devastating. Please learn from my mistakes and hear my words. For our God is a good Father and is ready to help you. However, you must do your part, and God will do His part.

During the **summer of 1987**, my life had abruptly changed in many ways. I had begun to realize that my drinking and life were out of control, and I yearned for something else in my life. That something else came in the form of two friends, Ted and James. We were all friends from high school; and when we returned home that summer, they had something I was looking for. Ted and James had become "born-again Christians" while at school their freshman year. I had previously known no other way of worship except what I was told as a young Catholic child.

Through the grapevine, I had heard that Ted and James were acting odd and preaching at parties and were not themselves. However, this made sense to me. I, too, had an interesting freshman year – to say the least. After having the vision in the Canisius College quad, I began to look for answers, and perhaps Ted and James had what I was looking for?

Ted and James were both eager to hear my story about my journey, and they shared theirs. They told me that — through a Christian group on their Albany University campus — they had come to know Christ. I wanted what they had. I wanted to know Christ as well. They led me in a short, small prayer that went something like this: "Lord, I am sorry. I am sorry for the life I have been living. I want You to become the Lord and leader of my life. Teach me Your Way, my God." And for a summer, the three of us had Bible studies, and we changed our lives – at least for that summer.

I decided to stop drinking that summer and brought six packs of soda to parties instead of beer. I was changing and, with change, came change of friendships. Growing pains are hard and don't feel good. Once a best friend, my friend Herb and I drifted apart. His family was my "adopted family," who kept me sane in the chaos of my upbringing. To lose their closeness broke my heart even more than words can express; but the tug in my heart – of my Father God calling me – held out hope for me. The loss of relationships would be replaced with more love. I began to trust and to follow.

Thoughts of the priesthood continued to come to mind, and I wanted to explore that life. I had, after all, promised God that I would become a priest. That summer I also called our family priest, Father Yeazel, and told him of my interest in the priesthood. I shadowed him for a day and saw the lifestyle that he lived. To be honest, it is a very attractive way to live. Prayer, quiet time and helping people in their time of need. Then there is the liturgical aspect of saying mass.

The lifestyle of a priest is still very attractive to me – even to this day. To be a part of that world, that Way of life, was very attractive to me; but my family had mixed reviews. My brother and sisters thought I was a bit crazy. My brother hid my "priest books" – as they called them. My mom and dad were proud, but they wanted to make sure I was making the correct decision. I was back and forth in my decision-making, but I was not ready for the priesthood.

I would like to say that, when I returned to college, I lived the life of a saint and continued to live a "born-again" Christian lifestyle. Unfortunately, when I returned to Canisius for my sophomore year, I continued with drinking, partying, smoking pot; but I still went to church on Sundays.

To be honest at that time, I wished I had not had any vision. I wrote off that freshman-year vision experience as a crazy drug-induced state, and I thought my summer experience with Ted and James was just a passing stage of life.

However, one night while sitting in my friend Mike's dorm room smoking pot to excess, I had a very rude awakening again. As my head fell back against my friend's couch, I awakened to the feeling of being unable to breathe. I panicked and ran out of the room. *Not again! This can't be happening again!* I thought to myself. Once again, I knew I had to go to my friend Herb's from high school. He attended the University of Buffalo and lived off campus with some friends on Niagara Falls Boulevard. It was about 7 to 10 miles away, and I knew I could run there. No problem. Like the year before, I got dressed in my sweats; but this time I was going to run there. A friend of ours went into the Army instead of returning to campus, and I put on his sweatshirt that he gave me.

Inner-city Buffalo is not anywhere you want to be by yourself at 1 a.m. I ran down the middle of the road and moved to the side of the road when I saw cars approaching. This way of running down the road made me feel safe. I was petrified. I was a young, white college kid in a predominantly black part of town. I did not intentionally mean to be prejudiced. I just had very limited interactions with anyone of color. I had two friends in high school who were black, but they were just part of the crowd. I didn't think of them as black; they were just Dave and Doug.

People are stupid, and I unfortunately fell into that category. I thought that, because I was in a predominantly black part of town, I would be safe when a young white guy pulled up in a car next to me as I was jogging. He said, "Hey, where are you going?" I told him, "I'm jogging to my friend's house down the road." He said, "Do you want a ride? It's a bad part of town." I gladly accepted. As I got into the car, I was suddenly aware that I made a mistake. He sped down the road and reached over and grabbed my sweatshirt. "Army crew. Do you row?" I instinctively lurched backward in the seat. "No, this is a friend's sweatshirt." He said, "You're a pretty strong guy. You work out?" In my mind, I saw headlines in the newspaper: "College kid killed by unknown attacker." I played it cool. "Yep, I exercise and lift some weights." The guy then said, "Do you want to show me anything?" All I knew was that I wanted out of that car, and I continued to remain calm. I replied, "Oh no, that's cool though. I've got nothing against gay guys or anything; but no, I'm all set." I went on to say, "You can drop me off right here." He said, "No, I will drop you at your friend's house."

My thoughts raced. I thought to myself, *Did this guy have a gun, a knife? Play it cool. Be calm.* I didn't like the control that this guy thought he had, and I knew he was up to no good. It wasn't because he was gay that bothered me. Literally, that thought was irrelevant. I have never been the one to discriminate about one's sexuality. Unfortunately, I learned a hard lesson about discrimination of one's skin color. This guy was creepy with a capital C. He was a predator, and I was prey. I was bigger and stronger than him, but he had a confident assertiveness that led me to believe he was going to hurt me. I gave him directions to my friend's, and he dropped me off without further incident. I quickly ran into the house, told my friend and his roommates; and they ran out of the house ready to kill this guy. They told me that the description I gave was similar to a guy who had been around their campus, stalking college students.

I thank God that evening did not turn out worse than it did. I let my guard down – thanks to being high, being stoned. I decided to stop smoking pot. It was obviously a lifestyle that I knew would someday literally kill me if I continued down that road. My Father protected me that evening and taught me a valuable lesson about prejudice.

I have since become more aware of people's race and ethnicity. As a firefighter, I have had many friends who are black. What I have learned throughout my life is that people are people are people. Whether it is a person with a disability, whether it is a person of any color, whether it is someone who identifies as LGBTQ or other, male or female, people are people are people. We all want to love and be loved. Some people are more like cacti, but even cacti can yield fruit. We are all God's children; and as children of God, we all have the same Father. We all have that in common.

My sophomore and junior years of college were all more of the same. I played lacrosse. I drank too much. I had fun, and I got poor grades. However, I still had one foot in the church and one foot out. I began to serve as an altar boy on Sunday candlelight service. The service was always beautiful and brought me a sense of peace in the chaos of college life. I was self-destructing. I knew better but still behaved in ways that I knew were meaningless. Lacrosse had begun to lose its flavor, and I began to realize there was nothing in it for me any longer. During my junior year fall season, we were playing U.B. It was raining; it was cold; and there were about 10 people in the stands. I thought to myself, *What am I doing? I have a paper that is due tomorrow, and I'm freezing.* It took everything in me not to walk off the field. Lacrosse had been my life. I was captain, and we were moving from a club team to Division 3 – just like I had been recruited for in high school. But something was missing.

In the spring season 1988, I got a terrible concussion while playing in a game. We played Canton College at Coyne field in Syracuse, New York. We were dominating the game. There were a large number of fans in the stands, and many of the players were from this area. In fact, the referee was my freshman lacrosse coach from high school (F-M), Mr. Mercer.

I remember saving the ball and running down the field. I dodged a couple of opponents and was running toward their end of the field. I then remember waking up on my back on the field screaming. I remember being on the ground on my back; and my dad standing above me on the field yelling back at me, "Danny, stop swearing." I remember feeling sick to my stomach and extremely dizzy and then waking up in the hospital. My entire family had come to see me play, and my dad was there to reign me in while I was laying on the ground swearing.

The Canton State player who hit me was ejected from the game. We had won the game, but that was of no consolation to me. I sat in the hospital spinning and nauseated. I was taken to the hospital on a backboard and stretcher; and coincidentally later in my life, I would work for that ambulance agency.

Unfortunately, I have always had a strong, competitive side. My Canisius coach told me that I didn't have to play the next game. However, I never wanted to give another goalie a chance to win my spot. There was no concussion protocol back then, and I now wish there were.

We played a small team from Keuka College. We should have handed them a very large loss; but I played awful, and they beat us. They had one player with a tremendous shot. It was the hardest shot I have ever faced in my lacrosse career. I knew my lacrosse life was over. The attackman shot, and I ducked. I had never ducked in my life. Never in a fight and certainly never in lacrosse. I always stood and took whatever was thrown at me. I ducked, and the other team saw it. Embarrassing is not the word. More like cowardice and embarrassment wrapped into one thick weight dropped on my ego. I had lost whatever grit I had been given. That was the culmination of my college lacrosse career. That was the last season I played lacrosse for The Canisius Golden Griffins.

Entering college, I knew how my life was going to progress. I had a plan. I would major in business, graduate, work for my dad's company, marry, buy a convertible Saab because that was success to me. I had my life planned out, and I knew my direction of travel. I had it all figured out. My life was mapped out for me before college. I knew where I would be working after college. College was a four-year fun ride to get to where I was going – or so I thought. The owner of Bennett Resources, also known as Aloha Leasing, was E. T. Bennett; and he was grooming me to come into business with him and my dad. My dad was in upper management within this company behind E. T.'s two sons Patrick and Michael. It was difficult for me to watch the sons of the owner treat my dad without respect, but Mr. Bennett and Mrs. Bennett always treated my dad with respect. E. T. told me what business courses to take in college, and I was set up to do a summer internship during my sophomore year (1988) of college at their office in Syracuse.

However, God had different plans for me. I had an overwhelming sensation not to work for my dad and E. T. Bennett at Aloha Leasing. In addition to turning down the internship, I changed my major from business to psychology. I had a burning desire in my heart to figure out my mom's psychological health problem. Why was she hoarding; and more importantly, how could I help her?

After my decision to change majors and turn down the internship, my dad was to say — at the least — very disheartened with me. Changing my major and turning down the internship to work with his company were not easy decisions. I was saying, "No thank you" to my ambitious career. I was saying, "No thank you" to my dream of a convertible Saab and living the life of a successful businessman. My world around me was crumbling, but I began to see that the buildings I had constructed were just facades. The buildings of my world were a movie set; and behind the movie set were tall green trees, waterfalls, sunshine and a deep blue sky. I had been living a lie, and God was revealing to me — step by step — a much bigger picture.

I got "knocked down and woken up" by my Father God. After my experience in the Canisius quad, it was like a seed had been planted in my heart. I had begun to change. You know the sound a bike makes when it is shifting gears, but it can't find the right sprocket? The chain rattles and makes a loud noise. My heart, mind and soul were all in between gears; and the Holy Spirit was making a loud noise within my soul. I was beginning to wake up.

Anthony DeMello, Jesuit Christian author, writes about the process of waking up. It is similar to the movie "The Matrix" with Keanu Reeves. Everything we once believed to be true is turned on its head, and one has a sense that this world – and everything in it – has suddenly shifted. Anthony De Mello SJ writes, "Spirituality means waking up. Most people, even though they don't know it, are asleep. They're born asleep, they live asleep, they marry asleep, they breed in their sleep, they die in their sleep without ever waking up. They never understand the loveliness and the beauty of this thing we call human existence. You know all mystics, Catholic, Christian, non-Christian, no matter what their theology, no matter what their religion, are unanimous on one thing: that all is well. Though everything is a mess, all is well. Strange paradox, to be sure. But tragically, most people never get to see that all is well because they are asleep. They are having a nightmare" (*The Spiritual Wisdom of Anthony De Mello*[4] by Anthony DeMello SJ).

I had promised God that I would become a priest. Now what do I do? I contemplated becoming a Jesuit priest. However, I rarely, if ever, told any priest of my vision in the quad. I did not want them to judge me, to minimize my experience or think I was crazy. I met with various priests and told them of my interest in the Church, in God; and I wanted to know what direction I should go.

It was December 1989 — my senior year of college, and I had one more semester to go. I completed the fall semester, but something inside of me did not feel right. I had a nagging feeling of anxiety. *Was I going crazy?* I was still drinking to excess with my friends. I was in relationships with girls that were not wholesome, and I knew I should be behaving better. At that time in my life, unfortunately, I saw women as a conquest. It was a game to inflate my ego and see if I could attract women. However, I knew that the lifestyle I was leading was bankrupt. I was partying too much, engaging in premarital sex; and I was not committed to my studies. I was blowing this college opportunity. I had one foot in the church, serving as an altar boy, questioning life — and one foot in the "fraternity lifestyle," living the wild, crazy college side. I was confused. I could not get a restless feeling out of my mind. I made a decision to leave college before I was kicked out for bad grades or had a nervous breakdown.

In the spring semester of 1990, I was supposed to be graduating from college in May, but I had a burning desire to leave school. It did not make sense, and my entire family warned me not to leave college. Everyone in my family said something to the effect, "If you leave, you will never go back." I tried and tried to convince them I was making the right decision in my life. My family had always been my sounding board; and I loved them, felt close to them but did not feel their collective support. At that time, I thought, *Am I making the right decision?* I called the L'Arche Syracuse director of operations with whom I had become friends while volunteering over the previous summer. *L'Arche* is a French word that means the Arc – as in Noah's Ark. L'Arche is an international community of homes throughout the world that serves people with developmental disabilities.

I told him of my college struggle and that I was thinking of dropping out of school. I asked him, "Bob, I'm wondering if I could work at L'Arche for a semester or two?" He graciously accepted me but told me that the dog I had rescued from the pound could not come with me.

I packed up my 1976 Chevy truck with all my belongings, said goodbye to my friends in "The Lacrosse House" on campus and cried as I backed out of the driveway. Irie, the dog I rescued from the pound, my best friend, was in the window, tail wagging; and she wanted to be in the truck with me. We were inseparable, and I had raised her from a pup. She would now live with my friends in the lacrosse house; and one of my friends, Mark, stepped up to take her. She was a loyal dog, my best friend; and it hurt desperately saying goodbye.

I drove home alone on a very dark night in December down the New York state thruway. I thought as I drove, *What am I doing? I left my girlfriend, my dog, my friends; and I am almost done with college, almost graduating!* But I knew, if I had lived with one foot in and one foot out of the lifestyle God was calling me to, I would break. I had to figure life out. Did I want to be a priest? What about my girlfriend? Was my family right? Would I never go back to college? Every one of my family members told me I was doing the wrong thing. I tried to convince them that this was, in fact, the correct thing for me; but try as I may, they never supported my decision.

Irie, my best friend, was left behind with my friends at Canisius.

CHAPTER 4

"Do Not Worry"

I moved into the L'Arche home on James Street in Syracuse, New York. I had no idea what I was doing and was just running by the seat of my pants. *Was my family right? Would I go back to school someday?*

It was 10 p.m.; the L'Arche home was quiet; and H. B., a person with disabilities who would become a dear friend, roamed around the home, performing his nightly routine. The rest of the home had already gone to bed, and my college friends had not even started to get ready to go out to the bars yet.

The Buffalo bars were open till 4 a.m.; and here it was 10 p.m., and all was quiet. I laid down on the living room floor, and I looked up at the ceiling and counted the dots in the ceiling tile. I prayed quietly, "God, why am I here?" Specifically, why was I now in L'Arche? I went from living in a "lacrosse house" fraternity-type setting with five housemates and my dog to now living with seven people with developmental disabilities and two Roman Catholic nuns.

My life was flipped on its head. God did not directly answer my question that night, and life would soon take a turn for the worse. Chrisie, my girlfriend of two years, ended our relationship shortly after I left Canisius. I now felt stuck in a commitment of working at L'Arche and wanted to run back to my girlfriend – back to the life I left behind at Canisius. I decided to stay at L'Arche and complete the commitment I began. I would never again quit something I started, and I learned a valuable lesson as an athlete in high school.

No girlfriend, no dog, no lacrosse team; and I now had responsibilities of working in the L'Arche home. I knew, in my heart of hearts, that I had made the correct decision – as hard as it was. During the first month of my L'Arche experience, I cried myself to sleep every night. I was homesick. My heart was broken, and I missed my dog.

Back at Canisius, the new housemate, John, took my spot in the lacrosse house, took my girlfriend and took my dog. Well, my dog actually was adopted by another friend in the house, Mark; but in my mind, John had stolen all things I loved in this world. When he moved in on my girlfriend and literally took my place in my house, I was enraged. I imagined fighting John, and I had hatred in my heart. It hurt so very much! My life was upside down, but I could feel God's presence still calling me....

Then one night, about a month into my decision to leave Canisius and work at the L'Arche community, I laid in bed and once again cried myself to sleep. However, on this special night, I was visited by Jesus in a dream. He wore a brilliant white robe, and He sat in the middle of my room. I was so excited to see Him. I asked Him if I could get Him anything to drink, ran around trying to clean up and had a sense that I must do, do, do. I biblically acted like Martha. In my dream, I spoke as Jesus spoke, and I busied myself with this and that. What I remember from the dream is this: Jesus had a very simple yet profound message for me, "Do not worry." I wished I had sat still — like Martha's sister Mary — and listened to all He had to say. I wish I had just sat with my Lord and been content in His presence rather than trying to clean up and "figure everything out."

> "'Martha, Martha,' the Lord answered, 'you are worried and upset about many things, but few things are needed – or indeed only one. Mary has chosen what is better, and it will not be taken away from her'" (Luke 10:41-42, NIV).

After that dream, I never cried myself to sleep again and stopped my month-long tear journey. Jesus had – in a moment, in a dream – spoken to my heart and freed my soul. I now realized that all was indeed okay. I had a peace in my heart that surpassed all understanding.

Jesus told me not to worry, and the hatred I had for John turned into understanding. I wrote John a letter because back then we did not have texting or email. I wrote something to the effect, "John, I thought about bashing your head against the ground. However, of all the guys at Canisius that Chrisie could have picked, I am glad it was you. You're a good guy. Please take good care of her." That is paraphrased, but what is of more importance is my relationship with John and Chrisie when I returned to campus the next fall. The three of us became friends. We hung out together, protesting the war in Iraq, going on a mission trip to Kentucky with approximately 10 other social justice-minded students and living and hanging out in similar circles. I liked John, forgave him; but our mutual friends thought we were all crazy. I knew, in my heart, that the forgiveness I felt did not come from me but was a gift from God. I would have handled things much differently if left up to me, but I had an overwhelming sense of "it's okay" and not to worry. I felt a peace beyond all understanding. God had someone else in mind for me. Someone who He handpicked and whom I had been waiting for and thinking about since my childhood. She would be an answer to my prayer as a young child.

What I have learned on my journey is that God hears our prayers. Please know, God hurts when you hurt. "Jesus wept" (John 11:35). He has emotions, and He wants the best for you and your life. It is not too late. Whatever road you are presently on, examine yourself and change for the better. Do good. Be the best you can be. Start small. Stop lying, stop swearing, start thinking and praying. Exercise, eat right, help others. Take a holistic approach to becoming the best you. God has literally placed within each one of us the endless possibilities of goodness. You are God's temple, and the Spirit of God lives in each and every one of us. It is our duty to water and feed the Holy Spirit within us so that God's love may be made manifest in our lives. The Bible is a road map – if we let it. God tells us, His children, not to do certain things because He wants the best for us.

A good Daddy always wants the best for His children – always. Imagine the best dad you know. A dad who is honest, loves his wife, has a good job and lives life with integrity. Our Father is all that and more. He literally created creation.

Live life to the fullest. Live each day as if it is your last but with integrity. Be honest, be polite; live as if God is watching you because He is. Do not be fooled. You are not alone. You're never alone – even in your loneliness.

In my loneliness at L'Arche, I was beginning to realize — as a young man in my twenties — that decisions I had made regarding my future were the correct ones. The decisions I made — based upon a stirring in my heart — came from the Holy Spirit, who was trying to guide me.

Regarding the Aloha Leasing company that E. T. (Bud) Bennett and my dad were grooming me to enter while I was in college, unfortunately that same company was involved in one of the nation's largest ponzi schemes in U.S. history. My reluctance to enter their business and take the internship during my sophomore year of college and my decision to change my major from business to psychology now made perfect sense. In hindsight, the decisions I had made regarding my future were coming to fruition. I was more grateful to God than ever before for numbering my steps. I look back and also thank the young man inside of me who listened to his intuition and listened to the calling of the Holy Spirit. When all the dust and chaos settled from the Aloha Leasing/Bennett Funding group scandal, my dad was cleared of any wrongdoing. He had left the company prior to any wrongdoing, for I know my dad to be a man of strong ethical principles.

In my short time at L'Arche Syracuse, I had grown to love many of the core members (people with developmental disabilities) and considered many of them close friends. Some of my peers and coworkers — assistants as we say — had become close friends as well. *Assistant* is a term we utilize to indicate our position within the community. We assist those in need. Ironically, many come to L'Arche to assist people with developmental disabilities; and in turn, they come to realize it is they who were really assisted by the core members.

L'Arche and the people there enriched my life beyond what I thought possible. I learned many, many valuable life lessons during my years at L'Arche. God, in His infinite wisdom, healed many of my wounds from living in a family with divorcing parents and with a mother who was a hoarder.

L'Arche was a simplistic, wholesome family life experience. We ate dinner together and said grace before meals. We cleaned up together after every meal. Life at L'Arche was structured, loving, fun and prayerful.

L'Arche taught me functional fundamentals like cooking, cleaning and living within a healthy family lifestyle. I was there to help and assist people with developmental disabilities, but I actually received a vast amount of education.

What L'Arche taught me about my heart and about love is that we all want to love and be loved. I initially came to L'Arche as a volunteer in 1989, and I literally was worried about my interaction with someone with a disability. I felt a large pull from God to start service work at this organization, but I had no experience with someone with a disability.

I will never forget my first experience at the L'Arche community. I went to visit my girlfriend Chrisie, who was volunteering at L'Arche before I made a decision to volunteer for the summer.

While driving my pickup truck to the L'Arche home for my first-ever visit and my first experience with someone with a developmental disability, I thought to myself, *What do I do if they attack me? What if they get upset when I walk in?* To my utter shock and amazement, I was greeted with love, hugs and almost instant friendship.

I met a man named David, who was a core member, about 40 years old, about five feet tall, about 130 pounds, had glasses and had been labeled with mental retardation. However, what I learned was that David was beyond labels! David was someone I admired, and I inwardly wished I was more like him. David had a wonderful way about him. People naturally loved

David. With David, there were no pretenses, and only love and enthusiasm exuded from his being.

I initially judged David's outward appearance; but what I learned — as I grew to love David — was that he had a profound faith in God. David loved people the way I only wish I could love. David had a way to unite people together in friendship of which psychologists should take note. It was his simplistic, yet rich, way of loving to which people gravitated. I capitalize the word Way because Jesus came to teach us a Way to live. David role modeled The Way in which to live in this world: he loved, cared for people and had a deep love for God with strong faith.

"However, I admit that I worship the God of our ancestors as a follower of the Way, which they call a sect" (Acts 24:14a, NIV). Paul said these words while on trial. Before the term *Christian* was a word, they referred to following Jesus as "The Way" — The Way to live life. Christians were called Christians at Antioch. "… So for a whole year Barnabus and Saul met with the church and taught great numbers of people. The disciples were called Christians first at Antioch" (Acts 11:26, NIV). David called me his "M&M buddy." Whenever we went to the movies, I would always buy David M&Ms,

and we would share them. I became affectionately known as "My M&M buddy." David would smile from ear to ear and often raise his arm in praise to God or when he was saying hello to friends and family. What a great way to be greeted! I felt loved. He had a great Way about him.

I refer to David in the past tense because he went to be with our Father about five years after I met him. At the hospital, his friends, family and his community were gathered together

David giving me a big hug.
I was his M&M buddy

70

to be with David as the doctors attended to his illness. The hospital staff were transferring him upstairs to his room on a stretcher. The last thing David said to me was: "I will see you up there, Dan." I believe David was referring to upstairs in the hospital but maybe not. Maybe David knew he was passing on soon, and we would see each other "up there" in heaven someday? David died shortly after they transferred him upstairs. I look back and think of his last words to me in the elevator at St. Joe's Hospital in Syracuse, New York, "I will see you up there, Dan." We grieved as a community, and I felt pain as I had once felt before at the passing of my high school friend, Pam. Today, almost 25 years later, I write, "Yes, David, I will see you up there someday. But for now, I must finish this book."

As a naive, young college kid, I came to L'Arche unaware, but God guided me step by step. One cold and snow-filled night, I walked to McDonald's with my new friend Ted. A core member at L'Arche, Ted is very outgoing and has an extensive social calendar. His speech can be challenging to understand at first, but that is Ted. This was my first outing since newly arriving from Canisius College to live and work in the community. As we were walking single file on the snowy sidewalk toward Ted's beloved McDonald's, for he was the "mayor" there, Ted stopped talking mid-sentence. I turned around and saw him staring into the distance and grabbed him as he slumped into a snowbank. Cars drove by as I tried to contain Ted as his extremities flailed. To witness this seizure for the first time — not knowing his history — was unnerving for a young, naive college kid.

After a few minutes of seizure activity, I was able to get Ted moving, and we walked slowly back to our house. Sister Jane — the head of our house, the manager — greeted us at the door and helped us into the kitchen. Sister Jane explained to me that this is normal for Ted. He had an extensive seizure history, and he unfortunately was prone to these periodic episodes. My friend Ted is difficult to understand verbally. But as I spent time with him, I began to understand his language. Ted stands hunched,

71

and he has one arm that is contracted and smaller than the other. Ted limps, and he immediately can be recognized as someone with a disability. At first, Reader, you might see core members and see disability; but after you get to know Ted, David, H. B., Pat, Eugene, Jeff, Genevieve or Eric, you would come to realize we are all the same. People are people are people.

What I learned in my time at L'Arche — over my five-year experience — is that we all have disabilities.... Some disabilities are just more apparent or have a prominent diagnosis. More intellectual individuals may be able to hide their disability more easily, or they may not be aware of it yet. No one is perfect. Except, that is, for a dear friend of mine, Jesus.

I came to L'Arche afraid and without a lot of life experience; but I soon learned the routines of L'Arche: meal preparation, cleanup, getting lunches ready for the next day, dispensing of medications, assisting with ADLs (activities of daily living), prayer, lots of fun, recreation and travel. I had found the rhythm of L'Arche, and God was healing my soul — one day at a time — through this invaluable life experience.

In the fall of 1990, I returned to Canisius College. After working nine months at L'Arche, I had begun to change. I had done a 180 in my life. From jock, party animal, dollar-driven business major to psychology major, contemplating the priesthood, protesting war, changing of friendships; and I dropped off the lacrosse team.

Throughout my college career, I became an altar server/altar boy and went on a school "mission trip." Upon returning to campus — after my hiatus at L'Arche, I lived in what was called The Arrupe House. It was named after a Jesuit priest named Fr. Pedro Arrupe. Pedro Arrupe was a Jesuit priest, and he was in the Hiroshima area during World War II. He ministered spiritually and physically to the people ravaged by the nuclear bomb.

When I returned to school, my ex-girlfriend, her new boyfriend John and I organized a peace protest rally in the middle of our Canisius College quad. This was the same quad, where I had a vision of God in the Buffalo night sky during my freshman year.

We protested The Gulf War in Iraq. We lit bonfires in the brick fireplace in the middle of the quad between Bosch and Frisch dorms, and we handed out hot chocolate. We coordinated with the campus ministry staff, the Canisius administration and the college food services. We obtained the necessary campus permissions and invited the television news stations. What more did we need to do? All the details were set.

My friends and I planned all the logistics of the evening. We had several cords of firewood delivered to campus; we had free hot chocolate from the Canisius food services in five-gallon containers and we made signs for the rally. We woke up early, placed signs throughout campus and wrote messages on college classroom chalkboards regarding the rally on campus. We did it, and we were ready. Everything was planned and coordinated – every "i" dotted and "t" crossed.

My professor, Fr. Moleski, showed up to the protest and asked what I had planned? "What's on the agenda, Dan? What do you have planned?" I replied, "Planned? There is a roaring fire, hot chocolate and hundreds of students; and the Buffalo news is here." What more did I need to do? Fr. Moleski was another guardrail in my life. He knew me as a student; and as my teacher, he knew that my follow-through was not my strongest attribute. He asked me, "Now that you have everyone here. What's next?" I gulped. I thought we were ready? The crowd grew impatient. Fr. Moleski pulled some notes from his pocket and began to address the crowd.

Fr. Moleski was prepared, and he was a gift from God. We sang songs and prayed for the troops and those touched by the ravages of war. The news interviewed me, which is perhaps archived in the Buffalo news rooms? The cameraman put a newspaper picture of George Bush on the bonfire, and they filmed it. I told them, "That's not what we are here about tonight." To their credit, they did not "run" the burning of the newspaper, and they got our message accurate – a blessing for those affected by war. There was uncertainty on campus, and tempers flared throughout our country against any who opposed the war. I thank God for Fr. Moleski that night at our peace protest rally. The night could have turned to chaos if he had not shown up with his notes, with his agenda and "a peace that surpassed all understanding."

I took two religious education classes with Father Moleski. One day he came into the classroom, carrying a box of books. He told us that the box was full of books from a friend of his. His friend was also a Jesuit, and one of his favorite books was *The Screwtape Letters*[8] by C. S. Lewis. Fr. Moleski said, "My friend used to give these books away because he wanted to share the message within."

With a heavy heart, Fr. Moleski said, "My friend died while bicycling recently. As my friend was bicycling in NYC enroute to Fordham University, he pounded his fist against the side of a van as it brushed past him. The van stopped; the driver got out and murdered my friend." Fr. Moleski told us this story and then handed out the books in a lottery fashion. I was privileged to get one of the copies, and I found the book to be a tremendous Way of looking at the world. I highly recommend reading it. The sudden death of Fr. Moleski's friend speaks to my life as well. Sometimes I let my temper get the best of me. I pray that I may mind my tongue and my actions at all times – especially when I am upset. I pray this prayer in Jesus' Name.

The
ARRUPE
HOUSE

AT

CANISIUS

The Jesuit College of WNY

My new housemates and I lived in this house on the Canisius campus named after Pedro Arrupe. We lived in community and celebrated Catholic mass one night a week. We were like-minded individuals who appreciated social justice issues. On our spring break trip, we went to Kentucky on a mission trip.

The mission trip was a fun experience. Approximately 10 Canisius students and a Jesuit novice (priest in training) went to a remote location in Kentucky to help families in need. We stayed for a week on a Roman Catholic Jesuit-run farm. We spent one week in a farmhouse that assists local rural families in the area. While we were there, we cleaned out and painted the cistern for a rural family. Imagine a gallon jug of milk buried in the ground; but instead of milk, it contained the water supply for the family. And instead of one gallon, imagine it could hold a large family van. Maybe 50,000 gallons? I'm not exactly sure of the size of the cistern, but it was large enough for four to five adults to be in there at once. Crawling down the ladder into that space certainly triggered some anxiety; but through the grace of God, I was able to do it.

The projects that week kept us relatively busy; but in our free time, we went swimming in the farm creek. There were no showers, and we had to clean up outside in a wash station. So the thought of swimming had a real good appeal.

There was a rope swing, and several of us went into the chilly 50- to 60-degree water. The current was relatively slow, and the water was deep brown in color. The guys went in first, and we all agreed not to tell the girls it was cold. We came out of the water and were like, "That's refreshing. Boy, does that feel good," trying not to laugh or yell about the frigid water. Some of the women from the trip asked about the temperature. "Is it warm?" We said, "Oh yeah, it's awesome." We had our first "victim." She swung out off the rope swing and into the water. From our vantage point from the shore, we could see only her head as she came up out of the water crying. She cried and said, "You guys lied." She tried to swim, but the cold water was taking its toll. I walked in and scooped her up and carried her up onto shore. I had taken a lifeguard course in high school, and I knew not to wait till we had a drowning. Perhaps she would have gotten out fine. Perhaps she would have swum to shore, but something nudged me to go in. I like to think it was the Holy Spirit. I am glad I listened that day!

Similarly in some ways, this book is like that cold-water experience in Kentucky. I feel nudged to write. I am being prompted to go into the cold water, tell my story and not second guess myself. For after I let go of the rope, after I write, everyone who reads my book will know my story. This, for me, is frigid water. However, I trust God and know He is my lifeguard.

On the mission trip, we also had prayer time. A priest from the farm led us in mass and times of quiet reflection. At one point, we were told to go off into the woods and contemplate our time with God and nature. The farm was surrounded by thousands of acres of rolling hills, valleys and forest. I decided to climb a large hill and look down to the valley below. I climbed up the steep embankment about one mile up to the ridge. The view was spectacular, but I imagined that the view from the towering pine would be even better. So I climbed up another 75 feet to the top of one of the largest pine trees I have ever seen. The wind was howling, and the branches were swaying. I was holding on tight, but I was not scared. The beauty of that moment filled my soul. I felt at peace and alone with God. I saw as far as my eye could see – from valley to forest peaks were covered with evergreen and trees in bloom. God's awe and wonder stirred my soul; my cup overflowed, and I knew I was on the right path now.

"The LORD is my shepherd, I lack nothing. He makes me lie down in green pastures, he leads me beside quiet waters, he refreshes my soul. He guides me along the right paths for his name's sake. Even though I walk through the darkest valley, I will fear no evil, for you are with me; your rod and your staff, they comfort me. You prepare a table before me in the presence of my enemies. You anoint my head with oil; my cup overflows. Surely your goodness and love will follow me all the days of my life, and I will dwell in the house of the LORD forever" (Psalm 23, NIV).

On our last day of our mission trip, one of the farm hands advised us that he was going to shoot the stray dog that we, the group of students, had befriended. In his deep, thick Kentucky accent, the farm hand said, "That dog will keep coming around here now that you kids fed it." He told us he was going to shoot this beautiful black-and-white young pup. She was about one year old. Perhaps we were being manipulated by this farm hand to take the dog with us, but we didn't want to chance it? We decided to take the dog back home with us to Buffalo. I cared for her like she was my own. I named her Manger because she had the mange, a skin disease; and I liked the biblical reference.

Manger was a loyal, loving friend. I walked her around campus without a leash. She was friendly, but she stayed by my side. I took her to the vet and nursed her back to health. Her coat came in beautifully, and she put on some weight. I loved that dog, but I knew I needed to find a home for her. I was going back to L'Arche after I graduated; and I knew that, once again, I could not bring a dog. One of the girls on the trip ended up adopting her; and Manger now had a loving, new home.

Within a short college career, I had changed friendships from lacrosse players and the party crowd. I now placed myself on a new trajectory with new friends, who were social justice-minded students.

I graduated in May 1991 and walked with my classmates and friends to receive my diploma. My family came to this graduation – unlike my high school graduation. We would have dinner after at a nice restaurant, but I told my family I had given away most of my clothes. I literally had four shirts, a sweatshirt, two pairs of pants and no dress clothes.

My stepmother, Christine, called me on the phone when I was living at L'Arche to tell me she loved me. She told me she loved what I was doing with my life and where I was working. She brought me new clothes to wear before graduation, and I felt the sincerity of her words from her previous phone call at L'Arche months prior.

I met my family in the parking lot before the ceremony and changed my clothes in a guard shack. I had not had new clothes in years, and I felt good wearing them. I placed my graduation gown and cap on with humility and wonder. *How did I make it through, and how did I get here?* Where I had come from in childhood and what I was doing at that point in my life I never could have never imagined. God was leading me, calling me; and I was following.

A little aside — I want to take a moment and thank The Canisius College faculty and staff, and the Jesuits (The Society of Jesus) who spoke into my life as a young man. Thank you — I pray that the narration of my experience as a student is received as it is intentionally written — in love and in awe — of the goodness of God.

Lastly, I want to thank Canisius College for allowing me to "walk with friends" to receive my diploma in May of 1991, but I want to ensure accuracy in as much as possible for this entire book. My diploma reads 1992. I took a summer class in 1991 to fulfill the last of my credit hours. Unfortunately, I was told that diplomas were only printed once a year. Therefore, the date on my diploma is 1992.

Manger rescue pup from Kentucky.

CHAPTER 5

Facing fear head on

The Northern Cross

I returned to L'Arche after graduating from Canisius College; and I was promoted to Head of House at Butternut Street house in Syracuse, New York. I worked in the L'Arche community for another four years – almost five years in total, and I continued to learn many valuable life lessons. I loved my time at L'Arche; but I knew it was time to move on; but where? I held my anxiety at bay, but it was always present. Unfortunately, it would soon rear its ugly head as I transitioned careers.

Through 15 years of counseling and therapy, I finally was able to be free from the chaos that was my childhood. In addition to counseling, what I truly know as healing were opportunities God gave me by way of bicycling across the United States (twice) and commercial salmon fishing in Alaska. Facing my anxiety and panic attacks head on allowed me to be free. Psychologists would term this as a type of immersion therapy.

I intuitively knew what I needed to free me from anxiety and panic attacks. In conjunction with prayer and counseling, I began an immersion type of therapy that lasted almost four years. "Cast all your anxiety on him because he cares for you" (1 Peter 5:7, NIV).

In 1993, I left L'Arche, and I bicycled across the northern part of the United States. I immersed myself in exercise and travel, and I began the work of deprogramming my brain.

Before flying out to Seattle to start my journey, I visited Gramma Connors. She was seated in her apartment, saying the Rosary when I went in to see her. She gave me her Rosary beads that day, and I carried them across the United States twice in my bicycle bag and had them in my locker in the fire department for the past 20 years. They are much more than "luck." They are a reminder of my grandmother, and they are symbolic of her faith. I believe they are a meditative way to commune with God. If done correctly, they can be a weapon against the evil one.

I raised approximately $14,000 for the L'Arche community for which I had been volunteering, working and living. It was time to move on and begin a new season in my life. I had grown to love many of the core members as family (people with developmental disabilities), and I consider them all friends.

On my own, I would not know how to fundraise outside of a small network of family and friends. The director of the Syracuse L'Arche community, Bob and I decided to form a fundraising committee. It consisted of board members from L'Arche, my dad (Jim), a priest named Ted Sizing, a family member of two of the core members and myself. Together, we brainstormed how to most effectively help the community. We decided that we must market this bike trek and pitched the idea to Phil Markert, a local news radio celebrity.

Phil liked the idea a lot, and we decided to have a radio call-in session every day of my bike trek. Every day, all the way across the country, I called and spoke with Phil on the air. In 1993, the technology was not as it is obviously like today in 2021. We were granted a "military grade" cell phone that weighed approximately 15 pounds, and I carried it in my bike bag. I would have to charge the phone each night when we had power in our campsites. When I returned home from my bike trek, family and friends from high school said, "I heard you on the radio. It sounded like a lot of fun." Unfortunately, the "military grade" cell phone did not prove all that reliable in the Rockies, the plains of the Midwest and many other remote locations. I would have to utilize pay phones as I called in to the Phil Markert Show each morning. We met for months prior to the ride as a fundraising committee. I was interviewed on television, and I had a couple of newspaper articles written about me. The media exposure was fun, and I reminded the viewers or readers that the purpose of the bike trek was to help L'Arche. As a committee, we decided that 90% of the proceeds would go toward L'Arche Syracuse and 10% of the proceeds would go toward Latin L'Arche communities. (After expenses – all said and done, we raised approximately $14,000 for L'Arche; and I was glad to do this for my friends.)

I flew out to Seattle, Washington by myself and would stay for a week in the Seattle L'Arche community. I had to force myself to board the plane to Seattle. The flight itself was unremarkable; but each second of every minute of every hour, I was aware that I could have a panic attack. I didn't know when it would strike, and I didn't know how to ward it off. I was learning to combat the anxiety once it began, but I was still very new at these life skills.

When I arrived in Seattle, the L'Arche community could not have been nicer! It was great to be with another group of like-minded individuals when I was so far from home. One of the assistants invited me to go with her to visit the Tacoma L'Arche community for a day, but I couldn't. I was debilitated with anxiety, but I couldn't tell her.

I did my best to get around Seattle, which is beautiful. I toured the city with a good friend from Canisius College, who came to visit me. She was living in Canada, and she was working in a social justice-run organization. We toured the Space Needle, fishing piers and various markets. I sent postcards to friends and family back home, and I attempted to remain calm before my adventure across the country. However, anxiety and panic were always right there with me, hounding me and ready to show their full colors any second. I kept thinking, *How the heck am I going to bike across the country?* I was petrified.

I was grateful that I would not be doing the ride alone. I also was grateful that a professional bike touring company planned the details of the event. The logistics of the trek were all taken care of by a tour group called Tim Kneeland and Associates (TK&A). For a nominal fee (approximately $4,000), this organization provided daily route guides (directions) for each day of our trip, daily breakfast and lunch, lodging, bicycle mechanic, a SAG wagon, support and gear. The SAG wagon was a vehicle that would stop and pick up bike riders. If a rider could ride no longer that day, they would raise their arm into the air. The van would stop, pick up the rider and carry the rider's bicycle on the roof carrier. I am happy to write that I did not use a SAG wagon once while crossing the country.

After multiple days on the road, one's body gets beat up! Achilles tendons swell; your back side gets numb and blistered; and your knees feel decrepit. After a while, your hands can begin to become numb as well from constant pressure of the handle bars. Add to these physical ailments, general sickness, bike accidents; and you can see why having a safety vehicle, or SAG wagon, is critical. Unfortunately, one of the downfalls with going with a large group is your day is predetermined. We knew that today we would be riding 60 miles; tomorrow we would ride 86 miles; the day after that, 100 miles. Every day of our 48-day bike trek was planned out from lodging to food to daily bicycling distances. Therefore, one of the advantages of a self-contained bike trek is that you can be a little bit more flexible.

When we met as a group of riders in Seattle before the trek, Tim Kneeland of TK&A, introduced himself; and he led us in our introductions as a group. There were approximately 40 riders and five staff, and we would spend the next 48 days together. In 48 days, you can tell a lot about someone; and I found there are a lot of great people from all over the world. We had riders from all over the country, including a female bicyclist from Germany and a staff person from Australia.

Tim Kneeland and Associates (TK&A) did a tremendous job with logistics, and Tim did double duty by also bicycling with us. Tim and his team took great care of us, and I would highly recommend this organization if you ever venture to Hawaii. Tim has set up residence in that state and runs a bicycle tour company there. I also utilized his service when I bicycled across the Southern U.S.

Our lodging consisted of campsites, church halls, school gymnasiums and motels. Some of the campsites were picturesque – like in West Glacier. However, most campsites were simplistic in an open field or a baseball park with a 10'x12' men and women's bathroom and shower. When we did get a motel, it was two to three bicyclists per room. However, after a long, hard day of cycling, I learned to sleep anywhere.

Reader, I was scared to ride across the country. What if's flooded my mind. In my heart, I knew that my inner journey of debilitating anxiety was unhealthy. I suffered in silence and did not tell anyone. What I didn't realize at this time in my life is that God was riding along with me the entire 3,392 miles and was leading me somewhere. At this point in my life as a 25-year-old man, I was trying to be healthy physically, emotionally and spiritually. Unfortunately, I was failing miserably emotionally.

"In their hearts humans plan their course, but the LORD establishes their steps" (Proverbs 16:9, NIV).

Every part of every day since boarding the plane in Syracuse and flying to Seattle, I was on the verge of a panic attack. Every hour except for when I was bicycling and physically exerting myself, I felt like I couldn't breathe well.

On one of our first rides from Seattle in a very remote area in Washington State, a car pulled up alongside us as we biked; and the driver screamed, "You're all going to die out there!" I cannot make this stuff up! It scared me, but I didn't let my inner Dan out. Instead I yelled back some obscenity. Inside I was scared beyond belief and thought to myself that this guy, whoever he was, may be right.

The anxiety was excruciatingly (emotionally) painful, so I stopped into a health clinic by myself. It was a very small emergency room in a fairly remote part of Washington. I told the doctor in the clinic that I was having trouble breathing. He listened to my lungs, took my vitals and determined

I was fine. My lungs were clear. I couldn't bear to tell him that I was anxiety ridden. I wanted to say, "I'm freaking out inside, man!" I carried an inhaler around with me like a security blanket. The thought of biking across the country was unsettling and was getting into my mind. Back home in Syracuse, I may have had a small amount of anxiety daily 2/10; but I was now experiencing 8/10 constant anxiety.

The further we bicycled from Seattle, the further from help we would be. We would soon be bicycling across the Rocky Mountains and then be in the remote plains of Montana. This country is vast; and until you venture into this land, it's hard to express the vastness of our country. I didn't know anyone, and this was all unfamiliar to me. I had recently been diagnosed with asthma, and I was concerned about my breathing. I was homesick. I missed my family, and I missed L'Arche. The security of my routine and job back at home in Syracuse were no longer present. I had resigned from L'Arche. I was now in between jobs, and I would be going to nursing school when I returned – if I returned from the bike trek. I needed a routine to keep me stable and at an even keel at that point in my life. I functioned well in life – if I had a routine.

I wanted to throw in the towel. I was ready to fly home. I imagined telling Tim (TK&A), "I'm not feeling well, and I think I need to go home." Reader, I have been there; and I have done that enough in my life. I smashed my hand with a bat to try and get out of wrestling in high school. I would not go down that path of desperation again. I learned enough basic psychology at Canisius to know I must face my fear. I would face my fear head on, or I would die trying. There was also my inner drive, knowing this was a fundraiser and I was doing this trek for my friends at L'Arche. This bike trip was a fundraiser for them, and I needed to get out of my own way. I would not let them down! Before I left Syracuse, I asked each of my friends to give me a t-shirt to wear as a reminder of them as I biked, and that helped ease my anxiety a bit.

"When anxiety was great within me, your consolation brought me joy" (Psalm 94:19, NIV).

I came to this bike experience so naively. I didn't even know how to change a tire. My first flat tire was in Washington State. We had just started our trek, and it was approximately day three or four. I had all the right tools, but I had no idea how to get the tire off the rim. I saw a group of riders go into a restaurant for some food; and 40 minutes later when they came out, I was still on the side of the road, trying to change the tire. One of the cyclists grabbed my bike rim and said, "Give me that." He proceeded to change my tire for me in less than three minutes. He was a Godsend. I think I might still be there if not for him. I can honestly say that — toward the end of the trip — my friend Steve and I were like an Indy pit crew. We could change a tire in less than two minutes flat (pun intended). I think, all in all, I had about 10 flats or so. If you, Reader, are planning on bicycling for any great length, I will give this sage, unsolicited advice: Be prepared to change tires; and know that if you bike on two wheels, you will eventually fall; so wear a helmet!

This is a mural in Poplar High School- the bicyclists stayed in their gymnasium - 1993.

I experienced the miraculous wonders that our Father created. One day as we biked up the Rocky Mountains, early in the trip – approximately 613 miles in, we had to cross a summit called Going-to-the-Sun Road. We were told by (TK&A) Tim at our meeting at breakfast that we had a small window of opportunity to bike up the road; and if we were not to the summit in time, we would have to get into the Park Ranger vehicle or SAG wagon. I was one of the last riders out of camp that day, and I had to sprint up that road. This extra push helped me because of the extreme panic I was having while biking that day. Most days, I did not have anxiety while riding; but this day was different. Reader, if you are one who is afraid of heights, then you can appreciate what I was feeling. It was a beautiful ride mixed with sheer terror. The road was fairly steep – maybe 8-10% grade as it switched back and forth up the mountainside. As I biked, I could see in the distance the beautiful snowcapped Rockies all around. We spotted mountain goats on a steep cliff, and it perplexed me how any animal has the ability to stand on such steep terrain. All around me was God's beauty, but man had sliced into this mountain. A straight drop of 1,000 feet was on my right side with a stone guardrail that – if I hit it – would send me over the side. I had battling emotions going on – terror, awe and wonder. I made it to the summit without incident and without falling to my death. (Reader, there is a beautiful, short four-minute video on YouTube regarding Going-to-the-Sun-Road that shows this picturesque scenery. It is worth Google searching.)

68 miles to Poplar, Montana from Fort Peck. We will have traveled 1,109 miles on bicycle from Seattle, Washington. At this point in the trek, friendships had formed and were solidified like friends of old. The biking that day was a short ride, and it left us ample time in camp to explore the area when we got into town. The town was in a remote area of Montana – the site of The Corn Festival and present-day Poplar, Montana Native American Days. TK&A had advised us there was a "Corn Festival" in town with Native American dancers, so we decided to explore the area. We walked down the street from Poplar High School, where we were staying for the evening.

What we found has been a story I like to tell friends and family for the past 28 years. It was a culture shock to say the least and one in which I feel very appreciative to have partaken. There were four of us bicyclists who ventured down to see the Native American Days Festival.

There was a football field-size area – part of which was sectioned off for ceremonial worship. I was in disbelief as I saw men with pierced skin, hanging from trees by their chest. We were informed that it was a ceremonial process; and the Native Americans, who were partaking in this event, had been fasting for a week. They had been ceremonially cleansed by fasting prior to entering this sacred area. As we were standing outside the secured area, a man, in his approximately mid-twenties, approached us. He said, "I do not know why, but the Elders have invited you men to have a sweat."

To enter into this part of the festival, we were supposed to be cleansed and prepared beforehand but were granted access by the Elders of this group. We were ecstatic and graciously entered into the event. I was intrigued with these men, who commanded a strong but quiet presence, seated a distance away. I looked at them and nodded in their direction as a thank you as we were led to the sweat hut.

The sweat hut was about 5 feet in height with a diameter of approximately 40 feet. The outer layer of the hut consisted of animal skin, and the main supportive structure was made of long tree limbs. We stripped to our underwear and crawled in on our hands and knees. My friends and I were excited, and I didn't feel the least bit anxious. This experience felt peaceful, and we were being shown extreme hospitality. As I crawled into the hut, the heat and the smell of smoke were apparent but not overwhelming. In the center of the hut was an opening that let the smoke escape. We crawled in on hands and knees as directed and followed the person in front of us in a circular motion around the fire. We then sat circular around the fire with legs crossed. To my right was a Native American man in his forties. He was strong and much bigger than me. His chest was pierced with antler bone, and he did not speak. The flap to the hut was shut, and the fire and red embers lit up the area around us. The music began and stirred my soul. The sound of the drum was loud and in perfect rhythm. I will phonetically try to express the beat and chant that have lasted in my mind and soul for these many years. In a loud and rhythmic fashion:

Drum beat-

Bum! . bum . bum . bum … Bum! . bum . bum . bum …Bum! . bum . bum . bum … Bum! . bum . bum . bum …Chant-

Ayyyy … Yi … Yah! ... Yi ... yi … Yah! ... yi ... yi ... Yah! ... yi ... yi ... Yah! … Ayyyy … Yi … Yah! ... Yi ... yi ... Yah! ... over and over and over again.

The drumbeat – in conjunction with the chanting, smoke and incense – lifted my heart, mind and soul. I felt God's presence among us. A deep peace stirred within me. The flap was opened; and superheated red, glowing rocks were brought in on long wooden poles into the center of the hut and placed in the fire. Their warmth was immediate, and perspiration flooded over me. We were told – as the ceremonial rocks were brought in – that these sacred stones had been in their tribe for many, many centuries.

Heat, sweat, drumming and chanting began to work within my body. I began to think of my friend David who had recently passed away. David was a core member at L'Arche and a very dear friend, who I missed very much. I had a realization, while sitting there, that David was more than "okay" and was in heaven. All is well.... For many months, I had been grieving the loss of my friend and did not function at full capacity – as I should have – as head of house, which means the manager of the home. I felt broken somewhere deep within me. The experience in the hut allowed me to understand that David was "okay" and that I, too, was going to be okay. It was also a realization that my friendship with David was a gift from God. For David was my "M&M buddy"… (see previous chapter on L'Arche).

As the chanting and drumming beat on, I was in a sacred space in my mind with David. This sweat hut experience was mystical, and it is hard to describe in words the beauty and majesty of that moment. I felt gratitude to the Elders who invited us into their sacred ceremony and appreciation for the members who partook in a sweat with us that now fills my heart, mind, soul and memory. We crawled out of the hut together and realized we had each partaken in something very special.

Through all of the anxiety that I was experiencing daily, I also found beauty and peace in much of the experience. I knew I was not alone. Yes, I bicycled with 40 others; but I also began to sense that God was with me, encouraging me to go through this valley experience.

"Even though I walk through the darkest valley, I will fear no evil, for you are with me; your rod and your staff, they comfort me" (Psalm 23:4, NIV).

With each pedal stroke, I got closer to Asbury Park, New Jersey, and closer to my goal of facing my anxiety head on. I knew I had a bleak future ahead of me if I couldn't learn how to handle this present struggle.

When baby birds are learning to fly, they do not just stretch their wings and soar. There are unfortunately many bumps and bruises before they can soar like eagles. I was beginning to fly, but I had many falls....

July 4, 1993, heading from Minneapolis, Minnesota to Wabasha, Minnesota. We were 1,878 miles into the trek. I was growing in strength, confidence; and I felt a little less anxious. At that point in the trek, all the riders were tripling their caloric intake. We would sit down for a large breakfast and have another breakfast on top of the first. I have never eaten like that in my life. The amount of calorie expenditure was enormous. We would bike — on average — 70 to 80 miles a day. We were on our bikes between six to eight hours every day. I did not lose any weight, but I packed on some serious muscle in my legs.

After breakfast on that 4th of July, it had just rained, and the roads were still saturated with water. The smell in the air after a rainstorm is one of my favorites. However, I soon would learn to use more caution when I smelled this scent in the air. A group of riders and I came hurling down the road. The hill was steeper and more slick than I imagined, and I ended up in the ditch on my back. It happened faster than for what I was prepared. One second, I was biking; and the next, I was literally on my back in the mud. The crew stopped to see if I was alright, and we had a good laugh. I have a picture of myself with a small American flag sticking out of my helmet covered in mud in the weeds. I humbly got back on my bike and said an internal prayer of thanksgiving for not being injured. The fall was a reawakening of the dangers that were all around us every second of every day that we were riding: train tracks (are extremely slippery wet or not), vehicles, distracted drivers, dogs off leash, pedestrians, uneven roads, potholes, metal grate bridges (oh my, what a hazard) and wet roads, of course. The oil from the road makes the surface like ice when it rains. These are just a few of the daily hazards we had to navigate in an attempt to be safe while we biked.

Francesville, Indiana day 36 approximately 2,500 miles. Each day of our ride, we would check in halfway through our bike trek with TK&A. They would have a checkpoint, and the riders would sign in. It was an attempt to keep track of the riders and regroup for the next leg of the day. As the days passed, I grew comfortable in my skin and made fast friends with other riders. One day my friend Steve and I decided to regress to our college lifestyles…. We formulated a plan to surprise TK&A, Tim and Karen-Ann, at the checkpoint that day. About 300 yards or so before the checkpoint, Steve and I stripped down to our birthday suits except for our helmets and shoes. Usually, I was a faster rider than Steve; but on that day, I unfortunately was a little slower than Steve. Maybe it was the adrenaline he felt or less wind resistance (lol), but Steve was faster than me for that short time period. I have forever etched in my mind Steve's backside swaying in the breeze. It was not a pretty sight.

We biked into the checkpoint, announced our names and rider numbers and sped out of the checkpoint as fast as possible. What we didn't count on was that the checkpoint was at a Dairy Queen, and the Dairy Queen was full of other members of our society. They were not in our bike-trek bubble, and they would not understand our humor.

On our bike trek, we formed an insular community, traveling in single mindedness, and almost forgot that there is a world still operating around us. We shocked many patrons that day, and Steve and I realized that our "joke" was not perhaps as funny as we imagined. As we bicycled down the road, we stopped, threw our clothes on and burst into laughter. Our laughter would soon turn into pain and regret. As we biked down the road, I instinctively reacted as something whizzed past my face. I turned my face to the side as a bottle was thrown at us from an oncoming car. The bottle smashed on Steve's handlebars behind me and sent him tumbling to the ground. His hands were cut from the glass, and he was banged up from the fall. We were given a very brash message that day: "Don't do that in our town." Putting two and two together, we instinctively knew that the patrons at the Dairy Queen did not like our antics, and we were paying the price for it.

Reader, I was learning that people reap what they sow. I am very certain that, if Steve and I hadn't pulled our naked riding stunt, then we would not have upset the person who threw the bottle at us. In fact, most sin in my life was never intended in malice or harm. However, the end result always has had a similar outcome: hurt, anger, jealousy, sadness, bitterness, regret.

"Do not be deceived: God cannot be mocked. A man reaps what he sows" (Galatians 6:7, NIV).

The organizer of our trip, TK&A, asked us later on if we ever saw where those naked riders went; and we said, "They are long gone and would not return." Fortunately, TK&A had a good sense of humor. However, Steve and I realized we are not in a bubble and couldn't mix the antics of our bike trek with the real society around us.

My bike friends were awesome. We rode together and grew close. We talked about family, life, God and future goals. We pedaled, bonded together as a family unit; and we had fun along the way. I was being stretched in my spirit, and it was beginning to feel good. Practical jokes, as described in Francesville, were part of the bike trek. We were adults; but during this particular adventure, I again regressed to my childhood. We were in Chambersburg, Pennsylvania; and we were biking to Lancaster, Pennsylvania. We had traveled 3,160 miles so far. We had an 88-mile trip ahead of us, and my friends and I decided to play a practical joke on the other riders. I had come out of my shell. Anxiety was not as persistent, and I was feeling like "me again."

One of the logistical aids to help us navigate odd turns "here and there" on our daily route guides, maps, are directional arrows painted on the road called "Dan Henrys" or "Dan Henry Arrows." TK&A (Tim) and his crew occasionally would mark the road with these arrows and help us navigate difficult areas of the country. The road markings are utilized by bicyclists and were named after Dan Henry who invented these symbols.

My friends and I woke up early and left camp before breakfast. Sometimes cyclists in the group would do this to get to the next campsite early. However, we were leaving early to play a practical joke on our friends and mark Dan Henry arrows on the road. We marked the road with the same fluorescent spray paint that TK&A (Tim & Karen-Ann) used and mischievously navigated our group of riders to a dead end in Gettysburg National Park. We climbed a tree and waited for them with water balloons. As the unsuspecting bicyclists rode below our tree, we threw water balloons at them. Our practical joke was not funny to anyone else except us. Not only did we end up apologizing to the group at camp later that evening, but we also were directed by park rangers to clean up our mess. We were fined for marking the road, and we had to scrub the road with wire brush to get the paint off. We had not considered the ramifications that small arrows being painted on the roadway might offend people. We kneeled on the road and scrubbed with heads lowered as tour buses drove through the park. Naive and embarrassed are nice expressions, but I sensed others had more foul adjectives in mind. The road was cleaned; we were given our tickets; and we were allowed to stay on for the remainder of the bike trek. Some proposed sending us home. However, as they stepped back from the incident, they saw that the idea was intended to be humorous, and the joke was actually on us. Our fine and manual labor helped lighten the mood.

The last few days – I didn't want to stop riding. I came a long way emotionally and physically. I had made great friendships along the way, and my anxiety was crumbling around me. I faced my anxiety head on, and I was beginning to realize it was not as powerful as I was giving it credit.

I began to understand that anxiety and panic attacks were not some outside force acting upon me but an internal force that I was creating. God, in His goodness, was allowing me to unravel the toxic knots that had formed around me. I was beginning to understand that I had control over anxiety and that God — through the Holy Spirit — was there with me, helping me.

"Cast all your anxiety on him because he cares for you" (1 Peter 5:7, NIV).

Reader, I had to do my part; and God would do His part. Together, my life would become as God originally intended – filled with love. However, I was far from done with my inward journey; and I had unfortunate life lessons that I would still have to learn.

We spent many nights camping along our bike trek, and each member brought their own tent. After a long day, it was actually excellent to lie down in a sleeping bag and rest. During each camping experience, I would organize my belongings, rest after a long day of cycling and also meditate utilizing a technique called biofeedback.

Mrs. Guarnieri, a good friend and guardrail in my life, taught me about biofeedback. I applied the lessons she taught me to help calm the anxiety within me. Essentially, biofeedback is a term that means self-understanding through body awareness and understanding how one holds their stress in their body. Mrs. Guarnieri was getting her Ph.D. in Psychology, and she gave me a biofeedback tape cassette that she made and produced for one of her psychology classes. I listened to the cassette tape that Mrs. Guarnieri gave me over and over, and I eventually felt my body relax. Her voice was calming as she walked the listener from head to toe to understand the difference between tension and relaxation.

I recommend trying this biofeedback exercise as you sit reading this passage:

Start at the top of your head. Tense your eyebrows and scalp, and hold this tension for 10 seconds. Squeeze, squeeze, squeeze and relax those muscles. Now feel the difference between tension and relaxation.

Tense your cheeks, face, mouth; and hold this for 10 seconds. Squeeze, squeeze, squeeze and relax those muscles. Now feel the difference between tension and relaxation.

Tense your neck muscles for 10 seconds. Squeeze, squeeze, squeeze and relax those muscles. Now feel the difference between tension and relaxation.

Asbury Park finish line

Tense your shoulders and chest for 10 seconds. Squeeze, squeeze, squeeze and relax those muscles. Now feel the difference between tension and relaxation.

Tense your arms and fists for 10 seconds. Squeeze, squeeze, squeeze and relax those muscles. Now feel the difference between tension and relaxation.

Tense your stomach for 10 seconds. Squeeze, squeeze, squeeze and relax those muscles. Now feel the difference between tension and relaxation.

Tense your legs and feet for 10 seconds. Squeeze, squeeze, squeeze and relax those muscles. Now feel the difference between tension and relaxation.

Mr. and Mrs. Guarnieri treated me like part of their family. I was welcomed into their home — with open arms — when I visited their daughter on school breaks. I felt loved. Mrs. Guarnieri told me once – clear out of the blue, "Danny, I would pay for your wedding; but you two are too young right now." It was such a nice compliment. Mr. and Mrs. Guarnieri were a beautiful couple who modeled their love for each other well for their children. They were both very intelligent, and they had exceptionally bright kids. Mrs. Guarnieri was like a mom figure for me at that time in my life. She was a psychologist and a "guardrail" — all wrapped up in one. During the summer of 1988, I sat in the Guarnieri family farmhouse in their kitchen, talking with Mrs. Guarnieri about how I was doing, about school and about my mom. I started to complain about my mom and the hoarding environment I had been living in. Mrs. Guarneri looked me square in the eyes and strongly said, "Danny, love your mother! Do you understand me? Love your mother. She needs you!"

In remembering this moment, writing this down literally brings tears to my eyes. I sit here today, 10/15/20, 32 years have passed; and I thank You, God, for Mrs. Guarnieri in my life. Mrs. Guarnieri was the arms and ears and mouth of Jesus as she spoke words from God that I needed to hear. The words she spoke brought me into a new way of thinking and a new direction of travel. Life up, to that point, was the "poor me" concept. I was expecting Mrs. Guarnieri to give me the "Oh, what a difficult life you have,

Dan" speech; but instead I got a strong tongue lashing. "Danny, you love that woman. She needs you!"

I was self-absorbed, and life was about me. I had not really stopped to think how awful my mom must have it. Yes, of course, I loved Mom; but was I loving her? All I did was complain how awful my living environment was and how I wished our family was back to normal. My mom needed compassion and love. Mrs. Guarnieri was there to show me a "mirror" and point me in a new direction as a major guardrail in my life.

Chrisie, my girlfriend, and I remained friends for years after we dated. However, we eventually drifted apart and lost contact. I think this was an unfortunate but good thing because it allowed space and mental clarity for God to bring the love of my life, my wife Veronica, into my life. I want to thank you, Mr. and Mrs. Guarnieri, for welcoming me into your family for a season in my life. God knew that I needed a family like yours to help me along the Way. Your family modeled for me what a good and loving family is all about.

And back to the bike trek -

Our last day of the event was filled with sadness and elation. I would soon be missing my friends from the trip, but I knew my family would be waiting with open arms. Elation and joy exuded from me in the form of tears as we entered Asbury Park's boardwalk. We made it! I crossed the country on my bicycle, and my family rejoiced in seeing me. I was swarmed in hugs, kisses; and I couldn't stop smiling. Gramma Connors and Concetta, my stepgrandmother, both made the trip along with my stepbrother, stepmother and dad. It was a storybook ending to a long and arduous journey.

I realized when I made it to the boardwalk in Asbury Park, New Jersey (home of Bruce Springsteen) I had been re-Born in the USA. Crossing this beautiful country of ours awakened a strong spirit within me, which God was filling with His awe and wonder.

The L'Arche community also came to greet me at the finish line. It was a true joy to see my friends from L'Arche after just traveling across the country as a fundraiser for them. I returned to Syracuse to begin my new career as a student nurse but with a lighter load, with less anxiety.

Asbury Park, NJ finish line, Daniel and Grandma   Dan and Dad finish line Asbury Park

CHAPTER 6

Emotional maturity

Nursing school 1994

We had a spokesperson from Hospice of Central New York come into our classroom and instruct us on the emotional understanding of death and dying. He said, "Your patients may know they have limited time left on earth. Do you? Have you ever thought about when you will die? It's important to think about because it allows you to think about the inevitable. It will allow you the opportunity to begin to empathize with your patient. Give yourself a number, a year. What is your death date?"

I chose the age 78, and I had never thought about a death date. We all have birth dates, and we all have death dates. I was 26 at the time; and this date seemed far enough away that I knew I could lead a very productive, fun and full life. It was the first time in my life that I began to understand that life is finite. The sound of a large "gong" sounded in my soul. Life is finite? I was 26; I was just ending my prolonged adolescence; and I had never, ever imagined life as FINITE.

I believe life would be a lot healthier if we collectively put in the forefront of our minds that this life we are currently living is not forever. I recently heard of a group of people starting a movement against death itself. People actually pay money to be frozen – in the hope of someday being thawed out and cured of their present illness. To me, this epitomizes the crazy thinking of this world.

"By the sweat of your brow you will eat food until you return to the ground, since from it you were taken; for dust you are and to dust you will return" (Genesis 3:19, NIV).

After nursing class that day, I returned to my dorm room. The thought of life and death got me thinking of my mother and her decision to attempt suicide when I was 13. All too often, people opt out of this gift we call life because of pain and depression. However, if we just hold out one more day, the Son will rise. Yes, a play on words, "Son will rise." If we place our hope in our Father and His Son, then we can flourish even in the pain. God will give us His grace through the Holy Spirit.

"In my distress I called to the LORD; I cried to my God for help. From his temple he heard my voice; my cry came before him, into his ears" (Psalm 18:6, NIV).

Nursing school was a great experience. Unfortunately, I dropped out of school during my second semester. I had enough credits to sit for my LPN license and passed on the first attempt. I also became a paramedic, and I found that lifestyle and that field of medicine more in line with my personality. It was the correct path for me, and countless doors have opened as a result of following my heart. The experience of nursing school was a tremendous benefit to my paramedic career, and the knowledge I gained in one field has certainly filtered over to the next. In addition, the friends I made in nursing school, I would later live with as roommates when I met my wife Veronica in the same apartment complex. God has an amazing Way of weaving the fabric of our lives together.

In 1994, I moved out of the college nursing dormitory and moved in with dear friends of mine, Kevin and Emily. I transferred to a different nursing school, was attending school part-time and was completing prerequisites. I met Kevin and Emily at L'Arche, where we worked together for approximately five years "caring for" people with disabilities. We became lifelong friends, and I am godfather to their oldest child. They are friends who have become family. Perhaps it was the strength of our friendship? Perhaps it was my age – then 26 years old? I was now emotionally ready to deal with the destructive behavior imposed on me as a young boy. I decided to confront an adult male who acted sexually inappropriate toward me. It was part of my journey and part of the mental health and healing that God was calling me toward. One day, I went to the house where he lived to confront him and rang the doorbell.

My mind, in an instant, flashed back to my youth. I was 14 years old and in ninth grade. I remembered cleaning the windows inside this old stone house. It was a cold, dark house. The house was oddly unique. He had built secret doorways throughout his home that looked like a wall but opened into another room. For example, the garage wall could push open into the dining room. Also, he had removed the receptacle from his bathroom to the adjoining room but placed the outlet cover over the void. He had made a peeping hole from the bathroom into the adjoining room or vice versa. My friends and I discovered these things as we cleaned his home and washed his windows. One only knows what else he had in this house? We were flies in his spider web. He offered us snacks and drinks and had the biggest television I had ever seen. He paid us well. My friends and I knew there was something "fishy" with this guy. He was a little too friendly, and his house was very peculiar.

One day, we had finished a little late while raking leaves; and the guy asked us if we wanted a ride home. My friend and I agreed to a ride, but I was nervous. I knew that I would be dropped off first because it was the most direct route of travel. I lived about two miles away, and Mike lived about five miles away. I envisioned us driving directly to my house and then to Mike's house, and he would then loop around back to his house. My friend Mike was bigger and stronger than me, and he could handle this guy if he was what we perceived him to be. The guy went out of his way to drop off Mike first. A huge warning sign flashed across my mind, but I hesitated. "Get out of the car with Mike," my now adult mind is yelling. This guy dropped Mike off at his house, and Mike looked at me with a "Are you okay?" type of expression. I must have looked like a deer in the headlights. After dropping off Mike, this guy drove toward my house but decided to take a detour. He drove to a gas station and drove us into a car wash. The car wash was the type on a conveyor belt that you put the car in park. The terrible thing is I remember this experience up to the car wash, and I remember being dropped off at my house. However, I do not remember the time alone with this guy in the car wash and right after the car wash. My memory is gone for that time period. I remember getting out of the car at my house and walking by my parents who were in the kitchen, and I went directly to my room.

For years after that event, I was unable to remember that short time period in the car wash. I have brought this event to therapists as a young man and wrestled with that memory for many years. Now that I have many decades in between me and that troubled older man, I say this: Perhaps it is the best thing that I do not remember this experience? Perhaps God sent His Holy Spirit to be with me, shielding my eyes and memory from the ugliness that pervaded this man? I am now grateful for my lack of perception for that time period in my life. Thank You, God.

I rang the doorbell; the front door opened; and I asked if Mr. _____ was home. The owner of the house advised me that he no longer lived there and that he had sold them his home. I inquired who the realtor was, and I got the company name. At the time, we had phone books and yellow pages to research phone numbers. I was able to get the realtor's number and visited the realtor. I requested the phone number of the previous owner. Initially, they did not want to give me the number because of confidentiality; but I told them I was friends with the family. They eventually ended up giving me the number, seeing as though I was a kind-looking, young man.

I drove back to my friend's house (Kev and Em) and sat with the number for a time. I felt like a young boy again as I muscled up the courage to call. I finally called the number. The phone rang a couple times; and as I was about to hang up, a woman's voice answered the phone. I asked if this was the _____ residence? She replied, "Yes, it is." I asked, "Did you own a big stone house in Syracuse, New York?" She replied, "Yes, we did.

Who is this?" I said, "Oh ok, never mind." She said, "No, no, don't go. Don't hang up!" I hung up the phone. I could not bring myself to get into a conversation with this woman, who I imagine was either the wife or the daughter of the man I worked for. The guy, at the time, was much older than me – probably in his late seventies; and 12 years later, he was probably deceased. I had this present moment of clarity while talking to his family member and understood that he was, more than likely, deceased. I could not bear to bring up the past, and that is today why I do not write his name in this book. His family does not need this legacy. However, I am fairly certain that his family knows. Given the fact that the outlet in the bathroom was a blank, one could see into the adjoining room. One can speculate that his dysfunction was beyond just the car wash.

I write to any abuser who is reading this book and echo my Father's Words, "It's not too late." It's not too late to say you're sorry. It's not too late to change your final destination and final resting place. It is not too late to repent. Forgiveness is freely given, and our God is ready for your repentant heart. It is time. Ask your Father for forgiveness, and make amends with the people you have abused.

It's not too late. The children you may be harming are God's children also, and He sees. There will be consequences to all actions. Be afraid. It is time to turn away from sin and repent!

"Nothing in all creation is hidden from God's sight. Everything is uncovered and laid bare before the eyes of him to whom we must give an account" (Hebrews 4:13, NIV).

CHAPTER 7

Southern Cross

On **September 15, 1996**, I began my bike trek across the southern United States. I entered into this experience more aware of what lay ahead, and I felt more comfortable than my first trek across the northern United States. In fact, I was overflowing with excitement. I left nursing school, but I did not burn any bridges in anticipation of returning to finish my degree.

Approximately six months before the trek, I reached out to Francis House, a local not-for-profit agency; and I proposed the idea of a fundraiser. Francis House is a hospice home, where someone goes to live out their last days when they are terminal. Francis House exudes love and is a very warm and welcoming environment. When one has to pass on, which we all do, this is a beautiful place during our final days and hours.

I love the Francis House; and my family was friends with Sister Kathleen, the director and founder of this unique, loving, little organization. Sister Kathleen thought the idea of bicycling across the U.S. was interesting, and we soon found ourselves knee deep in planning the fundraiser. We formed a committee of approximately seven members, and we began our task of fundraising.

Like the first trek when I biked across the northern U.S., we decided to have me call in to a local radio station each day of the ride across the southern United States. It would be good public relations and would help with donations. We ultimately raised more than $20,000.

I flew out to California, with my bicycle in tow; and I would soon be biking from Disneyland to Disney World. Much like the first trek, it would take 48 days with two days of rest and cover 3,200 miles from Anaheim, California to Orlando, Florida. I would be bicycling with approximately 40 other riders from the U.S., Britain and Australia. The riders were from various walks of life – professional men and women; and our ages ranged from 20 to 60's. What we all had in common was a sense of adventure and fun. During our 48 days together, we became family. In both of my treks across the U.S., each group became a cohesive unit, and we grew in a very short time to know each other deeply. Certain members naturally gravitated together more closely; but all in all, we were family.

I again chose TK&A as my bike trek company that managed the logistics of the ride. I found that the owner, Tim, and his partner, Karen-Ann, were fun and well organized. One cannot plan for each and every circumstance that occurs for 48 days and 3,200 miles; but Tim and Karen-Ann did their best.

This country is beautiful. The southern part of the U.S. was spectacular from the Pacific coast to the Atlantic coast. Reader, I can sum up my trip with one word: "party." When I was not bicycling or training for my marathon, I was partying. I once again had regressed into an addictive way of drinking alcohol.

Southern Cross - Daniel is riding up a steep incline in Arizona.

San Antonio, Texas is a beautiful city. It is the home of the Alamo, and another wonderful point of interest is the River Walk. I later learned when they say River Walk, they mean it. They mean walk. A friend, one of the staff members from TK&A, and I decided to run a handful of miles after our short bike ride that day. We weaved in and out of city streets and made our way to the River Walk. We were greeted with disparaging remarks:

"This is a walkway, not a runway." There were a few other, more colorful adjectives people yelled at us. However, instead of walking, we amped up our run and began an almost parkour type of jumping and running over railings and other obstacles. It was fun; and we thought people were overreacting, which made us increase our speed and intensity.

Reader, as you can see, I was regressing once again in my life. I knew this way of being in the world, and it came very naturally to me. I was being rude and self-absorbed. I wasn't thinking of others as well as I should have been.

Three steps forward and two steps back. Back and forth from a spiritual mindset trying to grow closer to God to living in this world and finding all the trappings that come from "living in the world."

"Do not love the world or anything in the world. If anyone loves the world, love for the Father is not in them" (1 John 2:15, NIV).

Our bicycling gear hung to dry after a long day of riding.

Later that evening — after a night of drinking with my bicycling friends, I had passed out on a bench near the Alamo. I was abruptly awakened by a park ranger who advised me, "Keep on moving. You cannot sleep here."

Reader, I stumbled back to the hotel where we were staying; and I was grateful it was a park ranger who woke me rather than someone with bad intentions. Was God watching over me? Does God only love those who love Him? Was God concerned with my behavior? A good daddy always cares and always wants the best for his children. And we have an omnipotent Father; so yes, He is watching.

Reader, I have grown to know this: God sent His Son to die for me, a sinner. Jesus sacrificed Himself so that I could be free from the sins that bound me. If God didn't love me, would He allow His one and only Son to die for me? Reader, from the depth of my heart, my true being, I know now that I have been set free from my sin. This understanding would not come for about a decade from this bike trek experience. But I now understand that God, through His Holy Spirit, has been with me all along – even when I was at my worst. "Amazing grace, how sweet the sound that saved a wretch like me. I once was lost, but now am found. Was blind, but now I see." (Lyrics are from *Amazing Grace* by Pastor John Newton.)

Unfortunately, there were many, many more failures to come in my life – as you can read, Reader. Life is a beautiful journey. I do pray that you continue to read on and come along for the ride.

The night before we finished the bike trek, we had one last meeting as a bike group. Tim and Karen-Ann (TK&A) said their congratulations and well wishes to all of us. I then stood up and said, "Raise your glass. I want to make a toast." My friend Kevin pulled on my arm and said, "Dan, we are the only ones drinking." Unfortunately, that didn't stop me. I went on to say, "May the road rise up to meet you. May the wind be always at your back." I couldn't find the rest of the words in my drunken state; and one of the riders, Diane, said, "May the sun shine warm upon your face, the rains fall soft upon your fields." And together we said, "May God hold you in the palm of His hand." I meant every word of that beautiful poem. I didn't want this to be the last days of our ride together. I met wonderful people, and I wanted to stay in that moment in time.

However, staying in that moment in time is not what God intended for me. God was forming me and remodeling me — one pedal stroke at a time. I had a much longer trip ahead of me — an inner journey that would be starting in my near future.

The next day was a beautiful, sunny day; and we would be entering Disney World. We would be grouped together as a unit and cross the finish line 40 riders strong. However, when you put 40 riders together into a tight, roadway accidents can happen. My first fall of the trip was less than two miles from the finish line. I was cut off by a rider who wanted to be next to her close friend. I get it. I get the fact that she wanted to be next to her friend as they crossed the finish line, but I also get that two objects cannot occupy the same space at the same time. I went head first over my handle bars, landing on the cement. It hurt, but nothing was broken – except for my bike. The rear bike rack was now protruding through my spokes. I grabbed the metal rack and yanked it with all my strength. I was able to ride my bike. I quickly put my chain on and sped after the group. We were all nervous with excitement to finish this trip and see our loved ones at the finish line.

I was deeply looking forward to seeing my dad and my family once again at the finish line. The first bike trek was an epic family reunion, and having them here in Disney World would be fantastic. My family could easily afford airline tickets, hotel accommodations; and this would be a great vacation for my grandmother. My dad told me, "We have a surprise for you at the finish line." I was expecting nothing short of fireworks when I crossed the country for my second time. However, what I found was that they were not there and that they sent two representatives from the Francis House to greet me with a banner that had my name spelled wrong. The feeling I had was reminiscent of high school when no one from my family showed up for my high school graduation. I was happy to see the representatives from Francis House, but it was far short of the emotional experience I was hoping for.

Reader, I had become a fundraising annoyance to my family and my parents' friends. My uncle Don, the priest, even mentioned his "concern" during our (my wife Veronica and I) wedding ceremony several years later. He stated during his homily at our wedding, "When I opened their wedding invitation, I half expected to see a fundraising request in the envelope." What was meant as a slight or a fun-loving joke at my expense was actually a wonderful idea –in lieu of gifts, to make a donation to a charity. I love it. I wish we would have thought about that sooner.

Shortly after my Southern Cross bike trek, Gramma Connors gave me a card with a bicycle on it and let me know how proud she was of me. She was my rock and let me know when I needed to "knock it off and wake up" or when I was on the right road. Through this symbolic gesture of her card, I knew I was on the right road. Today we have her card framed, and it adorns our exercise room.

See the finish line at Disney World.

CHAPTER 8

Alaska

The third part of my immersion experience into emotional health came in the form of fishing. I had always dreamed of fishing in Alaska and heard stories of young men going to Alaska to work on a fishing boat. I never pursued this dream when I was younger and just out of college. I thought it was just a pipe dream and out of the realm of possibilities. However, "I can do all this through him who gives me strength" (Philippians 4:13, NIV).

In the **summer of 1997**, I went to Anchorage, Alaska to run a marathon as a fundraiser for the Leukemia Society; but I found my emotional footing while fishing in Kenai, Alaska. I, three other runners and a coach — provided to us by the Leukemia Society — flew to Anchorage, Alaska. I was still dealing with constant anxiety and mild panic daily. I was able to mask my anxiety by flirting with the female runners I was with and self-medicated with alcohol while flying. I had not met Veronica, my wife, yet; but nevertheless, my actions of flirtation were not wholesome. The female runners accompanying me were both married and showed little to no interest in me. Thank God.

1997 Mayor Midnight Sun marathon finish line

I had friends in Anchorage from both The Northern Cross and The Southern Cross bike treks. I met up with them, reminisced with my friends and, after the marathon, ended up staying with my friend Katie and her parents from The Southern Cross bike trek. Katie's sister knew a fisherman on the Kenai Peninsula, and he was looking for a laborer. My marathon friends flew back home after the race, but I extended my stay for the remainder of the summer. For about a week or so, I played tourist. My friend Katie, her mother, sister and I flew up across the Arctic Circle to a remote fishing village named Kotzebue. The Arctic was not what I envisioned. I thought we would land in a vast snow-filled landscape and glaciers would be floating in the sea. When we landed in Kotzebue, I was shocked. It was the summer; there was no snow; and the ocean was not frozen. I saw no polar bears, and the landscape was unappealing. The town was a depressed, barren, flat land that stretched for as far as the eye can see. There were no trees, no mountains; and the land was a rocky desert. Small houses dotted the landscape, and a small hospital and school were the largest buildings I saw. We visited a museum that describes life in Alaska and the vastness of this state. The museum was impressive; and I am certain — if I spent more than a day in this remote village — I would have found God's beautiful Spirit within the people of this village.

On a map, Alaska usually is indicated near Hawaii and is drawn as a small replica of the state. In fact, the state of Alaska is about two times larger than Texas – to give you an idea of the immensity of this state. And it is between 1,500 and 3,000 miles from Hawaii, depending on which island you measure from.

Alaska is vast, and the majority of it is beautiful. I have traveled across the U.S. twice by bicycle and have witnessed some spectacular scenery. However, Alaska is majestic and still very wild. You can drive 15 minutes outside of Anchorage and be in a very remote area. It is still very much a wilderness, and Mother Nature lets you never forget that she could take back this land in a heartbeat. One of the largest earthquakes to ever be recorded was in 1964 in Alaska with a magnitude 9.2. Alaska has over 1,000 earthquakes a month; but most are just mild tremors. When I was there,

I experienced several small earthquakes. As you, Reader, may be aware, they can be somewhat off putting. As the earth mildly shook, I thought to myself, "Is this going to stop?" The excitement of the earth shaking and the realization that we are not in control are humbling.

In addition to earthquakes, melting permafrost and various wildlife that kill humans (bear and moose), there is also the danger of mudflats. I was warned by the locals not to venture onto the mudflats by the water. The beach areas can be beautiful; but where the beach meets mud, the silt deposits are the areas that can turn deadly. There is a place near Anchorage where the mud is like quicksand, and the suction force of the mud is like an extremely powerful vacuum. Unfortunately, many people — mostly tourists — have died in these mudflats. They get stuck and drown when the tides come back in. More on the mudflats in a minute...

The week with Katie and her family was nice, and they were a very hospitable family. However, I was itching to start my next adventure. The sound of being a commercial fisherman sounded appealing. However, I had no experience in this industry – other than recreationally fishing as I was growing up. My anxiety was about a 4 out of 10; but I forced myself to say, "Yes" to the commercial salmon fishing offer. I had no idea what to expect;

In 1997 Daniel picture with a 16' skiff and a work truck.

but in my heart, I knew that I had to force myself to do things that I was afraid to do. I wanted to overcome my fears. I did not want to be bothered by anxiety and panic any longer. Every day I had to get my mind right and not be overcome with fear or apprehension. I intuitively knew what I needed to do to rid myself of this debilitating psychological symptom.

The Kenai Peninsula, where I would be fishing, is like nothing I have ever encountered before. It is beyond beautiful and very remote. This is brown bear and moose country. The property I lived on was situated between the town of Kenai and Soldotna. I would be living in a small 20' x 20' cabin which had multiple bunk beds, a small, basic kitchenette and an outhouse. The outhouse was situated approximately 20 feet from the cabin, and there was a path leading to it with six feet of high grass all around. Walking to and from the outhouse made my mind race, and I thought of bears every time I had to use the loo. This cabin would be my home for the next month and a half. The property had a main house where the owner and his wife lived and a couple of barns that stored the fishing nets and equipment. It is a beautiful piece of property on a bluff that overlooks Cook Inlet. On the opposite side of Cook Inlet are three mountains. The mountains are actually three active

I lived in this cabin on a bluff overlooking Cook Inlet. It was picturesque. Across the way were three active volcanoes: Mt. Redoubt, Mt. Illiama and Mt. Spur.

volcanoes – Redoubt, Illiama and Spur. I received room and board for free in exchange for labor. I also received a small stipend at the end of the summer, depending upon the amount of fish we caught per ton. However, I had to buy my own gear: waders, arm guards, gloves and a fishing life jacket. The equipment purchase ate up most of my earnings for the summer. I had, however, seen Alaska for free and felt very fortunate to have had such an excellent experience. Also, how can I put a price tag on healing anxiety and panic attacks? That was priceless!

We used life vests that would inflate if you pulled the cord. Otherwise, it just looked like a regular vest. If you didn't pull the cord on the jacket, the CO_2 cartridge would not inflate. They told me, "Don't worry about drowning because the water is 38 degrees, and you will die of hypothermia pretty quick." It was fisherman humor, and I was taking it all in. We would be fishing our nets about 1½ miles to 1 mile from shore and would pick our nets around the tides a couple times a day, and it was good physical work and good exercise. We would stretch the net across the boat, pick the fish and pull our boat down the line about 300 feet from buoy to buoy.

On one hand, I was in awe of God's beauty all around me. On the other hand, I was anxious, scared and out of my element! I just met these guys; we were fishing 1 mile to 1½ miles from shore; the water was 38 degrees; I had to pull a cord to activate my flotation jacket. What if's flooded my mind. Orca, Beluga and shark could be in the water as I reached in to grab the buoys.

"When anxiety was great within me, your consolation brought me joy" (Psalm 94:19, NIV).

As time went by, my anxiety minimized. After a while, I wished to see an Orca or a Beluga. That would have been spectacular! I got used to the routine and began to fit in. The guys were great, but Aaron treated me like a servant every day. He was technically my captain, and I had to follow his order while on the boat. I also had to do the menial tasks when we got to shore as well: wash the gloves, wash out the boat and be at his beck and call. Chris, my boss, was aware of the situation between Aaron and me. Chris treated me like a man and was appreciative of my help. It was Chris' hospitality that made dealing with Aaron day in and day out worth it. JP and his brother, Dave, and Lilly were all excellent people; and I felt well taken care of. Aaron was also a good guy, but his upbringing beat him down. He would take out his difficult life on others, but he did not realize he was doing it. Aaron's attitude was worth putting up with because he was a good man inside.

In the mornings, Dave and Lilly would prepare breakfast, and I was told to eat a big meal. They said, "If you eat a lot, it will help with the sea sickness." I thought they were playing a practical joke to see if I threw up. I played along and gorged myself. However, true to form, they were right. When we had a big meal, I was never sea sick.

In my down time, Chris told me I could take the pickup truck and go into town. Town was a generous term for it. I had no desire to go down to the pub and drink. I preferred to read at the cabin, walk on the beach, write letters and attempt to whittle. I never got the hang of whittling wood, but it passed the time. My friends Kevin and Emily shipped me my bicycle through the mail, and I could now ride my bike around on my downtime.

One day Dave, the owner of the property, said, "Dan, there is a large bull moose down the road on the left side. You should take your bike and go take a look. You can't miss it." I rode down the driveway and out to the main road. I didn't see a thing. I turned right, heading toward Seward. I biked maybe a ½ mile and was looking left the entire time. I glanced to my right; and standing, maybe 20 feet from me, was an enormous bull moose! Its rack spanned at least 8 feet, and it stood bigger than an elephant. It was much bigger than any large horse I had ever seen. I now can understand how these animals can hurt or kill humans. Moose can be territorial and protective of their young. It has been reported that moose outnumber bears 3 to 1 in Alaska and injure more humans than bears each year. When I saw the moose, I turned my bicycle around as quickly as possible and pedaled as fast as I could back to Dave and Lilly's. It was the first moose I had ever seen – and the first one I almost rode my bike into.

We had a small black-and-white TV in the cabin, and it got a station or two. The television shows I did watch had multiple advertisements for depression and suicide. Seasonal affective disorder (SAD) is no joke. When I was in Alaska, it was daylight for about 20 hours a day with a short period of dusk. It could be 2 a.m., and you would think it was 8 p.m. The daylight was a bit disorienting, and it took some time to get used to. On the flip side, during the winter months, it is dark the majority of the time with a little bit of dusk/daylight. Couple the loss of light with the cold of winter, and now I could understand why every other commercial revolved around combating anxiety and depression. I was only in Alaska for the summer, and I had never experienced darkness on a daily basis. I hear that the northern lights are beautiful, and I believe this would be a truly magnificent experience.

"In him was life, and that life was the light of all mankind. The light shines in the darkness, and the darkness has not overcome it" (John 1:4-5, NIV).

In my life, there has indeed been much darkness; but what I have come to realize is that when I place my trust in God, in Jesus, in the Holy Spirit, I am free. When I let go of my control, place my control where it belongs – in God's hands, then life has a Way of flowing very well. When I am intentional with time, focus my mind in the present and trust in my Father, all is well – always.

I worked closely with four and sometimes five other guys – all seasoned fishermen. I was the new guy, and my position was the bowman. I would be responsible for reaching into the water, grabbing the buoys, hoisting them into the boat, tying a special knot called the bowline from buoy to net and throwing the 3-foot buoy back into the water. The nets were stacked next to me four feet in height, and they would fly off the back of the boat from front to back (mid-bow to stern). It was daunting! The fishing we were doing was called set-net salmon fishing.

There were large buoys that were anchored to the ocean bottom. Aaron and I would then go to our next set of buoys and do the same process. Each set of nets required a permit; and the permit, dates and times of fishing were all regulated by the government – the Fish and Game Administration. My boss Chris and his bowman JP would be fishing on three other nets with three separate permits that were owned by Dave and Lilly in whose home I was residing.

We would "pick the fish" (a fishing phrase, meaning to remove the fish from the net) from the nets by stretching the net across the width of the boat. We would set pins in the designated slots to keep the nets in place, then pick and remove the salmon from the net. We would drag our boat down the net and move onto the next set of buoys. We would toss the salmon in the bottom of the boat and work around them. We would then take the ocean water and pour it over them to keep them cool and fresh. The salmon we caught would then be brought to market and shipped to Japan for sushi. This particular area of Alaska was known for its sockeye salmon. Sockeye is the best salmon and the most expensive by pound.

Aaron and I fished out of a 16-foot skiff. Essentially, it is a large row boat with a big engine. On stormy days, the two teams would get together into the bigger boat, the 20-foot skiff, with four guys and fish all five nets. My job, on the stormy days, would be to steady the boat by holding the lead line down as the other guys picked salmon and I would yell, "Wave" when a big one was coming. The lead line was the bottom of the net and hung toward the ocean floor, and the buoy line had multiple small buoys evenly spaced and would float on the top of the water. The net would be stretched approximately 300 feet to the next buoy. The waves occasionally would splash over us, and we knew we could not take on much water. With four guys, the weight of the fish and water, we could sink. Most often though, the sea was calm and tranquil. During this time, it was much easier to appreciate the beauty all around me.

Reader, it did not go unnoticed by me that I was doing similar work as Jesus' friends. I could not help but think of Jesus and of the apostles' fear during violent storms. To see Someone walking on water and rebuking the wind and the sea should have solidified their belief! Who walks on water and rebukes the wind and the sea but God? My faith was weak also. I had experienced God at the Canisius quad in college. And I was visited by Jesus in a dream while working at L'Arche. But I wrote off these experiences. *Who am I? I am no one special. I was just intoxicated, and I was just dreaming.* Like the apostles in the storm, I too had weak faith…

> "Now faith is confidence in what we hope for and assurance about what we do not see. This is what the ancients were commended for. By faith we understand that the universe was formed at God's command, so that what is seen was not made out of what was visible" (Hebrews 11:1-3, NIV).

When we were done picking our nets during high tide, we would take our catch back to the beach and drive our boat right up onto shore. We would then bring the pickup truck down onto the beach and throw the fish from man to man and into the container in the back of the truck. After the fish were offloaded from the skiff, we would drive the fish to the fish market for sale. It was a commercial fish market; and the price was established by species, poundage and market fluctuations. By price, we sold our fish at the market: sockeye or red salmon at $1.60/pound, king at $1.20/pound, then pink salmon at $.25/pound.

During low tide, our delivery to market was a much different process. If we waited till high tide to drive our boat onto shore, we would be waiting for hours for the tide to come in, and the fish would spoil. On low tides, we would take our catch by boat and go as close to the fish market as possible.

The fish market was along the shoreline, and sometimes we would be as far out as ¼ to ½ mile from the shore. It was a sandy beach, and the owner of the market would drive his airboat out to us. We would tie off our skiff to the airboat, and he would pull us and our load back to shore. For me, it was a novelty and a fun experience; but the guys were used to this process.

One day, we sat in the boat, waiting for the airboat; but the owner of the market did not see us. It was overwhelming, sitting in the scorching sun, wearing all our gear. We started to heat up, and Aaron and I had nothing to drink. I was done waiting. I told Aaron, "I'm going to run in." Aaron looked at me sideways and said, "I wouldn't do that if I were you." I had just finished my marathon training, and I was in good shape. It was about ¼ mile through the mud and sand. What's the worst that could happen?

About 10 minutes into my run, I was halfway between the beach and the boat, and I started thinking more and more about the mudflats in Anchorage. Locals told people not to walk on the mudflats because of the danger! This was not Anchorage I rationalized and thought I would be safe. However, mudflats were not just located in Anchorage. Usually, I could run a mile in seven to eight minutes; but running through this sand and mud was like running through snow up to my knees in fishing waders. The mud was deep, and each pull of my boot was like lifting 40 pounds. It was exhausting! I started thinking about quicksand and people dying in Alaska related to the mudflats. I thought to myself, *What did I get myself into?* Fortunately, the waders were connected to my boot; or I am certain I would have lost them in the mud. I made it to shore as the owner was getting his airboat ready to come get us. It took me more than 20 minutes to run less than 1/4 mile. When I came into the shop, he said, "Where did you come from?" I told him, "I ran in from the boat." He said, "You did what?!" Apparently, this was not the common-sense thing to do; and I was greeted with a back-and-forth head shake of disapproval. I was just glad to be in the cool shade of the fish market, drinking a soda.

Aaron and I eventually became friends. One day while we were picking our nets, I felt a very heavy object in the water as we pulled our net. I said to Aaron, "I think we have a big tree limb in here!" We both groaned disapprovingly, thinking we would have to repair the net. Repairing the net is a tedious, time-consuming task; and the more time the net is out of the water, the less money you make. I reached into the water and hoisted a huge king salmon into our boat. Aaron and I looked at each other and started to hoot and holler. We knew we would be in the running for the largest salmon that summer. The fishermen along this coast wagered who would win the largest salmon of the season. Aaron and I won $100. It's not a great amount of money, but we had bragging rights. The fish was approximately 48 inches long and 77 pounds. I hope to include this picture of us in the back of our pickup, with me holding this fish by its gills. Aaron and I solidified our friendship with this experience, and I am glad that I tolerated his gruff demeanor until then. He had a tough exterior but a soft heart. God allowed me to see Aaron the Way He sees Aaron. God placed upon my heart, "Aaron is My child, Dan, and has had a rough start."

My friend, my boss, Chris was a master electrician; and he would be hiring an apprentice electrician after the fishing season. I had no clue about being an electrician, but I trusted Chris. I trusted my friend.

Here I am – at high tide – unloading a king salmon of approximately 20 lbs. to bring to market.

He told me he had a job waiting for me. We got along well over the summer, and I would be taking Aaron's spot as an apprentice. Aaron had a family, and he was eagerly anticipating working with Chris. The behind the scene was that Aaron had a temper, and he was hard to work with at times – most of the time. I liked him though. I could see that he had a hard upbringing, which contributed to his personality. Chris was looking for an apprentice who he got along with and was not hot tempered.

I am glad to have met Aaron's family because that helped me with my decision not to accept Chris' invitation. I did not want to negatively impact Aaron and his family. I also took into consideration that I would be on the opposite side of the world as my family of origin. At the time, my mom was alive, and my family and I all got along well. My family of origin was a very big factor as to why I did not relocate and live in Alaska.

I learned a lot about the fishing industry that summer and considered staying in Alaska. I had learned a trade, and there was ample work for a young man. Alaskans have a saying that I love: "We work to live, and we live to play." Alaskans have it right in my opinion. They play hard and work hard.

I wrote my friend Katie from Anchorage a couple of letters and shared my heart. I told her about meditating while on my downtime and about my spirituality. I also told her that I was considering staying in Alaska if I had a reason. I was rebuked. She did not find my spirituality interesting and also was not interested in me as more than a friend. What I didn't realize was that God had been preparing a very special gift for me, and she was waiting for me at home. I would be returning home to Syracuse, New York with no job, no direction, no place to live; but I was trusting God that I would land on my feet.

"'Come follow me,' Jesus said, 'and I will send you out to fish for people'" (Matthew 4:19, NIV).

What did Alaska teach me?

In retrospect, Alaska was a piece of the puzzle regarding my mental health. I was able to overcome debilitating panic and anxiety attacks by forcing myself to accept the job as a commercial fisherman. However, it was not by my force of will or determination that I credit the healing of my anxiety and panic attacks. I contribute my healing to God. I have been on this journey to find my Father for a long, long time. I said, "Yes" at my confirmation in eighth grade. I said, "Yes" by confessing my sins; and I had a desire in my heart to know God more. God heard my prayers as a young child, as an adult; and He has been with me in my struggles. With every further step in His direction, He has allowed me to develop my spiritual muscles. I first learned how to crawl at L'Arche. I then began taking my first steps when I returned to college after working at L'Arche. I walked on my own for the first time while biking across the northern part of the United States. I then walked confidently on my own while I biked across the southern United States. Finally, I began to run while I was fishing in Alaska. All thanks be to God.

"Trust in the LORD forever, for the LORD, the LORD himself, is the Rock eternal" (Isaiah 26:4, NIV).

Reader, if you are struggling in ways similar to what I have written about, I want to let you know that it's not too late ... to face your fear, to face your anxiety or apprehension and grow as an individual. Emotional health and healing are possible. Prior to Alaska, I could "cope" with my day to day, but I was not fully living as God intended me to live. I was anxiety ridden, and I was trying to fix the problem on my own.

We are social creatures meant to be with each other and to help one another along The Way. If you are struggling with panic and anxiety — as I did, I recommend you "walk with" friends and a trusted therapist.

Most importantly, I recommend facing your fear prayerfully and hand in hand with God. God wants the best for each one of us. Call out to Him, and He will answer. It may not be what we want, when we want it; but He is listening. Place your trust in God.

"The LORD is a refuge for the oppressed, a stronghold in times of trouble. Those who know your name trust in you, for you, LORD, have never forsaken those who seek you" (Psalm 9:9-10, NIV).

CHAPTER 9

Veronica, Love of my life

The healthy decisions I made in my life allowed God's grace to lead me to the love of my life, Veronica. God is good, and He provides us opportunities. If we choose well, we allow the Holy Spirit to flow in our lives and furthers the journey that God desires us to live. However, when we make poor choices in life, we veer off the path that God intentionally has laid out for us. I believe God had my wife Veronica in store for me. I believe she is an answer to my prayer as a young child. I asked my Lord and my God – as a young child of 8 to 11 years old – to provide me with a loving family. I asked and pleaded, as a youth, for Him to heal my family. "Please, Father, stop their fighting. Father, I want a family like my friends have. I want a clean home and clean clothes. Please, Father, help me. Help my brother and sisters. Please bring love to our home." I prayed this prayer time and time again throughout my childhood. The prayer always had the same themes: love and the restored love of family. It took my Lord God almost 20 years to answer my prayer, but He did. He heard me. I am 100% sure. Unfortunately, Reader, I almost blew it. I almost lost, destroyed and sabotaged the gift that I had been given.

I had multiple relationships, as a younger man, that could have ended in marriage; but I was not ready. God, in His wisdom, advises us to keep the wedding bed Holy. I now believe it is good for us to enter marriage pure and without knowledge of another partner. Sexuality can be very misleading. Emotions can manipulate our minds into believing that the person with whom we were intimate is our soul mate. Reader, be careful; for intimacy can lead one down a path that was not intended.

I had several girlfriends prior to Veronica, and their positive attributes make the sum total of my wife. It's almost as if I have been searching for her all my life and saw in these girlfriends a vision of what God had in store for me.

If you don't get anything else from this book, hold onto this: God hears you, and He hears your prayers. He does not work on our timeline, but He answers our prayers in due time. Pray with an earnest heart. Don't pray to win the lottery or for selfish ambition. Pray selflessly with true love. Pray with the mind of a child who waits expectantly, knowing that our good and faithful Father hears you. Believe. God wants the best for His children. Reader, if you are a parent who wants the best for your children, then you know that God wants the best for you because you are His child, and good parents want the best for their children. God is indeed a good Parent, a good Father!

"I waited patiently for the LORD; he turned to me and heard my cry. He lifted me out of the slimy pit, out of the mud and mire; he set my feet on a rock and gave me a firm place to stand" (Psalm 40:1-2, NIV).

In **August 1997**, I returned from Alaska and applied to work for our local ambulance company. I had taken an EMT course at Rural/Metro Medical Services during the previous winter, and I was hired as their EMT intern when I came home from Alaska. I initially bicycled to work because I could not afford a car; but after I slid on my side through an intersection while riding my bicycle, I realized I must figure out a new way to get to work. I asked my good friend Chuck for a loan, and he readily gave me the money. He said, "Danny, I will give you the money; but one day, I will ask you to help someone out just like I am helping you." Chuck was asking me to pay it forward.

I was initially making $5.25 an hour or minimum wage. Among rent, car insurance, a small car payment and food, I was barely squeaking by. I had to work much over time to make ends meet.

At that time in my life, I lived with two friends who I met in nursing school. We lived in a large, brick row apartment complex. It was a three-story apartment building, with new carpeting, fresh paint and an alarm system. It was convenient to downtown, bars, restaurants and markets. It was everything three young (20-something) friends could want in an apartment.

On one beautiful, sunshine-filled January day in 1998, I saw a beautiful woman coming into our apartment complex. As fate would have it, she lived on the first floor in the downstairs apartment – directly below our two-story suite. I can still vividly see her in my mind's eye. She wore a white, down winter coat; and she had brown, short hair to her shoulders. For a week or more, we would randomly bump into each other in the hallway, and I longed to get to know her. One day as I was going to grab a coffee, we again crossed paths. I said to her, "I am going for a cup of coffee. Would you like to join me?" Veronica was so cute, and she dropped what she was doing to come with me. We hit it off from the start. We sat at "our coffee house" down the road and talked for hours. We became friends that day, and I learned that Veronica was no stranger to a difficult life.

Veronica told me of her tumor, recent brain surgery and her challenges surrounding her loss of hearing. Veronica is deaf on one side due to an acoustic neuroma. It was a benign tumor about the size of a golf ball that grew on her brain stem.

She had begun to feel symptoms about six months before the surgery. Initially, the pins-and-needle feelings in her extremities were dismissed as anxiety. Then one day after a Dave Matthews concert, it left her temporarily deaf on one side. Again, Veronica felt that something odd was going on with her brain; but the symptoms were dismissed as normal for going to a loud rock concert.

After several weeks of not feeling well, Veronica said her parents decided to ease her mind, and they were able to get her an appointment with a neurologist who ordered a MRI. Unfortunately, the MRI revealed a three-centimeter tumor and would require surgery. The first doctor advised Veronica and her parents that the surgery would last approximately 11 hours and that she would have facial droop related to the nerve around which the tumor had grown.

Veronica was a stunning 22-year-old woman, and the thought of having unilateral facial droop was excruciatingly painful to hear for her and her parents. Veronica's parents were in the medical field. Her dad was an urologist, and her mom was a Registered Nurse. Together, they researched various surgery options and, through a family friend, found a specialty clinic in Los Angeles.

Veronica and her parents flew to LA and had her surgery scheduled at the House Ear Clinic. The surgery – that would have taken 11 hours for the original surgeon – took four hours with the specialist in LA. Also, Veronica did not suffer any facial droop but had to relearn to balance. She had suffered trauma to her balance nerve during surgery, and it took several weeks of therapy for her to learn to walk again. In addition to her balance nerve damage, Veronica also was now deaf on one side. These deficits were a challenge that led to her growth. Veronica's physical beauty initially attracted me to her; but her positive attitude, perseverance and humor are attributes of hers that set her apart from any other woman I had ever met.

As we sat drinking our coffee and as Veronica shared her story with me, I realized – right then and there – that she was a very special person. I knew she understood that this life is temporary, and she was not absorbed with material possessions. She had depth of character and resiliency. And she was beautiful, intelligent and funny. What more could I ask for? We sat and talked about family, friends and life experiences. Time flew, and it seemed as though I had known her my entire life. We returned to our apartment complex, and we said our goodbyes.

I had just returned from Alaska a couple of months prior and had the freezer stocked with salmon. I had planned on surprising my roommates with dinner. Fortunately, I needed a can opener for the fish stew I was making but could not find one. I went downstairs to Veronica's apartment, and I asked to borrow her can opener. I also invited her to join us for a meal. At dinner that night, my friends were a no show; and it seemed as though I could not have planned it better; but to this day, I contend these were not pickup lines. However, the salmon stew worked its magic. Veronica loves a good meal, and this too was very attractive to me. The night was wonderful. It was a storybook evening with laughter, good food (if I may say so myself), bread, wine and an abundance of conversation. Hours seemed like minutes, and we were becoming good friends. I was smitten.

A couple of weeks had passed, and Veronica and I were falling in love. God had answered my prayer and literally brought my soon-to-be bride to my doorstep. Our dates were always entertaining and fun, and we decided to meet family.

Veronica invited me to lunch with her mom – test #1 inspection from her mother. When I met Cathy, Veronica's mom, for the first time, I politely shook her hand. Cathy responded, "Oh, my God, my hand!" I had shaken her hand with my usual, firm handshake; but my nerves got the best of me, and I squeezed too tight. We were off to a great start...

Several months later, I would be meeting Veronica's dad. This would be the test #2 and a much more difficult challenge. Veronica had warned me that her dad is protective and has scared off many a boyfriend. We met Veronica's parents for dinner, and we went to their friend Stavros' Greek restaurant. It was a wonderful meal, and Greek food has now become my favorite. The evening was great. Any apprehension I had of a protective, dominating, strong-minded, critical dad and doctor lording it over me – a lowly EMT, "want-to-be boyfriend" – did not exist!?

At dinner, Fotis said to me, "Eat, my son. Don't be shy!" We ate and drank and had a good time. "Opa!" Veronica and I shared glances during the meal and nonverbally said, "Where is the criticism? Where is the protective daddy behavior?"

129

Several years later while playing golf together, I asked Fotis about the first night I met him. I said, "Fotis, the first time I met you, at the Greek restaurant, you welcomed me right away. How come you were so nice to me?" Fotis nodded slowly several times, turned down his bottom lip slightly — as he was accustomed to doing — and said matter of factly, "I wanted to put you at ease, so you would screw up." He wanted to see my true colors, and he gave me enough rope to do so. I learned early on that Fotis, my soon-to-be father-in-law, was much more intelligent and much more cunning than me. I knew that Fotis often would test and challenge me, but I would just continue to focus on loving his daughter the best I knew how.

Six months after meeting Veronica's parents, they invited me to NYC to meet the Greek community and their Greek family. I was a little apprehensive because I could not afford the trip. They allowed me to stay in their hotel room with them, but I would have to sleep with Fotis, Veronica's dad. The Greek party would be attended by several Greek families — hundreds of people — and hosted in a very nice, very large reception hall in New York City. (A little aside, yes, we live "My Big Fat Greek Wedding." In fact, when I first met Veronica, I was a vegetarian like Ian Miller in this well-known movie. And true to form, Fotis said, "Eat sum lumb Doan." I spelled the previous sentence phonetically. My father-in-law has a very strong Greek accent. Needless to say, I ate some "lumb," and the rest is now history.)

This party was a time to show one's accomplishments. The Greek party was mostly first-generation immigrants from Greece. They were all now very successful entrepreneurs, restaurant owners, lawyers and doctors. They exemplified The American Dream. At this formal event, Fotis unfortunately forgot to pack his "good" shoes. As we were getting ready for the party, he started to hit his forehead with the palms of his hands. Fotis repeatedly struck his head with strong, forceful, painful strikes. I thought to myself, *What in the world is he doing?* There was no time for shoe shopping. Fotis looked great at the party, and no one mentioned his shoes. His outburst or

CHAPTER 9 | **VERONICA, LOVE OF MY LIFE**

head smacking was something new to me. It was a part of his persona and something I would learn to understand.

I was introduced to friends and relatives as Veronica's boyfriend, "the psychologist." I went along with this introduction. Most people just smiled and nodded. I did, however, have my bachelor's degree in psychology; but it was a white lie told by Fotis to avoid judgment from others. I was, after all, "just" an EMT. To my girlfriend's father, the doctor, I was not worthy of his daughter.

The party was wonderful – filled with dancing, laughter and great food. We went back to the hotel; and the next morning, I awoke next to a Greek man – inches away from my soon-to-be father-in-law's face. I opened my eyes and blinked hard several times, trying to remember where I was…

Reader, I think this trip was how they realized that I had sincere feelings for their daughter. It is today one of our go-to stories for fond memories and a good laugh. It is part of the glue that binds us.

After the NYC Greek party weekend, I realized — if I was a doctor, a lawyer or a successful business owner, that still would not be enough. Fotis was not materialistic; he was just a doting and very protective daddy, who wanted the best for his little girl. Having two daughters of my own, I now understand, and I can respect where he was coming from. One day while visiting Veronica's parents at their home in Utica, New York, Veronica, Cathy (Veronica's mom), Fotis and I sat by their pool. Veronica's dad received a phone call from his friend in the village of his hometown in Greece. He spoke to his friend in his native Greek tongue and laughed and carried on. When he got off the phone, Veronica asked her dad, "What were you talking about with your friend?" Fotis turned to me and said, "I asked my friend if there were any good Greek boys in the village for my daughter." I just shook my head, swallowed hard and held on for a bumpy ride…

One day, Fotis said to me, "Doan, before you ask to marry my daughter, you will have a good job — one that you can afford a family." I promised Fotis that I would not ask for his daughter's hand in marriage till that day.

At that point, I was still working at Rural/Metro Ambulance. I had started a social service program at the company called The C.A.R.E. Program. As EMTs and Paramedics, we go into homes and see a vignette of people's lives. We treat our patients' medical conditions and see a glimpse of their lives. Unfortunately, we often encountered people living in dire circumstances. I created The C.A.R.E. Program to ease a feeling in me that we were not doing enough when we treated people medically.

With the blessing of the general manager of the company, I was given an office and some designated time out of the ambulance. When EMTs and Paramedics had a challenging social service type of situation, they would fill out our newly created C.A.R.E. form and write down their concerns regarding the patient's living condition.

I would contact the patient on behalf of Rural/Metro Medical Services C.A.R.E. Program and attempt to meet their needs. I utilized the systems previously established within the county to meet the client's needs. More often than not, the answer was already there; but many times, people's needs fell through the cracks of the system. That is where we, The C.A.R.E.

My friend, Fotis, and I playing golf.

Program, attempted to meet the additional social service needs of our patient. Often people in need lacked transportation. It is very challenging to bring children on a bus, then go to a grocery store or food pantry and return home with bags of food and children in tow. Also, people, who are elderly or have medical conditions, may have difficulties getting groceries. If we encountered people in need of food but who lacked transportation, we would deliver food. We created a mobile food pantry, and we would deliver food in our service vehicle.

Another aspect of the C.A.R.E. Program was client/landlord mediation. Unfortunately, many tenants are taken advantage of by landlords. I often would act as an in-between for tenants and landlords. One referral from one of the Paramedics regarded a single mother living with her children, and they had no refrigerator. So with her permission, I called the landlord and said, "Hi, my name is Dan Connors; and I am Rural Metro's C.A.R.E. Program director. I understand that your tenant does not have a refrigerator?" The landlord replied, "I will get one there tomorrow." And he did.

In a short time, we had helped hundreds of people in small but meaningful ways. I enjoyed this work very much, and I was given the Star of Life Award for EMTs throughout the nation for going above and beyond the call of duty in their agency. Approximately 50 other Paramedics and EMTs throughout the country were treated to a trip to Washington, D.C. and met their local Congressman and Congresswoman.

I had found my passion, but my passion did not pay well. I had doubled my initial pay to now make $10.50/hour. I decided to try and fast forward my managerial track and asked for managerial pay for the work I was doing. I got shot down hard; and with this rebuke, I now knew I had to find another career if I wanted to marry Veronica.

Emergency Medical Services (EMS) work closely with Police and Fire. Firefighters and EMTs partially overlap in their job descriptions, and I saw an opportunity to further my career. Firefighters make a good income, and this career would lend itself to satisfying my soon-to-be father-in-law's requirement. I had to choose. I had to choose between a career that I loved or a job that was more financially secure. I made the right decision at that time in my life, and I became a firefighter... (I hope to rejuvenate my former C.A.R.E. Program now that I am retired from the SFD.)

So, with my new job as a firefighter, I now could ask Fotis for his daughter's hand in marriage. I called Cathy and Fotis and drove to their home 45 minutes away. A perfect distance away for in-laws, so I thought. Not too close but not too far away either. I asked Fotis to breakfast and said, "I love your daughter. I want to marry her." He said, "You two are best friends?" I replied, "Yes, we are best friends." Fotis replied, "Because you are best friends, because you are now a firefighter with a reasonably good-paying job and because you love my daughter, I give you my blessing."

I asked Veronica to marry me on December 23, 2000. I called her girlfriends, told them my plan and asked them for their help. I said to Judeanne, "Tell V you want to take her out to dinner at a nice restaurant." Veronica was dressed beautifully when I picked her up in the limousine. I had a dozen roses, and I got out of the limo in front of our apartment building. I knocked on her door, and she looked puzzled. I said, "Jude and Vicky aren't coming. Come with me. I have something I want to ask you." The limousine drove us to our church, the Cathedral of The Immaculate Conception. Our feet barely touched the ground as we entered the church. The church was candle lit, and I had arranged with Monsignor Champlin to have our engagement there. I gave my brother, who was waiting in the wings, a cue; and he started to play "our song" on the CD I had given him. We went to the altar, and I got down on one knee. I told Veronica, "I love you, V. You make me a better man. I want to spend my life with you. Will you marry me?" Veronica was so adorable and beautiful and said, "Yes!" Monsignor Champlin came out, blessed our engagement and told us, "You young love birds, go and have a wonderful marriage." My brother graciously photographed wonderful candids that we cherish.

Our engagement was wonderful and romantic, and we now had some decisions to make. I would be satisfied with a small backyard wedding, but Veronica was an only child. Her parents were ready to celebrate, and Veronica was ready to have the wedding of her dreams. One day we toured banquet facilities in Veronica's hometown. We found one that we both liked and went back to her parents' home to discuss the situation. I was on autopilot and would go along with my soon-to-be wife's decision. We did not have to pay for the wedding, so I felt reluctant to voice my opinion. Veronica was beaming as she announced, "Daddy, we found a beautiful place! It's the Twin Ponds Country Club." Fotis replied, "Oh, that's nice, baby." Veronica excused herself for a minute and left Fotis and I sitting in the family room together. Fotis turned to me and said in his deep, thick Greek accent, "Do you know how much that f---ing costs?!" I must have looked like a deer in the headlights. I had just received a small glimpse of what I signed up for. Veronica returned to the room and jumped back into the details of her plan. Fotis nodded and smiled at his daughter. Veronica is the apple of his eye, and he would do anything for her.

A couple of weeks prior to our wedding, Fotis broke his leg, falling from a ladder. He had to utilize a walker and had pins placed in his leg. The thought of using a walker, while walking his only daughter down the aisle, left Fotis feeling tremendous anger. My father-in-law is one of the most self-determined, strong and loving dads I know. The day of our wedding, Fotis put away the walker and walked his daughter down the aisle without limping. I imagined the pain he was feeling, and I am in awe of his resilience.

Years before our wedding, before Veronica and I met, in 1987, Fotis had a "pool accident." I place "pool accident" in quotes because it is how the family talks about it, and it is a painful memory for all. Fotis was found at the bottom of the pool unresponsive. Veronica, 12 at the time, decided to look out the family room window. She describes having a feeling that was not right. She saw her dad submerged in the water and screamed. Her mom and neighbor were able to retrieve Fotis from the pool, and an ambulance was called. Fotis was intubated; CPR was performed; and it was suspected that he had a heart attack. Fotis was in a coma for several days at St. Elizabeth's Hospital in Utica, New York. In 1987, the percentage of people who survived a heart attack was approximately 5%. Not only did Fotis survive a suspected heart attack, drowning and near-death experience; but he made a full recovery. Fotis went on to practice medicine as an urologist for almost 20 more years.

Reader, I am not sure if I am fully giving the astronomical percentage that was against surviving a near-death experience such as Fotis'. It got me thinking ... if Fotis had died that day in the pool, life would be tremendously different for Veronica. Her mom may or may not have remarried. At any rate, the tremendous influence of her father would not be around to influence Veronica's life. Veronica very well may never have gone to Elmira College. She may never have gone to LA for the surgery. We may never have met in Syracuse. The list of "may never haves" and "ifs" are infinite. I do believe I may never have met Veronica, and we would not have these two wonderful children who are upstairs sleeping as I am writing this book.

Not only would Veronica's life be different but my life, too. Veronica has changed my life for the better. She literally made me a better person. She

Wedding day 2001

loved me when other girlfriends/women would have given up on me. She loved me for better and for worse and in sickness and in health as in our 2015 experience. She and her parents nursed me back to health. She was meant for me, and I was meant for her. She is a gift from God. This I am certain.

Again, Reader, not all girlfriends or boyfriends are meant to be spouses. When we dabble with sexuality, it can be misleading and keep one away from our designated soul mate. Perhaps that is why the divorce rate is so high? However, once married to our soul mate, it is our continual responsibility to treat them as God sees them. Your wife, your husband is God's child. You, Reader – myself included, Veronica included – should treat each one as the gift that they are – a gift from God. It's Not Too Late to heal the marriage that you, Reader, professed before God and guests. As my good friend Don Maldari said, "If in doubt, follow love." Reader, let's clarify love for a moment. Don Maldari SJ did not say if in doubt, follow lust or follow what feels good at that moment. Love is an action – not always an emotion. We can love others in loving actions; and this, in turn, can bring about loving emotion. Once-futile feelings of a broken marriage can be brought to life again through love in action. Love in action is saying NO to other extramarital relationships and energy that takes away from your spouse. Perhaps it's not another person that garnishes your attention from your spouse. Perhaps it is your career or your hobby or your depression or your ... fill in the blank.

> "Love is patient, love is kind. It does not envy, it does not boast,
> it is not proud. It does not dishonor others, it is not self-seeking,
> it is not easily angered, it keeps no record of wrongs. Love does
> not delight in evil but rejoices with the truth. It always protects,
> always trusts, always hopes, always perseveres. Love never fails..."
> (1 Corinthians 13:4-8a, NIV).

This passage from the Bible is not just a wedding announcement; it is our duty as married couples. We are asked to live what is instructed; and by doing this, we will have a love-filled life. It is a recipe for a wonderful meal, and thanks be to God – something I learned.

In 2001, Veronica and I decided to buy a house. After several months of looking and researching, we finally found our starter house. It was a three-story townhouse in a small middle-class development. It was near the river, and we could launch kayaks or fish. It was a good location and in a good school district. It had all the makings of a wonderful first home.

After Veronica and I shook hands with the couple and verbally agreed to the deal, we invited Veronica's parents to come and see our new home. They toured our prospective new home and were not impressed. Fotis said, "If you fart, the person next door could smell it." He went on to say, "What if there is a fire and the attached home next door catches fire?" Fotis was starting to encroach on my profession as a firefighter as well as offend our decision to buy our first home. We thought they would congratulate us, but we were wrong. Both Veronica and I decided to disregard their opinion and moved forward with the sale.

Later that week, I drove to our "new house" and gave the owner a "good faith" down payment of $1,000. That was a lot of money for us, but we were so very excited. We had no problem securing our loan, and our credit history was reasonable for two younger professionals.

Literally 10 seconds after I handed the owner a check, I received a call from Veronica. She said, "Don't give him the check!" I replied, "What are you talking about?" Veronica went on to tell me that her parents decided to give us a very large sum of money as a down payment for a different home. I drove home excited, confused and not sure of what I should do. Should I be grateful for the money or feel manipulated by their gift? In the end, we accepted their gift; but it came at a price.

One weekend while returning from a ski weekend with friends, we drove through a small development on the way home to our apartment. We had not found a house to buy yet and had lost our "good faith" down payment. We pulled up to a home with the "For Sale" sign in the front yard, and Veronica audibly gasped. We had found our new home....

The house needed work, and we have been doing little by little for the past 19 years. It is now very much our home; but for many years, I was resentful that we took the gift from her parents. I blamed them for our financial troubles, for buying a home that we were not financially ready to buy. Our taxes were not accounted for in our decision process, and we were saddled with taxes that we had not escrowed into our mortgage payment. I was blaming them, but it was me who was to blame.

I was young in my mindset and perhaps stunted in my development related to my upbringing. I should have felt grateful, but a very large piece of me felt manipulated.

My in-laws and I have been through many lows. One day after working at the firehouse, I came home to find Fotis painting our kitchen. I asked him, "Fotis, what are you doing?" He said, "My daughter told me you're having a party, and you need your kitchen painted." I told him to get down off the ladder and that I would do it. Fotis said to me, "You Irish have sticks up your asses." I bit my tongue and did not respond to his aggression.

Veronica and I got our home ready to have the party. We also rented a hot tub, which you could do back at that time, and literally rolled it into our backyard. We had a very large bonfire, karaoke, food, beer and music. We were the fun, young, new couple in the neighborhood. I was not the man I am today. I drank to get drunk, and I looked too long at attractive women. Unfortunately, at that time, I disliked my in-laws.

I sat in the hot tub, intoxicated, after I had just done cannonballs off the deck and watched neighbors of ours singing karaoke. The couple, Bob and Marsha, seemed different. I couldn't put a finger on it; but this older, mature couple were in love, having fun and were completely sober. They sang, smiled and radiated love. I was mesmerized, for some reason, at the obvious bond of their marriage. They would soon become our very dear friends. Bob was a Christian man who would have a life-changing impact on me.

I would like to say that life always has been roses for Veronica and me in our walk together. Unfortunately, we have had our struggles. My inability to get my "stuff" together early on in our marriage almost derailed us. I thought I wanted out of our marriage. The first four to five years of our marriage were the hardest part by far. We had to learn the dance of living together, and we would have to learn how to live close to in-laws.

Fotis and Cathy decided to move into our town and moved 0.4 miles from us. The 45-minute gap from their original home, a perfect distance, became a 45-second car ride. No longer would there be physical distance separating them from us. My mind reeled and my heart pounded as they told us of their recent purchase.

Veronica is an only child, and she brought issues to our marriage that I did not understand. I am one of four brothers and sisters, and I have a stepbrother and stepsister. There are more than enough of us to go around for my parents to concentrate on. The time is equally split; but for Veronica's parents, she is the apple of their eye and has 100% of their attention. I was not used to parents stopping by multiple times a week and multiple phone calls daily. Not to mention the groceries they would bring us, without asking, sent shock waves into my system. They were doting on their daughter, and I did not understand. Unfortunately, neither Veronica nor I understood this complicated, normal family dynamic. It is one many couples go through; but to be a healthy couple, we needed a little daylight between the two families.

"Therefore shall a man leave his father and mother, and shall cleave unto his wife: and they shall be one flesh" (Genesis 2:24, KJV).

When my in-laws decided to move down the street from us, it was a very large adjustment process. Unfortunately, in that process, I thought I wanted out. They were too much! There was constant competition for Veronica's attention. I often had to hear what was going on in my wife's life by overhearing her talk with her mother on the phone. They had a close-knit relationship with their daughter. Ironically, this was one of the reasons I initially fell in love with Veronica. She loved her parents so very much, and that was attractive. Through the first four years of our marriage, I stumbled to adjust to married life, and our marriage of intertwined in-laws.

Unfortunately, I began to sabotage our relationship. I was impacted and influenced by my unresolved family upbringing; and with the stress from our marriage, I acted in unbecoming ways. I thank God for good counselors who weeded out the turmoil of my mind and helped me unravel my thought processes. I was a walking, talking mess; but I did not realize it.

Unfortunately, I met a woman at the gym, who was a trainer at the gym and very attractive. We became friends, and I learned that she was going through a divorce. Unfortunately, we kissed and I was very tempted to pursue a further relationship with her. I was at a precipice, and I had to make a decision. A good friend of mine is a Jesuit priest; and one day, Don said to me, "Dan, if in doubt, follow love." That expression saved our marriage. I was in doubt; but I knew that I had made a vow to my wife before God, and I was going to fight for our marriage.

I knew that I must end any romantic interest in this woman at the gym. I was driving and thinking about what to do. I pulled into an unknown, empty parking lot and called my friend from the gym. I told her that I could not work out with her any longer and that we could not be friends. I told her that I love my wife very much.

Reader, unbeknownst to me, the church parking lot I pulled into would be the same church where I would be baptized 11 years down the road. That church became our home, and the pastor became a dear friend of ours. God works in mysterious ways...

"No temptation has overtaken you except what is common to mankind. And God is faithful; he will not let you be tempted beyond what you can bear. But when you are tempted, he will also provide a way out so that you can endure it" (1 Corinthians 10:13, NIV).

Unfortunately, I was sabotaging our marriage. My life was a mess, but it was great at the same time. I had a wonderful career, a beautiful, loving wife; but I was my own worst enemy. I loved my wife with my whole heart, but what I didn't realize was that my heart had much room to grow. It was only through God's grace that our marriage was healed, that my heart grew and that I became the man who God has called me to become. Thank You, Father!

My childhood development and lack of development allowed me to think that this type of behavior at the gym was alright. I have since learned that it is not okay. In fact, I would say that it is sinful; and I am very grateful for a forgiving Father and a very forgiving wife.

I was a good guy, but I had baggage. My baggage was becoming out of control, and it could have directly impacted our marriage. I would like to say that this friendship with the woman at the gym was my only sin, my only sabotage; but I would be lying. Unresolved physical needs between Veronica and I resulted in me getting massages. I exercised frequently and ran long-distance races. I justified getting massages frequently for keeping my muscles healthy. However, I desired more than just muscular manipulation. I found several massage therapists who helped me drown in sin and several others who I offended. I am truly remorseful about this conduct and my behavior.

God had been hounding me and disciplining me along my journey. When I sinned, it was as if a billboard – with my face and my sins – was broadcast for many to witness. Living in a small city has its good and bad qualities. In 2007, I had the "honor" of being on the Fire Department's calendar cover page. My picture and the firefighter calendar were splashed across the county. I placed honor in quotes because being on a cover was a tremendous headache. I was asked to help sell the calendar and make appearances in the local mall. Not only was it a headache, but it was a source of tension for me at the firehouse. Some of that tension I now contribute to my Father God as part of my discipline process that has brought me out of darkness.

"Because the Lord disciplines the one he loves, and he chastens everyone he accepts as his son" (Hebrews 12:6, NIV).

One evening just before dinner, early in our marriage, Fotis asked me, "Do you want to end up in my garden?" It was not a veiled threat. Fotis was physically threatening me. I get it. I was not a great husband. I now respect what he was saying. He was being a strong, protective father to his lovely daughter. It is a small community, and word of my indiscretions had gotten around.

Through therapy, I learned to curtail impulsive and toxic behaviors. I undid and relearned appropriate boundaries. It took several years; but through God's grace, I have learned the proper ways to interact with women.

I learned that I must fight any impulse – especially when I am tired. I learned that I must always make my wife the number-one woman in my life. She is my best friend, and I must always move forward with that thought in my head and carry this thought forward in my actions. This understanding applies all the time - even during arguments. I learned that I am not designed to be close friends with women. I have a wife; and my wife should always get the first fruit of my knowledge, thoughts, decisions and play.

I would like to say my relationship with my in-laws got better with the birth of our first daughter, but unfortunately it heightened the tension.

Veronica developed sports-induced urticaria as an adult after her brain surgery in about 2000. We are not 100% certain what brought about the urticaria and facial edema, but the allergist recommended taking allergy medicine prior to exercise. Essentially, when Veronica gets overheated during exercise, she develops a rash and hives throughout her body.

One day before we were married, Veronica went running and felt an odd sensation in her face. She ran by a bus stop and looked at her reflection in the glass. Her face had swollen, and she looked unrecognizable. Her lips, ears and face were so swollen that her eyes were swelling shut. She called me, and I raced home to find an ambulance in front of our apartment. I jumped in the back and knew the crew members (Sandy and Jeff) who were working on her. Veronica had her face covered with her hands and was crying. When the ambulance pulled up, Veronica ran out to the ambulance with a picture of herself to show the paramedics. She was unrecognizable due to the swelling. She was treated for a severe allergic reaction, which was a precursor to anaphylaxis. She had what is known as angioedema; was treated with IV epinephrine, Benadryl and oxygen and placed on a heart monitor.

At the hospital, she was given a steroid, continued with nasal cannula oxygen; and they monitored her closely for swelling of her airway. With Veronica's history and relatively recent diagnosis of sports-induced urticaria, we – as well as our OB-GYN – were reluctant to have a vaginal delivery and opted to have c-sections for the births of our daughters. We knew that, once the labor began, it would be a marathon of sorts. We were concerned with Veronica overheating and having an allergic reaction during the delivery.

Both children's c-sections were met with criticism from my in-laws. They had wanted to try and see how the delivery went naturally and then do an emergency c-section if there was a need. I did not feel comfortable with that opinion after seeing Veronica in her distress. We knew that – once Veronica's hives started – it was hard to control the itching, the facial edema; and we were concerned with anaphylaxis. Both of her parents, being in the medical field, knew of possible complications from c-sections and were more skeptical of that invasive surgery. I get their opinion. Veronica, the OB-GYN and I all agreed to have a c-section; but I received the in-law wrath. I had swayed their one and only daughter against their medical opinion. I was a thorn in their side.

When our first daughter was born, the anesthesiologist said to me, "Dad, you can take a picture now." I stood up from a seated position by Veronica's head and looked over the surgery screen at my wife's abdomen. The doctor lifted our beautiful, little girl from a surgical opening and removed her from Veronica's uterus. I went to take a picture but couldn't move my finger. I was in awe of God's creation and the miracle who was being held before me. Our daughter came into this world quiet and aware of her surroundings. She blinked and looked around — calm, cool and collected. Our first daughter! Joy beyond all joy ... Veronica and my love incarnate. The fruit of a good decision. "If in doubt, follow love."

After we weighed her, cleaned her, bundled her and held her, I went to tell our families in the waiting room. I walked into the waiting area and announced to friends and family, "We have a baby girl!" Exuberation and happiness flowed, and I was hugged and kissed. I said to my in-laws, "They are allowing two at a time. Follow me." While walking to see Veronica and our new baby, I said, "Our little girl is quiet but healthy!" My mother-in-law said, "She's not a loudmouth like her father!" I ignored the slight and remained in a happy place. They had just been panicked at the thought of their one and only daughter going under the knife once again. This experience was disheartening for them, but we had started the much-needed separation of daughter and parent. We needed a little daylight to grow as a couple and as a new family unit. Veronica and I made a family decision to have a c-section, but Veronica's parents were not on board. This decision was difficult – to say the least.

Reader, I get it. Veronica is their baby, and they want the best for her. I thank God for my understanding of where they were at emotionally. I was able to empathize with them and deflect their criticism.

I can honestly say that — by the time our first child arrived — I was ready to be a dad and our marriage was again on the right path. I had begun my present journey with God. I had managed the mess of my childhood, and I knew that the negative generational behaviors ended with me. Veronica, thank God, had an ideal childhood. It was not perfect – as no life is perfect. However, growing up, Veronica lived in a loving, caring, respectful family environment. An environment in which the parents chose to stick out the discomforts that married life can bring and worked through marriage difficulties. Their marriage was not the ideal marriage but was much better than my parents. In other words, Veronica brought less baggage to our marriage. Unfortunately, Veronica was doted on as a child and literally never washed a dish. She was not exactly spoiled but never did dishes. This was a little opposite of how I grew up. However, together, we have – through God's grace – created a wonderful home environment. Our children do chores, wash dishes and cook dinner on occasion.

The idea of a healthy marriage and healthy family life is to work on our negative past to not pass down generational baggage to our children. I can confidently say that we are a happy, healthy family; and I feel tremendously blessed by God.

I do not take this for granted. God does His part, but we have to do our part. As I did my part, Veronica did her part. I said "no" to sinful behaviors that ultimately could have led to the end of our marriage, and Veronica attempted to create healthy family boundaries between her and her parents.

If I had chosen to leave our marriage early on, we would not have been blessed with two wonderful children. But because I got my head on straight and learned the life lessons that were being presented to me at the time, God truly has blessed our marriage.

"… 'Though your sins are like scarlet, they shall be as white as snow; though they are red as crimson, they shall be like wool. If you are willing and obedient, you will eat the good things of the land'" (Isaiah 1:18-19, NIV).

By the time our first child was born in 2006, our marriage was better than it had ever been, and we were ready to be parents. In-laws can add a whole heck of a lot to the mix. When you bring people together, there inevitably will be a test. And test it did … I get it now. As a dad, I get the desire and the need to have your children in your life. A good dad, a good parent will always want to see his/her children; to be a part of their lives; to be there in times of plenty and to help in times of need. But I also have learned that new families need some daylight between themselves and extended family.

The birth of our second child was also like touching the beauty of God. As I waited to be called into the operating room, I prayed and thought of my wife getting prepped. I put on my surgical garments, which they required. I told the nurse, "I would like to go in with Veronica. I am a paramedic and a nurse. I can handle it." The nurse said, "You are husband and dad first, and I will be back in a moment to get you." They wheeled Veronica into the operating room. I had made a promise to Veronica that I would be at the head of her bed all the way through the procedure. Unfortunately, Veronica suffers from debilitating anxiety and panic at times. She has passed out into my arms on numerous occasions. Her body will drop in blood pressure, and the result is loss of consciousness. The medical professionals describe this condition as a vagal vagus reaction and can be brought on by stress and anxiety.

As I stood in the surgery suite changing room, waiting for the nurse to return, I started to get concerned. Five minutes passed, then 10; and finally, the nurse came in to get me. I walked into the operating room with the nurse, and there was almost a physical wave of tension throughout the room. I said aloud, "Did she give you guys a scare?" The tension eased; and the doctor said, "Yes, Veronica's blood pressure dropped." I said, "She does that sometimes." I could tell that Veronica had been given a relaxant and was groggy. Veronica's blood pressure had dropped to almost critical levels – 80/40. I wished I had asserted myself more with the nurse and come into the room initially with Veronica. Thank God for competent doctors and nurses. Again, witnessing the OB-GYN remove our second daughter via c-section from Veronica's uterus made me profoundly aware of God's goodness. I stood in awe and told Veronica we have a baby girl. They cleaned her and put her on Veronica's chest. Our second child was determined to let everyone within earshot know she was in this world! She let out some good, hearty cries that are music to medical professionals' ears. It is one of many assessments made in the delivery process. We had a very strong and healthy second child. Thanks be to God.

Renewal of vows – In 2011, Veronica and I decided to renew our vows. We had accomplished 10 years of marriage! Unfortunately, the first five years were tremendously difficult; but our marriage started to improve the next five. We, as a couple, were ready to say "I do" again. We wanted to say before friends, family and God that we love each other. We wanted to say to each other that I choose you again. On August 25, 2011, in our backyard on our deck – with our children as flower girls, we recited our wedding vows publicly in front of 50 guests. Our dear friend Father Don Maldari, SJ, my spiritual advisor, who prompted me several years prior "If in doubt, follow love," officiated our wedding renewal. Veronica and I were made for each other. She saw in me what my Father God sees in me. She sees my heart. She knows I am a good person and knows that I love her and our children with all my heart. My heart has grown exponentially, and I am now ready to love. I, too, see Veronica as God sees her. She is a beautiful woman inside and out. I knew she would be a wonderful mother someday, and I was right. God knew what He was doing when He allowed us both to be in the right place at the right time.

Therapy, therapy, therapy. I worked hard to right the ship, to right myself and behave accordingly. However, therapy can only do so much. For

Renewal of vows... Our ten year anniversary.

me, it was my relationship with God that has changed my life for the better. I feel healed. Thanks be to God for His strength, I now make good choices.

"I can do all this through him who gives me strength" (Philippians 4:13, NIV).

I make good choices today because my nose is in His Book and my lips are praising Him and giving Him thanks. I literally have been praying every morning for the past 10 years of my life. Prayer has made me a better person. My relationship with my Father God has healed me and freed my soul. However, when my nose is not in His Good Book or I am not diligent in my prayer life, I can falter. But if I fail, I get up. I dust myself off and ask for forgiveness. If and when I need to ask for forgiveness, it is always with a repentant heart and not a robotic mentality of "I can sin and get away with it."

Our hearts are the key to unlocking God's free gift of forgiveness. God will give forgiveness freely to those who sincerely ask, but forgiveness is not some formula that can be manipulated. God knows our heart. I do not take my newfound freedom for granted! I know I must be vigilant and always choose correctly. We have a wonderful life, and I know the enemy would rejoice in seeing us slip.

"So, if you think you are standing firm, be careful that you don't fall!" (1 Corinthians 10:12, NIV)

My father-in-law and I have always had Veronica in common. We both love her, and this is what binds us. Fotis, my father-in-law, is a doctor. I am a LPN, paramedic and firefighter. I will never measure up, and I know that no one would be good enough for his daughter. I smile as I type this because I now understand. I understand because I am now a dad. I once was threatened by his objection to me and my career, but now I get it.

As written in a separate chapter of this book, 2015 was one of the most challenging times in my adult life. It was, however, a time in which I felt extreme closeness with The Holy Spirit. Unfortunately, for a short time of that year, I was not eating well, sleeping well and had a PTSD-

IT'S NOT TOO LATE... | DANIEL CONNORS

type experience from years of secondary trauma while firefighting. I will never forget the kindness shown to me by my in-laws during that season of my life. I had lost 12 pounds in one week and I had virtually stopped eating. (See chapter 2015.) During my family medical leave from the fire department, my in-laws showed me extraordinary hospitality. In my 17 years of knowing them, I had not felt such lovingkindness from them. My mother-in-law fed me soup and made me sit down and eat. This is exactly what my mom would have done if she had been alive. My body was screaming for help, but my mind resisted. My mother-in-law insisted that I take good care of myself, and I ate.

My father-in-law and I developed a coffee-and-conversation routine at their kitchen table. For my two-month leave from the fire department, Fotis and I developed a regular daily routine. We must have had 20 or so coffee-and-conversation get-togethers in that time period. During this season of my life, I grew to love them as true family. They were there for me in my time of need, in my time of distress....

I now call Cathy, Mom. Cathy has been so very motherly to me, and she is a devoted mother and grandmother! It is truly impressive, and I am now in awe of her strength. I am not saying that our relationship is now perfect. What I am saying is that I love her through and through. God — in His infinite wisdom — brought our family together for a reason. Together, we have battled each other and learned to love, learned to forgive and learned the true meaning of family.

When I returned to the fire department from my medical leave, my coffee and conversation with Fotis stopped. This is something I now regret and wish we had never stopped our daily meetings. I do wish we could get those years back.

A month before Fotis died, I had the privilege of interviewing him. I told him it was for my book, and he graciously accepted.

It took me several years to understand Fotis and a couple more years to truly love him. But love him I do. He is a brilliant man, who lives a simple lifestyle. He does not flaunt wealth or live a lavish lifestyle. I love this about him!

One day after he was discharged from the hospital, I went to his house for a couple hours of respite for Cathy, his wife. Fotis described for me the essence of his life.

FOTIS

He came from very humble beginnings in Greece. His dad was a farmer, who sold homemade duffle bags made from woven fibers for extra income. They raised sheep, goats, chickens and rabbits as livestock. They made wine and olive oil from their gardens. Fotis' father, brothers and he took care of their local Greek Orthodox Church. He was a cantor in the church, and he could read the old Greek language. He lived through war and famine. He was a young child — approximately 5 to 7 years of age — during WWII when the Germans invaded and occupied Greece.

Unfortunately, he recounted stories of near starvation and going without adequate footwear. Perhaps Fotis' outrage of not remembering his shoes from the Greek party also was tied to that season in his life

A memorable day of golfing with his daughter, Veronica.

when he had limited means? Fotis recounted that, although they had little finances and little food during his childhood, they had fun as children. He and his friends would use a sheep's bladder as a soccer/football ball. The bladder would be tied in a ball, dried; and it would harden. It then could be used like our present-day soccer ball. Fotis was educated in Greece as a physician at the University of Athens. He sat in his chair with oxygen in place, shaking his head. He said, "I come from the mountains. How do I compete with boys who come from Athens? But I did and I became a doctor."

Fotis served two years in the Greek military on the border of Turkey. He stated, "There was never physical military conflict." He was a Lieutenant in the military, and it is a title that I share with him as a retired Lieutenant from the Syracuse Fire Department. His belt from the time he served in the Greek military, I now wear with pride as a remembrance of my friend. At the age of 31, he came to the United States to practice medicine. He knew approximately 1,000 English words prior to coming to the U.S. However, when he first arrived in the U.S., he often would get the words "chicken" and "kitchen" mixed up. Also, for the first month after his arrival, all he could order at a restaurant was "apple pie and coffee" due to his limited vocabulary. He came to the United States during the same year I was born, 1968; but he still had a very strong accent until the day of his passing.

I am so very impressed with this man. The more I get to know him, the more I love the guy. Can you imagine starting over in another country? Seems very daunting to me. He did it and did it well. He practiced medicine for well over 30 years in the United States.

He told me about how he raised Veronica. He taught her not to be judgmental about her friends. He said, "I would let her play with children of all economics." He knew it is not one's wealth or status that determines character. Throughout our marriage, Fotis often would give me little words of wisdom and parenting advice without sounding threatening – just matter of fact.

Fotis said, "We go into store, and Veronica see baby doll. I no buy her the doll." He said to his daughter, five or so at the time, "Veronica, before we come into the store, did you dream of having the doll? But now you want because you saw it." He went on to say, "If my daughter dreams of this or that, I get it for her; but I do not get it because she just saw it." My in-laws loved their daughter through and through and knew how to parent. They would not buy her everything and anything, but they would buy her things she needed and thought about. The gifts, in other words, were never impulsive purchases. Fotis was a wise man and an excellent dad.

152

However, it was Fotis' sense of humor that I adored about him; and in our difficult times, I would hold onto. Fotis told me the same stories throughout the years, but the one that I love is the story of when he was pulled over for speeding. Fotis said, "It was raining very hard, and I was speeding coming home from the hospital." A police officer pulled him over and walked up to the car. The usual "license and registration" question was asked by the police officer. However, Fotis was quick minded, incredibly humorous; and he splashed water on his glasses before the officer's question. Fotis said, "Heh, heh, what you say? What you say? I can't hear you." He said this, in his thick Greek accent, and looked around from side to side quickly. The officer repeated the question; but Fotis repeated his antics, "What you say? What you say?" The officer got frustrated in the rain, told Fotis to drive safe and went back to his police car. To write this story is not complete without my friend, my father-in-law describing it. However, this story makes me belly laugh to this day.

Unfortunately, Fotis became very sick in his 80th year. We thought we would lose him to congestive heart failure; but he is a stubborn, old Greek man. He was discharged from the hospital, and we had his 80th surprise birthday party at our home. All of his Greek relatives and friends came, and we celebrated this wonderful man. Opa!

Four years later, his health was again catching up to him, and he ended up in the hospital once again. Veronica and I visited him in the hospital; but due to the pandemic, we could visit only one person at a time. Veronica went first, and she was with her dad for over an hour as I waited in the lobby. When she came back down, I said, "Let's go. I don't want to overburden your dad." Veronica said to me, "He is waiting for you. Now go." I resisted for a second or two, but I went to find my friend. When I went to his room, he looked good for someone who had recently stopped breathing on his own. He was now seated upright and on oxygen. We had some small talk, and my mother-in-law came in. I knew it was my cue to leave when they began the "who's on first, what's on second routine"; but before I left, I turned and said, "I love you, Fotis." He stopped, turned to me and said, "I love you, too." Then I could see him thinking and once again said, "Yes, I do love you!" I smiled, waved, said my goodbyes to them both and went back to the lobby.

Fotis and I came a very long, long way together in our relationship. God has a truly magnificent Way. When we follow God's Way by behaving well within the circles that we are planted, God can and does His will in our lives.

On November 14, 2020, I went to my in-laws, once again, to rake leaves. When my father-in-law had been in the hospital the week before, I had cleared their one-acre property of leaves. I rode his tractor and made his yard beautiful for his return. My father-in-law had just been discharged from the hospital, and the prognosis was not good. He would remain on oxygen for the remainder of his life. We got him home before Thanksgiving, and we were planning on celebrating what we knew could be our last holidays together as a family. As I raked their yard, I knew time with my friend was short. I thought to myself, *I will ask Fotis if he minds that I call him Dad?*

Fotis told Veronica that he did not want any visitors that day because he was not feeling well. Since I was outside, we thought that would be okay. Veronica and our children stayed at home.

My mother-in-law called me up to the house frantically. She said, "Fotis fell, and I can't get him up." Fotis was coming out to yell at me to do the gutters instead and not rake the grass. However, he fell in their hallway as he was coming to speak with me. I ran up to the deck and into their home. I put on a mask and made eye contact with Fotis. He was lying face down on the floor. I bent down, rubbed his back and said, "How are you doing, my friend?" I sat him up, got behind him on the ground and rested his body weight against my chest. I positioned him seated in front of me, so he would not fall over. I rubbed his chest and prayed The Lord's Prayer. I told my mother-in-law that it was time to call an ambulance if that was what they wanted. Fotis was a DNR (do not resuscitate), and he wanted

NO CPR or lifesaving actions. His breathing grew quiet, slowed and then stopped. I asked for a stethoscope from Mom and confirmed his heart had stopped. He died in my arms, literally on my chest, as we sat together in the hallway; and I thanked him for the gift of his daughter. I rubbed his head and combed his hair with my hand.

My mother-in-law (Mom) and I stood in disbelief, grieving in the hallway. To have a loved one die during this pandemic has been daunting. We knew this could be the last time the grandchildren would see their Papou, and it was. We decided to place Fotis in bed, so they did not see him lying in the hallway on the floor. I picked Fotis up and carried him to the bedroom. I fell onto the bed with the load of his weight in my arms. We made him as comfortable and presentable as possible for his granddaughters and his child, my children and wife, to see him. I again checked his heart for any sign of life. Hoping I was wrong, willing him back to life did not work. Fotis had passed and was now with God.

I drove home in a fog to get my wife and our children to say their goodbyes. I pulled into the driveway of our home, and my wife and children were in the front of the house waiting. I made sure my car was in park because I was "out of it." I got out of the car and handed the cell phone to my wife. She said, "What, what, what!" Her mom was on the phone and told her of her daddy's death; and we all then drove to their house to say good-bye to Fotis, Dad, Papou, my friend.

This was one of the hardest deaths I have ever experienced in my life. His death was grueling and excruciatingly painful beyond words. Fotis and I had been on a long journey of forgiveness. We had learned to love each other. It took many years; but through God's good grace, we loved.

"… love covers over a multitude of sins" (1 Peter 4:8, NIV).

My friend, my father-in-law, a man I wished I called Dad, Fotios Constaninos Poulos died in my arms on November 14, 2020; and I have not been quite the same since. I have witnessed many deaths in my career in EMS as a Paramedic Firefighter and as a nurse. However, to hold someone you love and watch them die and not be able to do anything about it hurt me to my core. It breaks my heart to this day, and I cry when I type this.

I interviewed Fotis, my friend and my father-in-law, two weeks before he died. I got about halfway through the interview before he said, "Oy, oy, oy, oy. What do you think of that?" I knew that meant the interview was over for now. Upon leaving their home, my mother-in-law came home and Fotis said, "Cathy, I give Dan a piece of my heart today." A week before Fotis died, I advised Veronica to tell her dad things she always has wanted to say but has never. Veronica was adopted from Greece but always has been raised as their own. Veronica has never felt the pang of remorse from adoption and has always felt lovingly accepted as their child. I prompted Veronica to thank her dad and mom for adopting her. She agreed and had a loving conversation with her parents. However, Fotis confided in me later, "My daughter tell me, 'Thank you for adopting me!' She no tell

St. Patrick's Day Parade. Blessed to be with two wonderful women-
pictured left to right: Cathy, Dan, Veronica

me thank you! She is my daughter. She need not thank me." (I write that as he said it, but I only wish I could have the heavy Greek accent come through.) I encouraged Veronica to voice those words. I knew that Veronica needed to voice those words and not Fotis nor Cathy, who needed to hear them. Veronica needed to leave it all out "on the field" so that — when the unfortunate day came — she would have zero regrets.

Reader, she held onto her spoken words of love and gratitude as a beacon of light in the darkness when that fateful day came. She knew — in her heart of hearts — that her dad knew how appreciative she was for this life that they gave her. If not for her adoption, she would be in Greece and may never have had the surgery for her acoustic neuroma. Therefore, she may have died an early death. We would not be married; and we would not have our wonderful, beautiful girls – if not for Fotis and Cathy's wonderful decision 45 years prior.

The love of my life and my best friend, Veronica, on our 20-year wedding anniversary.

Veronica is still my best friend 20 years later. She has been in my corner and I in hers – through thick and thin. We have lived our vows. I often pray in thanksgiving for God hearing me as a small 8-year-old child while lying in bed at my home. God answered my prayers in ways I never could have imagined. God also has blessed Veronica and me with two children of our own. Our love incarnate. To know and experience the birth of children is to know the love of God. For me, there is no bigger miracle to which I can point to show the love of God for us, His children, than the birth of our two precious children.

CHAPTER 10

SFD 20-year career

God, in His infinite wisdom, gave me opportunities through bicycling across the northern and southern U.S. and fishing in Alaska to help heal the panic and anxiety that shackled me from my adolescence and early childhood. These physical and mental challenges, bicycling and fishing, strengthened me emotionally for a career that was to come in firefighting. If I had not challenged myself with these experiences, I never would have been able to put out fire for a living. As the saying goes, "When most people are running out of a fire, firefighters are running in." How could anyone with a panic disorder fight fire? It would be impossible to effectively do this job and hide a panic and anxiety disorder.

On **September 5, 2000**, I entered the Syracuse Fire Department. Unlike many of my classmates whose family or friends were firemen, I had no friends or family in the department and little idea of what I was about to encounter. I was naive about the firefighter culture, and I had very little idea what firefighting entailed. However, I was ecstatic and hopeful for the promise of my new career. Now I could ask my girlfriend, Veronica, to marry me. I had promised her father, Fotis, that I would have a "real career" before I asked for her hand in marriage.

My saving grace, during the academy, was that I had a background as an Emergency Medical Technician. EMS (emergency medical services) is a large portion of a firefighting career and, having that background, helped with some confidence in that area of my new job. For many of us firefighters, we come into the field unaware of the chaos that lies ahead. Yes, we get trained in the academy. And yes, it is excellent and effective training; but no one can prepare someone to see their first death, their first suicide by self-inflicted shooting, self-inflicted m80 firework in their mouth, first hanging, their first full cardiac arrest, first SIDS (sudden infant death syndrome), first fire fatality, first car pedestrian, firsts.… Not only are first calls problematic but more critical is the accumulative effect of years upon years of built-up visualized and experienced trauma. Unfortunately, many firefighters succumb to drinking in excess, gambling and other addictive behaviors. These vices can rear their ugly head and cause havoc in our lives if productive-coping mechanisms have not been firmly established. I entered the fire department somewhat naive about the goings-on in the day-to-day life of a firefighter, but I soon realized that firefighting is much like sports teams that I have played on my entire life.

I had the physical attributes that make up a good firefighter. At that time, I was bench pressing 275 pounds five times in a row; and I could do 20+ pull-ups and 80+ push-ups. I was running long-distance races (10-, 13.1- , 18.12-, 26.2-mile races) and participating in sprint triathlons.

The above stats are not phenomenal — as in world-class athletics, but they are solid for an average Joe. I was trying to impress the guys around me for a couple of reasons. I wanted to transfer to the Rescue Company. It

My graduation ceremony from SFD recruit class was in 2000.
My dad is pictured pinning my badge on me.

was the top company in our department, and it was each firefighter's goal. I also was trying to let guys know I was in shape because I feared when and if they — the powers that be — found out I had asthma that I would lose my job. That was my thinking, and I feared losing my job and my career due to health concerns. My career as a firefighter was financially supporting my family, and I did not want my medical history to negatively influence my family's future. As long as I could pass my yearly pulmonary function test, my doctor would sign off on my paperwork; but my mind thought the worst-case scenario, and I began to live scared. I had some stinking thinking; and I was worried that the Chief who, was hounding me throughout my career, may have some leeway to fire me. It was nerve wracking to say the least. As he got promoted, he was given the call sign 103 on the radio and was promoted to Deputy Chief. He now could wield his authority to make my day-to-day life miserable, and that is exactly what he did. However, God has a truly greater Way about Him than even the powerful Chief who was hounding me.

"'You intended to harm me, but God intended it for good to

SFD Engine, followed by SFD mini, and ambulance 2019 Open House and Parade Fire Station #2

accomplish what is now being done, the saving of many lives. So then, don't be afraid. I will provide for you and your children'...." (Genesis 50:20-21, NIV).

The Chief, who was hounding me, retired; and in his place, his designated 103 call sign was the city's nicest guy in our department. The 103 call sign that once gave me nightmares now became my friend. 103, our new Deputy Chief, treated each member of our department with respect. He is someone you would do anything for because he respects you and would go to "bat" for you. When he gives an order, you do it with a pep in your step because you knew he had no negative agenda. God used my time as a firefighter to discipline me.

"because the Lord disciplines the one he loves, and he chastens everyone he accepts as his son" (Hebrews 12:6, NIV).

During the first four years of my career, I behaved off the job in ways of which I was not proud. I credit all my healing to God, therapists and my desire to be a good daddy someday. Prior to children, my wife and I were having marital problems, and I was looking to get out of our marriage. I was sabotaging our marriage, but I did not realize it. The firefighter and emergency services careers lend themselves to self-destructive family lifestyles. We tend to drink our problems down and I did. Ultimately, this reaction can lead to alcoholism and marital problems. In addition to these problems, we tend to gossip like it's a prerequisite for our job; and unfortunately, I did. I was also on the receiving end of gossip, and it changed my life for the good. Yes, for the good. Before, I used to think I could keep my indiscretions quiet; but telephone, tella friend, tella firefighter, and all bets are off.

My sin, in front of others, made me look at myself in the mirror and take a moral inventory like I never had before. I was supposed to be the good guy! I worked with people with disabilities. I fundraised for Francis House (a hospice organization), the Leukemia Society and for L'Arche (home for people with developmental disabilities). I started the C.A.R.E. Program at

Rural/Metro (assisted with the social service needs in the community). I was a good Catholic. I was an altar server in college, and I was involved with social justice issues on campus. However, the dysfunction of my past family upbringing and my present family dynamic with my in-laws encouraged me to behave in ways of which I was not proud. Also, I was dealing with unresolved secondary trauma from EMS and firefighting calls.

I had begun to gamble, and I was out of control. I was going to the casino on my off time and justifying it to my wife because of winning. I never made money that was lasting from gambling. Everything I won would be lost in my next venture. In the end, I built a wing of the casino and lost part of my soul.

If my Father in heaven was looking down with an angry expression during my Canisius experience, I only could imagine how He was feeling now. However, a persistent theme in my life always has been a desire to help others. One night during my first two years on the job, I was tasked to drive the fire engine. We rotated positions in the apparatus, depending on experience and time on the job. The senior man was off duty that night. He was the full-time driver, and I was filling in. We were dispatched to "smoke in the residence – possible grease fire." Our officer held the assignment to one Engine, Truck and a Chief. If it was a structure fire, we would upgrade the alarm or fill the assignment to additional apparatus. For now, we would investigate. Upon arrival, there was no smoke or fire showing. However, there were two children and their mother seated outside on the front porch. Being the driver, I stayed outside and waited by the apparatus until I was needed to "man" or operate the fire pump. The guys went into the residence with their firefighting gear and brought in a water can. They were in for a short period of time; and from the radio dialogue, I could tell it was a "no-nothing" little stove fire. The guys ventilated the house, and the call was wrapped up in 10 to 20 minutes. However, when they got back in the rig, that's when I started to get uneasy. My overtime officer got in the rig and pulled off his pack. He said, "Those kids don't have a chance." The firefighters jumped in back, took off their packs and said, "Did you see all that stuff in there? There is no way out the back. If there's a fire, those poor kids." The guys reported dog feces all over the floor and a hoarding type of situation. The young children that were just sitting out front with their mom were living in a deplorable situation. Immediately, I was brought back to my childhood. I knew what it was like to live in conditions like that and wanted to help.

At that time in our department, we did not have the type of reportable child incident forms as we do now. I was not comfortable sitting back and doing nothing. My overtime officer was not going to follow up with paperwork. Having only about two years on the job, I felt uncomfortable voicing my concern.

I waited till the next day and called Child Protective Services, "I am a firefighter who was on a call last night that you need to look into. We just witnessed children living in filth and in a very dangerous situation. They have no exit out the back due to tremendous clutter, and there is dog feces throughout the residence." He asked me my name; and I said, "I would like to keep this anonymous." He persisted, and I gave him the address and details of our call but not my name. The call taker was upset that I did not give my name and assured me it was confidential. I was scared that I could lose my job or at the very least upset the Chief on the call.

The next day, I drove by the house and realized I gave the wrong address. I had transposed the house numbers. I called Child Protective back and reported the correct address. I said, "I called yesterday, and I gave the wrong address about two children living in a hoarder house." The call taker said, "Yes, we know. We went to the house and investigated but found nothing." I then gave the correct address, and this time I provided my name. I said, "I am sorry for the mix-up. My name is Dan Connors, and the correct address is xxxxxxx."

When I returned to work for our next tour of duty, three days later, we could all see something was visibly wrong with the Chief. It was 7:30

a.m.; and we were all having coffee, reading the newspaper and catching up before the morning bell hit to start the day. The Chief, however, was pacing back and forth. We all looked at each other; and someone said, "What's up with Chief?" The morning bell hit at 0800, and we would start the morning routine. We would get our uniforms on, do housework and check our apparatus and equipment.

However, on this day, the Chief said, "Everyone in the kitchen now!" The kitchen area is where we have some of our firefighter drills and is also our dining area. I was hoping this was going to be an impromptu drill, but I had the feeling I knew what this meeting was about. The Chief started out by yelling, "In my 20-plus years on the job, I have never seen such outlandish behavior! Before I begin, does anyone want to tell me who called Child Protective while they were off duty?" The guys looked around, and I sheepishly raised my hand. The Chief then screamed, "Connors, my office now!" My direct officer, my Lieutenant who was off duty during our call to the hoarder house, said, "Chief, being his officer, can I go, too?" The Truck officer also went with us, and the four of us met in the Chief's office. Chief began, "Who the hell do you think you are?! Do you think I don't care about my citizens who I am sworn to protect?" I said, "Chief, I am sorry. No, that's not it at all. I was just concerned about the kids, and no one was doing anything. I felt a need to call." Chief went on to say that I made him look bad. I mentioned that I used to run the C.A.R.E. Program at Rural/Metro, and this was what I would have done when at R/M. Chief said, "If you had that type of skill set, how come you didn't say anything?" I said, "Chief, I was nervous. I only have a couple years on the job. Chief, I grew up like those children; and I needed to help." I was then excused and gently shut his door while the officers talked.

"Consider it pure joy, my brothers and sisters, whenever you face trials of many kinds" (James 1:2, NIV).

Unfortunately, I made an enemy that day; and he has made it known to me in many ways that I made him look bad. Child Protective had called my Chief's superior to get more information on the recent referral that I made because of the transposed address numbers. The Chief, to his credit, did file some paperwork with our Code Enforcement and Fire Prevention departments, regarding the incident of the night in question; but a call to Child Protective — the correct thing to do — was done by someone under his command.

What I have learned subsequently is not to bypass the chain of command. I was wrong in how I went about trying to help the children on scene. If I had lived my convictions that night and not waited till the morning, things would have gone a lot smoother in my career.

One evening while I was making dinner at the firehouse, the Chief confronted me in the kitchen. Although he was shorter than me, he had every advantage over me. He walked up to me and stood inches from my face. He said, "Connors, as I rise in power in this department, I will get those who have gotten me." He named a couple of guys who he would "pay back." He glared at me and walked away. He got me alright and made my life miserable for the next 12 to 15 years on the job.

One day I asked a fellow firefighter to swap days with me or do what we call a "work-for." I filled out the appropriate paperwork, dotting my I's and crossing my T's. I gave the paperwork to my officer – as was the protocol. On the next shift, the firefighter, my friend, who I asked to work for me, showed up on time and was ready to start the day with the rest of the crew. The Chief in question came into the dayroom and asked, "Where is Firefighter Connors?" My officer replied, "He has a guy working for him." The Chief said, "I didn't get any paperwork. If he is not here before the morning bell, he will be AWOL!"

I was then called at home and asked where the paperwork was for the "work for." I raced into work, filled out the paperwork once again; and I was able to talk with the Captain of the house. I said, "Cap, I filled out the paperwork twice. What's going on?" He said, "Dan, always follow your paperwork to the Chief's office." That advice was not our regular routine;

and what I heard him saying to me — so to speak — was that "games" were starting to begin. He did not say it, but the Chief had intentionally "lost" my paperwork. I now know this, but it has taken me many years to understand the following scripture:

"And we know that in all things God works for the good of those who love him, who have been called according to his purpose" (Romans 8:28, NIV).

Yes, Reader, all things – discipline, cattiness, betrayal, unfairness – God can use all things. Not just the good in our lives but also the hurtful. God, Creator of the universe, can do mighty works in our lives – if, that is, we let Him in.

"And he did not do many miracles there because of their lack of faith" (Matthew 13:58, NIV).

I had interviewed to go down to Rescue – as was our custom; and the Captain of Rescue said, "Danny, you know your job at Hazmat; and you have skills in EMS. You don't have technical rope skills, but don't worry about it. We will teach you when you get here." We shook hands, and I was on cloud 9. I was *hoping* to get down to Rescue. It was my dream.

Unfortunately, for the next decade or so, I also was constantly putting out emotional fires that the Chief set in my name. He got a hold of some of my past mistakes and spread it like wildfire. A friend of mine from the Rescue Company called me at my firehouse and said, "Dan, the Chief is down here slamming you." My aspiration of going to the Rescue Company dwindled before my eyes. I went and talked with the Rescue Captain again; and he said, "Dan, when a District Chief says some derogatory things about you, I gotta listen." I was crushed. I knew I had to get away from that Chief.

One morning, my friends and I were talking before the 0800 bell; and our Chief walked by on the way to his office. He was singing a song as he walked by, "Jesus, take the wheel...." As he sang that verse as he walked by us, he walked into a recliner and tripped. There is a part of me that thanked Jesus for "taking the wheel." I say that in jest, but I do know that God has got our back always. Always, that is, when we walk with Him by walking in His Ways.

Reader, I also need to mention this about the Chief who was hounding me for many years. He has his redeeming qualities. He is a good firefighter; he is strong and intelligent. He was acting out of his truth. He believed he was justified in treating me and many men under his command as he wished. Furthermore, God used this man to wake me up. I was disciplined by my Father God, and I am a better man because of the difficulties I went through. God used negative in my life and turned it into a positive. However, it does not justify acts of negativity by me or the Chief I am writing about. We are called to live good lives and to treat all with love and respect and not gossip.

> "Likewise, the tongue is a small part of the body, but it makes great boasts. Consider what a great forest is set on fire by a small spark. The tongue also is a fire, a world of evil among the parts of the body. It corrupts the whole body, sets the whole course of one's life on fire, and is itself set on fire by hell" (James 3:5-6, NIV).

In fact, I believe many of us gossip all the time in our daily lives. We typically do not intend to hurt others or cause others anguish, pain or grief; but we do so under a "righteous" understanding that we are better than…. We also gossip because it is conversational. We gossip because we are trying to bond with another. We gossip because it makes us feel better about ourselves.

Do you gossip, Reader? Have you ever passed on juicy information about another? Do you have baggage in your closet that you don't want on billboards or in black-and-white ink? Of course, you do.

> "For all sinned and fall short of the glory of God, and all are justified freely by his grace through the redemption that came by Christ Jesus" (Romans 3:23-24, NIV).

I was working on my Paramedic certificate at this point in my career, and I had to get 10 intubations as part of my field work. I knew I would have a very hard time getting the "tubes" by working in my present firehouse, so I transferred to a firehouse that also had an ambulance. The Chief was out on medical leave from a motorcycle accident when I put in my transfer, and the transfer went smoothly. It was the first time in a long time that my career was operating without friction.

What I learned — and I have been living since 2011 — is that my Father loves me. He has called me, and He knows me by name. He says, "'Well done, good and faithful servant!'" (Matthew 25:21, NIV).

It has taken me many years to realize that — even though my Father, my Abba, was upset with me many years ago — it didn't mean that He didn't love me. As a dad, I have been upset with our children misbehaving, fighting with each other, etc.; but that never meant I did not love them. I would die for them. I would protect them with my life, for they are my children. God says the same thing to us. In fact, He sent His Son as a sacrifice for my sin, our sin and humanity's sin for all of time.

Although God may have had a disapproving look on His face at the Canisius quad in 1986 and although He did not approve of my various inappropriate actions, He, however, does forgive me. He now calls me His son and says to sin no more. I have learned right from wrong and now follow His Way. The journey has been long and arduous, but He has been with me all along. I thank You, Lord, my God, for the guardrails that You have placed along my journey and for disciplining me when I needed it. What was intended to harm me, You, my Lord, used for the good.

"You intended to harm me, but God intended it for good to accomplish what is now being done, the saving of many lives" (Genesis 50:20, NIV).

Considering the current 2020-21 social, racial and political climate, I will provide this story in my book:

To get on the job in Syracuse, firefighters have to take a civil service exam. In addition to scoring well, the city Common Council required city residency for all entry-level firefighters. There was a quota of minority firefighters who needed to be maintained. Sometimes not enough minority firefighters scored high enough. Therefore, scores needed for entry for minority firefighters were less than civil service scores of white firefighters. In essence, what was designed to assist the minority candidate, in fact, had caused an underlying tension. White firefighters, whose friends or family were passed over with higher civil service exam scores, sometimes felt oppressed. A system designed to help minorities became an instrument of racial tension.

For me, I do not care if someone is black, white, brown, yellow, red, purple, orange, pink, green, male or female, heterosexual or homosexual. If the candidate firefighter can do the job and do it well, we should hire the best candidate.

Can they pull my family, friends or myself out of a burning structure? Can they hold onto a hose with 200 psi pumping through? Can they climb a ladder, and are they not afraid of heights? Can they drive a fire apparatus? Can they take a blood pressure, pulse, respiration? Can they perform CPR and stop a bleed? Each of these skill sets can be taught to prospective firefighter candidates. In my opinion, physical ability far outweighs civil service exams. The cognitive portion of the exam should be a pass/fail, and the physical portion should be graded on objective data. How fast are they? How strong? How fast did they pull a hose, climb a ladder? How hard can they swing an axe? How accurate was their blood pressure, pulse and respiration count?

Many of my black firefighter friends did not score as well as me on the civil service test, but they were excellent firefighters! I would trust them with my life and with the lives of my family. The civil service test – designed to help obtain the best candidate – is antiquated and a potential source of tension.

Unfortunately, early on in my career because I was white, I witnessed firsthand the discrimination that pervaded the department. It sickened me. I have multiple family members who are minorities. My grandmother eloquently stated, "Our family is like a little United Nation." We have first-generation families from Senegal, South Korea, Cuba and Greece and descendants from Italy and Ireland. We also have a family member with Down syndrome. And we have family members and friends who are gay and one who died of AIDS. We are truly a multicultural family.

When I first entered the fire department, it seemed as though I was transported back to the 1950's. There was subtle and sometimes direct racial tension. However, I say with all honesty, every firefighter I know never objectively stated they were racist. We were all brother and sister firefighters – at least on the surface.

One night, early on in my career, we sat around the firehouse playing cards. The Captain of the house, who has long since retired, also was playing cards with us. He told a racial joke, and the guys all laughed except me. He had an unfair advantage over us because of his rank. So perhaps the guys who laughed did so more out of a group dynamic as opposed to a racial thing? I did not confront him or call him out on it which, in hindsight, I wish I had. I did, however, not smile and shook my head with disrespect. He caught on to my subtle expressions and called me out in front of the other white firefighters. He said, "You don't like that joke, Dan? Are you afraid to say the n word?" I said, "No, I am not afraid. I just don't say it." He went on to say, "Come on, Dan. You can say it. Let's hear you say it." I replied something to the effect of: "That's okay, Cap. I'm not going to say that word."

We had black firefighters at our station, but none were there that night. I find it cowardice that the Captain did not tell the racial joke when our black firefighter friends were there. I was angry. I felt isolated. I wished I had confronted him aggressively. A couple of days later, I had a discussion with a black friend of mine and told him of the "card" incident. He was sympathetic regarding my position that night. I would like to say this was the only time that racial jokes were told, but I would be lying. I would like to say I stood up and called someone out to the parking lot because of the joke. All I did was sit in silence. I did not smile and did not go along. I have regretted not doing more to call out the stupidity of racial joking, and I have regretted it ever since. I wished I had confronted and challenged stupidity.

When I was younger in high school, I said stupid stuff, too. I have used the n word before, and I am sorry. I am not perfect, and I know my Father forgives me. In addition, I learned that we are all equals in the eyes of our Father. My family has taught me that color perceptions are purely nurture and not nature. Our pigment may be different colors, but our blood is all red. We are more alike than we are different, and to judge someone by the outer surface is beyond ignorant.

This book is not a "tell all " and not a smear on the Fire Department. That is not my intention. Instead my intention is to shine a light in this dark age. That is, the light of Christ Jesus. God has done a mighty work in my life. From my using the n word in my youth, on rare occasions, and having prejudice and fear while running down Main Street in Buffalo, New York as a college student at 1 a.m. (See the third chapter.) My misunderstanding was plain and simply ignorance. And, Reader, by the Way, it was sinful... Jesus calls us to love.

God can and does change hearts of stone. He has created in me a new heart. I pray for you, Reader, if you hate me right now, that your heart of stone will be transformed into God's heart of flesh. For we (all of us) are made in the image of God: black, white, brown, yellow, red, pink, green, blue, orange. I pray this in Jesus' Name. Amen

"I will give you a new heart and put a new spirit in you; I will remove from you your heart of stone and give you a heart of flesh" (Ezekiel 36:26, NIV).

After about eight years on the job, my little four-year-old daughter said, "Daddy, I want to be a firefighter when I grow up – just like you."

I, in turn, said, "Honey, dream another dream. I will never allow you to be a firefighter." Up until that point, I had always encouraged our little ones to dream dreams; but now that I knew the culture, I was not going to allow my daughters to dream of this job. At that time in our firefighting culture, nothing was off limits with "ballbusting" and firehouse dialogue. As firefighters, we see too much; and consequently, we have a morbid sense of humor as a part of our coping mechanism. There was absolutely nothing that was off limits with joking in the firehouse. However, in the last seven years of my career, I saw a tremendous shift for the betterment of our Fire Department, regarding racial and minority inequalities.

Political correctness may be taboo for some, but I have seen a world of change for the good. We hired more female, gay and minority firefighters in the last years of my career. The laws that were administered during the Obama administration filtered their way down to the everyday workplace and into our Fire Department.

The new generation of firefighters is much more diverse, which is a tremendously good thing. I recently have apologized to our daughters. I said, "Your daddy told you two that you could never be firefighters. However, I have changed my mind. I will still be nervous because it's a dangerous job. But you girls can be firefighters if you wish." The firefighter culture has changed from night to day in my short 20-year career. The old guard is gone, and new thought processes are enforced for the greater good.

After the "card" incident with the Captain, early on in my career, I let out my political and religious beliefs. With other firefighters, I had conversations which I normally would not let out in public. I was done hiding my values. However, allowing oneself to be open for others to see can make you vulnerable. My Christian mindset has been attacked, but I also have had opportunities to witness my faith by actions.

Early on, as a relatively new Lieutenant, with about 12 years on the job, I was working Engine 6 on a rotating assignment. Essentially, I was filling in for the regular officer. My partner and I received an emergency medical call at the nearby Rescue Mission, a homeless shelter. It was a call for an assault in progress. We were dispatched by 911, "Mini 6 call for EMS – possible assault. 40's male assault may still be in progress." (This dispatch has been paraphrased, but it is essentially the gist). In approximately 15 to 25 seconds, we were out the door. Staging for the police. SPD (police), R/M (ambulance) and SFD (fire) all rolled up to the incident about the same time. This call left a searing picture in my mind.

There was a fist fight in progress among several homeless men. The fight got broken up in no time and left a couple of people bruised and battered. There were no significant injuries to speak of. My partner and I watched and waited to assist as the police subdued one of the homeless men – the agitator if you will. As the man was being cuffed by SPD, one of the R/M paramedics stepped on the homeless man's head while the officers were attempting to restrain him as he struggled in the prone position on the ground (face down). The homeless men — who were once fighting with this man, the agitator, who was now being arrested — now stuck up for him. One of the guys next to me yelled at the paramedic, "Get your foot off his head!" About six to eight guys were all shouting and getting verbally upset. I quickly bent down and pulled the paramedic's boot off the man's head. I told the paramedic, "I agree with the other guys." In a quick motion, the man was restrained, handcuffed and propped up on the stretcher with cuffs restraining his arms behind his body. He was seated face up and kept asking for his hat. I grabbed his hat and placed it on his head.

Having compassion is often not the norm in the field. Unfortunately, this field eats them up and spits them out. Someone can come into the field with a soft, golden heart; and their heart can become tarnished and calloused – if they do not protect it.

"Above all else, guard your heart, for everything you do flows from it" (Proverbs 4:23, NIV).

The reason that call got seared into my head was the audacity of the paramedic. He was new to the field; he had no right to step on the guy's head; and it made me angry. Sometimes the citizens we are called to help will try and physically assault us, biting us and spitting on us as we legitimately are trying to help. There also have been numerous instances where Police, Fire and EMS were shot and killed during various incidents. However, in this case – the homeless shelter fight, the Police had this situation well in hand, and they did not need any outside assistance. We were not in harm's way. The paramedic was copying what he had seen others do.

At this point in my career, I was trying to live out my faith on calls, in the firehouse and throughout the rest of my life. It was difficult. My partner and I got back in our vehicle, Mini-6, and returned to the firehouse. Much to my surprise, my partner agreed with what I had done on scene. I later found out that my partner — and now friend — is a Christian, too.

I am no saint (a friend of Jesus', yes); and I certainly don't have all the answers. However, to remain silent in times of injustice is to agree with the injustice. We are complicit by our inaction. It took me a long time to understand that notion and an even longer time to try and live it out.

What would Jesus do in that situation? He probably would intervene also; and Jesus — more than likely — would have a conversation with the paramedic after the call. Jesus would have made a friend or at least shown the paramedic the error of his way of thinking. Unfortunately, I just wrote that paramedic off and labeled him as a jerk.

In November 2014, we responded to a very large house fire. The call was at approximately 2 a.m. or 0200. Engine Company 8 had been dispatched to an outdoor fire which turned out not to be an outdoor fire but a house fire. The Engine 8 officer, a good friend of mine, advised fire control/911, "Engine 8 officer to fire control, fill this assignment. We have a 2 ½-story wood frame building with heavy fire. Signal 99." (paraphrased) "Copy Engine 8, 2 ½-story wood frame heavy fire. Filling the assignment, Engine Companies 3, Engine Company 1, Truck 8, Squad, Rescue and Car 3. Engine Co. 8 on scene reporting signal 99 with heavy fire. Multiple calls on this, with reports of several victims still inside."

I was working Engine 3 that night, and I had a brand new rookie. Her name was Carrie, and she was as good of a firefighter as anyone with whom I have worked. She was intelligent, hardworking and physically fit. She was about 25 years old, and she was my rookie. I had a seasoned driver with about seven years on the job driving, Steve, and a good pipeman with about two years on the job, Daryl. He was young and fit, and together we were a solid crew.

As we pulled up on scene, I reported, "Engine 3 on scene." I heard Car 3 state, "On my command, all firefighters exit the building. Exit the building!" The hydrant was next to our apparatus; and my driver advised me he could "make the plug," open the hydrant and supply water to the engine on his own. My rookie was assigned to the hydrant detail; but if my driver could "get the hydrant," we could use her help. The three of us were packed up, and we ran toward the burning building. I saw a wall of fire, and I grabbed the nozzle from the bumper of the first due engine. I pointed at Larry, the Engine 8 driver; and I gave the send the water sign, a sweeping circle around my head. He said, "The bumperline?" I gave him a loud, "Yes." Fire was blowing out windows, and the fence was on fire from radiant heat. Chief had given the verbal order: "All firefighters exit the building."

From the beginning of my training, we were always taught never to put water from outside the structure into the structure or you risk burning the firefighters and/or victims inside. This was the training we were given in the academy and maintained throughout most of my career.

However, about two weeks before this fire, all fire officers in our department had a department-wide drill. We met at the Syracuse Airport and had formal training regarding firefighting operations. We were taught to forget the training we were once given regarding firefighting extinguishment. The training lasted two hours, and we were told that the training we had been given regarding placing water from outside to inside the structure was incorrect. Underwriters Laboratories technicians and scientists proved, through various studies, that applying water in a straight-stream fashion in short bursts from outside the structure fire did not upset the thermal conditions to negatively impact interior victims or firefighters. This approach was a vast difference from what we were taught originally. It turned our firefighting mentality on its head.

The night of the State Street fire, I utilized the information and training given to me and applied it to the fireground. I sprayed water from outside to inside, with victims and firefighters inside – a huge "no-no" in years previous. Not all firefighters had received this training yet, and I was looked at and talked about later like I had two heads…. After we knocked down fire showing on the right side of the structure, I directed my rookie to grab a 300-foot attack line, so we could make an interior push. I now was acutely aware that my nozzleman was not with me. I did not know where one of my men had gone. My rookie and I ran to the front, and I was handed a charged line. My nozzleman had been inside, where he was assisting the Rescue Company. He had gone to the front of the building when I went to the right side of the building with my rookie. Fortunately, we met up again on the front step as we donned our masks and readied ourselves to make an interior fire attack. The three of us went in on the line; and my rookie stayed by the door, pushing hose up to us. I looked back, and she was not on my heel. I yelled, "Carrie!" She yelled back, "I'm okay, Lieutenant. I'm moving hose." My nozzleman's alarm bell went off, indicating he was running out of air. I sent him downstairs to the first floor to go outside and told him to send the rookie up the line to me. My rookie and I moved from room to room, flowing water on fire. Dark smoke and fire rolled above our heads. Our low-air alarms began to sound; and I indicated over the radio, "Engine 3 coming out. Need someone online up here." Before we exited, we had knocked down the bulk of the fire. Unbeknownst to me at the time, a Chief grabbed our line and continued to hit hot spots. We returned to our apparatus to get fresh-air bottles.

As my crew and I were packing up to assist with overhaul, a firefighter from Rescue came up to me and shoved me saying, "Get in there. There is a chief on the line." I was packed up and had changed bottles, but my crew was still getting their packs on. I pushed that Rescue firefighter backwards with all my might, and he fell backwards. I said, "Do you know how much f-ing fire we just put out?" I was beyond upset at this firefighter's brash rebuff of me. He laid his hands on an officer. He was way out of bounds in his thinking. My crew and I went to the front of the building and met up with the rest of the fire crews. The Command on scene took head counts, and we regrouped on the fireground to ensure all firefighters were accounted for.

I glared at the Rescue firefighter who shoved me as he was talking to his officer. I walked over to them, and I stuck my hand out. He shook my hand and apologized. I said, "That's alright. I am sorry, too. This is done right here." Tempers were flying all over the fireground. We collectively had just pulled multiple victims from the fire building, including an approximate five-year-old boy. One of my crew performed CPR on this child, and the boy went on to make a full recovery.

I told my story later to some firefighter friends back at the firehouse. I said, "Can you believe the audacity of that Rescue guy?" My friend said, "Yeah, Dan. It wasn't about what you think. It wasn't about the fire."

What I had learned is that 103, the Deputy Chief who disliked me, had empowered some guys to treat me anyway they like. My authority, as an officer, was undermined by the authority of a Chief. It made my working in the fire department as an officer a nightmare at times.

I would soon be transferred to a different firehouse, leading to a cascade of events that I have termed my 2015 experience. I was out of work on medical leave for two months. (See the chapter entitled 2015.)

When I returned to work after a grueling and life-changing experience, I would have to regain the respect of the men/women firefighters. Questions surrounded my capabilities and capacity to perform my job. I would silence their concerns with effort and fireground knowledge.

When I was out sick, I was truly sick, and I would not wish that feeling on my worst enemy. That time was, however, a gift from God; and I found peace in His arms. At this new firehouse and in my new assignment, I was determined not to worry about the rumor mill. I would deal with what was in front of me, live out my faith on and off the job and perform my duties with everything I had.

I have made my faith known at my new firehouse, my new assignment, by playing Christian music in my office and not shying away from controversial questions of faith. One day a firefighter acquaintance said to me, "I know how this works, Dan. I can do whatever I want now; and then just before I'm ready to die, I will ask to be forgiven." I just shook my head and said, "That's not exactly it." Unfortunately, what my friend was saying is that he will manipulate God's system and squeak into heaven with an "I'm sorry."

We can manipulate each other, but we cannot manipulate God. He knows our hearts and our minds. If my friend at the time of his death had a truly repentant heart, I know our Father would gladly bring him into His embrace. However, if my friend thinks he can manipulate God's system at the time of his death, he will be in for an unfortunate awakening. My friend is proposing to throw all the ingredients into the oven and call it cake. If you are baking a cake, you first get all your ingredients together (mise en place), preheat the oven to the specified temperature, mix the contents and follow the directions, according to the cookbook. You then spray the pan and add the mixture into the pan. You then place the batter into the oven for the appropriate amount of time and at the correct temperature. You let it cool and frost the cake accordingly.

For me, salvation has been a process much like the above analogy. The ingredients of my life have been placed on my countertop. The cleansing of my soul was preheating for many years. God placed me in the oven and baked my soul and spirit, fashioning unlike ingredients into a spectacular dessert. I now sit on the counter, waiting to cool before the frosting is applied. I know that my Father is not quite done with me yet. He has made a wonderful dessert for which I am truly grateful. I hope that my Father serves this cake soon and that He finds it enjoyable.

Do I find it ironic that a "punk" kid, me, who pulled a fire alarm in his youth, later became a fireman? Yes, I do. Please do not discount the children in your lives because of their current problematic behaviors. With the right influence, the child can thrive. Jesus has a wonderful Way about Him and turned water into wine. And He can turn a problematic, fire alarm-pulling, rebellious child into a fireman and follower of The Way, His Way....

"Being confident of this, that he who began a good work in you will carry it on to completion until the day of Christ Jesus" (Philippians 1:6, NIV).

CHAPTER 11

2015

The year 2015 was, for me, a very difficult one but also a year filled with God's grace beyond understanding. As I look back, I shudder but I also am strengthened. I now know — beyond a shadow of a doubt — that God is here with us through The Holy Spirit; but we also are engrossed in battle. May those who doubt be protected by His mercies.

The Armor of God

"Finally, be strong in the Lord and in his mighty power. Put on the full armor of God, so that you can take your stand against the devil's schemes. For our struggle is not against flesh and blood, but against the rulers, against the authorities, against the powers of this dark world and against the spiritual forces of evil in the heavenly realms. Therefore put on the full armor of God, so that when the day of evil comes, you may be able to stand your ground, and after you have done everything, to stand. Stand firm then, with the belt of truth buckled around your waist, with the breastplate of righteousness in place, and with your feet fitted with the readiness that comes from the gospel of peace. In addition to all this, take up the shield of faith, with which you can extinguish all the flaming arrows of the evil one. Take the helmet of salvation and the sword of the Spirit, which is the word of God" (Ephesians 6:10-17, NIV).

I began having asthma symptoms shortly after college; but I had not started treating them with steroids until I was a couple of years into the fire department or approximately 10 years after my initial asthma symptoms. I remember, on occasion, sitting at our firehouse table, having difficulty breathing. I would excuse myself from dinner or our fire department training, go up to my locker and use my Proventil inhaler or rescue inhaler. I had begun to realize that, if we were called out to a fire when my lungs were spasming, I would be in trouble. It was then that I realized I couldn't be on just a rescue inhaler any longer. I needed something stronger. My doctor prescribed a long-acting steroid inhaler – two inhalations both morning and night. I also continued using the rescue inhaler as needed. In 2015, I had been on inhaled steroids for about 13 years. The steroids were doing their job. My lungs felt great, and I could still do my job as a firefighter. I worked out regularly, and I ran in several long-distance running events and sprint triathlons. I was in tremendous shape for a 47-year-old man.

My doctor placed me on a new steroid called Symbicort. This medicine did wonders for my asthma after being on it for about a year. I felt so good that I began to question if I really needed any medication at all. I also had begun eating a gluten-free diet; and when I did not have gluten in my diet, I was able to run my mile quicker. My mile pace over longer distances went down significantly. For example, when I would eat gluten-filled foods and beverages, I would feel congested in my lungs and sinuses and would run approximately 10 to 11 minutes per mile. However, on a gluten-free diet, I had less sinus and chest congestion and began running a 7:45- to 9:15-minute pace without difficulty. Say what you will, but this was my lung litmus test. My doctor said, "If it works for you, keep doing it."

In February of 2015, my family and I went on a winter recess break to Florida. Syracuse is definitely in the snowbelt. It can get frigid, and fighting fires in the extremes of temperatures can be difficult. In addition to firefighting, firefighters also are called to the routine and the mundane as well.

On one wintry and brutally cold February night in 2015, my Engine company was called out multiple times for a water leak to the same residence. The call came in at approximately 0300 (3 a.m.) – our second time to this address during our shift. "Engine Co. 3, Truck-3, Car 2, water problem in a structure, possible involvement with electrical." This is a paraphrased dispatch but to the point. The windchill that night was -20° F. My Chief, Car 2, was dispatched to this address three times that evening; and Engine 3 was dispatched twice to the same address – all for the same reason. We were all miserable, tired, cold and annoyed with the issue at hand. I, too, was annoyed and thought we already took care of that issue earlier in the shift. I was not prepared for the chaos that followed.

Engine 3 arrived on scene first; and I advised dispatch, "Engine 3 on scene." Truck-3 and Car 2 were coming from a separate firehouse, and we beat them by a few seconds. I packed up (put on my SCBA) and advised my crew to put on their packs as well. This was met with resistance because they are heavy and "It's just a water leak, Lieutenant." More than likely, this was "just a water leak" – as we had been there earlier. I would rather err on the side of caution. I always operated on the premise of better to have and not need than to need and not have. I have been to fires where "just a water leak" turned out to be a bathroom fire that had melted the plastic pvc water lines, causing water to leak through ceilings. Unbeknownst to the occupants, there was a raging bathroom fire upstairs on the second floor, and they did not realize it.

Fortunately, on this night in question, we found that the water leak was again just a water leak and not a fire. We got out of our rig, trudged through the snow and onto the front porch of the structure. We pounded on the door and announced, "Fire Department." We heard, "Come on in" and went inside. Dad was on the couch playing video games in the dark and greeted us with "It's in there." We walked into the kitchen, and a heavy stream of water was pouring through the kitchen ceiling. Mom explained, "The upstairs tenants turned the water on again after you all left from last time." Her three young boys were huddled around the oven, trying to warm themselves. It was freezing in the apartment; and I told the mother, "It's not safe trying to heat your apartment with the stove and with the oven door open." She explained, "Our furnace is not working, and the kids are freezing." I definitely get it. She was trying to take care of her children the best she could.

At that point, the Chief came into the kitchen and loudly exclaimed, "Lieutenant, what do you got!" I attempted to tell him what we found, but I was cut off. "Lieutenant, take your crew, go to the basement and shut that water off!" The Chief was in a foul mood because of the weather, the hour of the night; and it was his third time that night to the residence. He proceeded to berate the parents and met us in the basement.

My crew and I went back outside and around the side of the house to the basement entry. The Chief came stomping down into the basement a couple of minutes after us and yelled, "Lieutenant, shut off the water and take off the valve; so they can't turn it back on!" I told him that the furnace also was broken, and the tenants were freezing. He said, "Lieutenant, you can't save everyone!"

I didn't like how he was handling the parents. I didn't appreciate his dismissal of me in front of my crew, and I certainly did not like the conditions in which he was ready to leave the families who lived in this structure. At a minimum, we could call for The Red Cross to find temporary housing for the tenants for the remainder of the evening.

As he abruptly turned from me in the basement, I yelled, "Chief, there are kids up there. We got to do something." No response. "Chief!" No response. "Chief!" Again, no response. I followed him upstairs and outside into the cold. The rest of the crews were huddled together, waiting for us outside. They had heard the Chief and I having a "go-around" in the basement. A fellow officer said to me, "You picked a bad night to piss him off." I continued after the Chief up onto the front porch. Once again, I called, "Chief!"; and he slammed the front door in my face as he went back inside to once again yell at the parents/callers.

I stood on the porch and yelled down to the crews standing in the front yard, "It's not right, and you all know it. We can't leave these folks like this." I pointed at a friend of mine and said, "James, you're a Christian. You know this is wrong." James was relatively new on the job; he was a firefighter, not an officer and had "no say" in the matter. James had no position of authority, and I placed him in an awkward and tough position. Sorry, brother...

The children came out of the house – bundled up with coats and hats. I asked them, "Where are you guys going?" They responded, "We're walking to Grandma's house down the street."

Chief came out of the house and asked me, "Where are those kids going!?" I told him what they told me, and we all got back into our apparatus – back to the warmth of our firehouses. I felt satisfied that the children were going to be safe with Grandma and would be warm for the night. However, we did not take care of the other occupants of the five-family house. We did the bare minimum, and that made me mad.

We "ran" your basic EMS and fire calls for the remainder of the evening. I was chilled to the bone; but I knew that, when I got off shift, my family and I would be going to Florida. My wife and I had planned a trip to Disney World with our children and my mother-in-law.

After the shift, I showered, shaved, jumped into my sweats and was ready for our flight. As firefighters, we are accustomed to sleepless nights, and I routinely would try to get onto my family's sleep schedule as my shift ended. We made it to the airport with time to spare and boarded our plane. As we walked past the first-class passengers, I heard a businessman — dressed in a suit and tie — say, "Look at that guy. I remember when there was a dress code on planes. He looks like he just rolled out of bed." I was being tempted to say something. I was tempted to argue. I was exhausted; but this was no time for a fight, and I was excited to be going away to Florida with the family. I now know that the devil often works on us when we are tired. I knew enough to know that any confrontation could end badly. For example, escorted off the plane, sued over injuring a person, inadvertently hurting someone not involved from tussling with this businessman. The list is endless, but the point is I swallowed my pride. The guy was obnoxious, and that was on him. I was comfortable in my sweats, and I was with my family – thanks be to God. We flew into Fort Lauderdale, and we would visit with friends for a few days before heading north to Orlando.

The above paragraphs have been a prelude to what my wife and I are terming my "2015 experience." Our good friends John and Debbie own a home in a development outside of Fort Lauderdale. In their front yard is a large palm tree approximately 25 feet to 30 feet in height. Being a firefighter, I am accustomed to judging height by the length of our ladders that we regularly use. One day after returning from a jog, the thought of getting a coconut from their tree "hit me like a ton of bricks." No, one did not drop on my head.

I told my friend John I was going to climb his palm tree and get some coconuts for our girls. I threw on some jeans and headed back outside. My little one came running up to me and asked, "Daddy, where are you going?" I told her, "I'm going to climb a tree and get some coconuts." My daughter was excited, and we went outside to meet up with John. My friend was on board with my antics, and he gave me a small saw. He told me the coconuts were like missiles during storms, and he would be grateful if I could get them down.

I have always been a good climber; and as a child, I climbed every tree on our property. Not always for the good.... The palm tree has become a symbol for my family and me. It is, for us, a symbol of fun, excitement, pain and new beginnings.

On that day, I began my climb with vigor and enthusiasm – 25 feet to 30 feet were nothing. I made it to the top in about eight to 10 seconds. I hugged the tree with my legs and bear hugged it with my arms. I reached into my back pocket while grasping the tree with my legs and left arm. I started to cut the palm; but all of a sudden, my energy was gone. I knew I had seconds before I fell. I placed the saw back in my pocket and slid down fast. Ouch! Being from New York and not seeing palm trees too often, I did not realize that their skin runs upward toward the branches. When I slid down the tree, it was like sliding down a cheese grater; but I made it to the bottom without falling. My daughter screamed and said, "Daddy, are you okay?" My arms and right calf were raw and bleeding. "I'm okay, honey. Don't worry." My daughter ran inside and grabbed Mommy. The cat was out of the bag. Our mission had failed, and John and I were about to get it from our wives. "What were you thinking? Are you okay?" Blood was not spurting but was just oozing from deep abrasions. Being a paramedic, I knew there was no arterial involvement. My good friend Debbie said, "Dan, you do realize we can buy some coconuts from the store today for about a dollar a piece, right?" As I recount this story, I sheepishly grin, shake my head and say to my wife, "Sorry, honey." It's sorta funny now. I sent the picture of myself on the top of the palm tree to my friends at the fire station, and my wife posted it on Facebook. My friends laughed and texted back some good "guy stuff." At 47, I was still a kid at heart, and I hope to always have that playful mentality.

Three fourths of the way up. My attempt to get coconuts proved unsuccessful.

However, my wife began to notice subtle changes in me. Veronica recounts noticing some signs that were outside of my norm and believes this was the start of the 2015 event in question. Maybe I was a bit more reckless than usual? For me, this was just another day in the life of Dan. I was a firefighter, and we regularly did much more dangerous tasks. When I was in recruit class, a Chief, for whom I have a lot of respect, lectured our class about the principles of risk vs. reward. He said, "We will take great risk when there is great reward. When life is at stake, we will put our lives in danger. However, we will take low risk for low reward. If it is a vacant structure, we will not run recklessly into the building to save nothing. Your lives are more important than a vacant structure." This Chief was a wise and seasoned firefighter, and I should have applied his advice before climbing the tree. I now buy our coconut milk and coconuts from stores. However, if we were on a deserted island, I know I could and would feed my family by climbing the palm tree and harvesting the coconuts. Therein lies the difference. Risk vs. reward. Chief, it took a while; but I will now heed your advice.

I cleaned up my arms and leg, and we walked down to the local pool in our friend's development. We laughed about the coconut incident and played in the water with our children. I soaked my injuries, and the cool water felt good. It felt good for the first hour; but then all of a sudden, six out of 10 pain struck throughout my arms and leg. The chlorine and water had started to affect my injuries; and I told Veronica, "We need to leave now." We went back to our friends and placed some aloe on the wounds. Today, six years later, I sit here and look at the scar on my right arm and thank God I did not get more injured. In our family, the running joke is: "I could climb that," but now wiser minds prevail. I now understand how my wife believes that the climbing event was the start of my "2015 experience."

A week before the palm tree incident, I decided to abruptly stop taking my steroid medication. My lungs felt so good that I didn't want to be taking steroids if I didn't need the medication. Without consulting my doctor and without tapering off the medicine, I stopped taking Symbicort. I was afterall, a firefighter, a paramedic, a nurse (LPN), with a bachelor's degree in Psychology; and I researched the side effects of withdrawing from steroids on the internet. I had a good head on my shoulders — or so I thought. Doctors only know what they have been taught and only know what they have researched. My internet search concluded that I may have some joint pain by discontinuing the steroid abruptly. I thought to myself, *I can handle a little joint pain.* But I had no idea what was in store for me.

I highly recommend that you, Reader, follow the advice of medical professionals who you trust. I have learned a valuable lesson and have been humbled. DO NOT ABRUPTLY STOP TAKING A STEROID. Consult your physician. (Reader, please be advised to not do what I did with this medication. Please learn from my mistake. Symbicort is great medicine for asthmatics, but do not stop taking it abruptly and without consulting your doctor.)

We had a great vacation with friends and family. We were sun-drenched and unfortunately returned to the stormy and snow-filled Syracuse Airport. One of the perks of being a firefighter is free storage of our vehicle at the airport fire station while away on vacation.

I left the family in the terminal and ran to the fire station a short distance away. I grabbed my keys from one of the officers on duty. "Hey, Dan. Did you guys have a good time?" I replied, "It was good to get away. Great weather." Ben then asked me, "Did you put in for the Truck?" I replied, "What are you talking about?" He said, "Oh, you're on the transfer list. You're going to Truck-4." I was shocked but was also a little excited.

Engine 3 ran all day and night; and as an officer, I had an abundance of paperwork regarding our probationary firefighter and entering the data from our medical and firefighting incidents. Truck-4, on the other hand, had no probationary firefighters and ran a lot less. Typically, more seasoned firefighters will transfer to the truck to hone and apply different skill sets.

I thanked Ben for my keys and for storing our vehicle while we were away on vacation. I then went and picked up my wife and children from the airport terminal. We got our children and baggage loaded, and I told my wife the news. "I'm going to the Truck." She was taken aback and said, "What are you talking about? How did you hear that?" I told her what Ben had just told me, and I shook my head in disbelief. I told my wife that I was glad to do a lot less runs and this could be a good thing on the way out toward retirement. I was being honest. This transfer was intended as a slap by the upper echelon. I was not notified personally or in writing or by phone, but I heard it through the grapevine. It was a way to discipline, and it sent a clear message by the administration. I had talked back to the Chief on a call. I had disagreed with a Chief regarding the handling of an incident regarding the five-family house. A house that had no heat and no running water on a bitterly cold night just before my vacation.

Prior to the evening, the Chief and I had a decent, cordial relationship. We would discuss fire incidents or various calls, after the fact, in a constructive feedback, mentor-type of relationship. He once told me to tell him if I had a different opinion and that he wanted to hear it. I took him at face value. Prior to that incident, I always had used decorum and respect when discussing issues with command on scene. That night in the frigid cold, I let my guard down and raised my voice.

My only regret of that evening was that I didn't call for The Red Cross. I would have usurped his authority on scene and found myself in trouble then and there. But it would have been the right thing to do.

Station #3 is a notoriously good firehouse, and Engine 3 went to a lot of fires. Truck-4 went on less calls and a lot fewer fires. In our city, Truck work has much different operations than Engine work. As an Engine officer, our main task is putting out fire. Engine officers and firefighters also handle EMS work. Although I was a paramedic and knew my way around an ambulance, I was getting tired, emotionally fatigued. The monotony and stress of 18 years of EMS was beginning to take its toll.

A great part of the job as a firefighter is our schedule, and I still had another week off work when we returned home from Florida. On my off days from the fire department, I was Mr. Mom and visited friends and family. I was able to get a lot of projects done around the house.

The day after returning from Florida, my sister and I went to a local restaurant to grab a bite to eat. It was good to see her, and I wanted to hear how she was doing. She was in the midst of finalizing an awful divorce. My sister is two years younger than me, and we always have been close. I was the stereotypical big brother. Growing up, I literally beat up boys for calling her names and threatened several other guys who were inappropriate. We always have each other's back.

As we sat waiting for dinner, Meghan began to explain the verbal abuse she was enduring. Her ex-husband had found another woman, and he had begun to live with her. The divorce was ugly – as divorces can be, and the bitterness from the two of them was toxic for their entire family. My sister confided in me that her ex had begun to verbally insult our family as well. He had said something about my niece, my godchild, that made me unravel. As I sat in my seat at the restaurant, I could not contain myself. I excused myself and went outside. It had begun to snow; it was freezing cold; but I felt nothing. We were in for a very large storm! I stood outside without my coat and began to pace. I called my ex-brother-in-law and left a message. I became enraged. I was beyond upset, and I never had felt this type of anger before. I wanted to kill. I didn't want to just fight. I wanted to kill him. He called me back, and we exchanged some expletives. I asked him to meet me. I told him I was going to bring 20 of my friends and stomp him out. He said, "One on one." I said, "OK by me. Where?" As I look back on this exchange, I am very grateful that my ex-brother-in-law's "cooler head" prevailed. He said something to the effect, "Okay. We got that guy stuff out. Now let's talk rationally." I still was not ready and was still seeing red. Cars drove by me in the parking lot as I ranted and raved on the phone, and people stared with mouths agape. When the call with my ex-brother-in-law ended, I was beyond mad. A wild rage boiled in my veins. I looked up toward the dark blizzard night sky and screamed, "God, I am going to kill a man tonight! God, help me! I am going to kill him if You don't intervene. God, I need You!"

"You shall not murder" (Exodus 20:13, NIV).

A very large part of me knew not to break this commandment, but I was out of control. As my wife, doctors and I now know, my rage was also part of the steroid withdrawal and a culmination of emotional triggers from years of post-traumatic stress. Looking back upon this night, it was, for me, the beginning of the "2015 experience"; but my wife would say it began in the palm tree a couple days before.

That night in the parking lot, I asked God for help, and He showed up in a big Way. I felt like I was unexpectedly hit by a 12-foot wave while walking on the beach. I was turned upside down and figuratively bounced along the sand. However, instead of sand, it was the brisk cold and snow of our Syracuse winter. Such were the next two months of my life.

That winter there were reports of homes in Buffalo, New York literally collapsing from the snow load. With this in mind, homeowners throughout the Northeast were eager to get the snow off their roofs. The snowstorms had been underway back home while we were in Florida, and we were that much happier to be in the warmth of Florida. However, now that we were home in snowy upstate New York, we were in for another doozy of a storm. We had an abundance of snow from the previous week's snowstorms, and more snow could prove dangerous. Therefore, shortly after returning home from Florida, I cleaned off my dad's roof, our roof and my in-laws' roof in that order.

It was a beautiful sunny but cold winter day as I shoveled snow from our roof. I was mid-waist in snow on top of our roof — shovel in hand; and I was working hard to clear the snow. At that point, I had been at it for about three to four hours. I had begun to have a euphoric feeling while clearing off our snow-filled roof. I heard the birds chirping, and the sounds of cars in the distance echoed in the air. It all sounded beautiful. A peace and a sense of tranquility flowed through me. As I finished clearing off the last part of the roof, I suddenly felt an abundance of energy. I felt light and agile; I danced on our roof — like Bert from Mary Poppins, and felt more alive than I ever had in my life. My body felt like I was a teenager again, and I literally was spinning around on the rooftop like a breakdancer. It was an intoxicating feeling, but I knew that something unusual was going on with my body. I had cleaned off two roofs in two days. It was back-breaking work, but it had to be done. I climbed down the ladder and went inside. I told my wife about my experience; and she was like, "Hmm, interesting?" She asked if I had anything to eat. I hadn't, but I wasn't hungry. I had no desire or urge to eat. Food was an afterthought. Not that I was trying to avoid it, but I didn't really want it.

We eat meals as a family. This is a cherished part of our family routine. We sit, say grace and eat home-cooked dinners. We will order out on occasion and sometimes fall into that routine as well. But for the most part, my wife and I take turns cooking, and this has been our rhythm. I love food, and cooking can be fun. However, during this week of snowstorms and roof clearing, time was of the essence, and family meals could wait. Or so I thought... The third roof in three days. My nephew Dillon helped me with my dad's roof; but besides Dillon, I was undertaking two out of three roofs by myself. The snowfall that season was the most I have seen in years. I was concerned with the weight of the snow and with structural collapse. If it can happen in Buffalo, it can happen in Syracuse. In fact, as a firefighter, I have seen the aftermath of buildings that collapse from fire, water, age and snow. Collapses do and will happen if structures are not well maintained. I was working hard to ensure this scenario did not happen to our family's houses.

The third roof

I was on my in-laws' extremely snow-covered roof. My wife, our children and my in-laws were down below having dinner. It was a beautiful, cold night. The stars were magnificent; and light, fluffy clouds drifted about in the deep, dark sky. My in-laws' neighbor walked by with his dog and yelled up to me, "Be careful up there." I thanked him and continued working on the roof. Again, the feeling of exuberation and euphoria flooded my body just as it had the day prior on my roof. I had been working long hours for the past two-and-a-half days. I was due into the firehouse in the morning, but I started to get the feeling that I wasn't well. I sat down on the roof, looked up into the starlit night sky and began to pray. It was about 7 p.m. I had been working for several hours, and I still had the other half of the roof to go. Exhaustion was an understatement.

As I prayed, I began to confess my sins to God and asked for His forgiveness. Anything and everything I had done wrong in my life came pouring out. I sat and cried and prayed. I looked up toward Heaven, into the night sky; and I knew I was not alone. God was there with me, was pleased; and it felt like communion. I sat there on the roof in prayer, in awe and wonder.

I also had the sense that the devil was looking down on me, but God had him at bay. I felt protected by my Father. I had the sense that God was with me, and I knew nothing could hurt me. I felt embraced in the warmth of His loving arms. I felt like a newborn baby in the arms of his daddy, being rocked and cared for. I was told in prayer, "Go down and have your family move away from the kitchen. It is not safe. There is too much snow up here." It was not an audible voice but an "internal voice" but not a voice. It was communication from The Holy Spirit. I was then told, "Call in to work tomorrow. Tell them that your Father needs you."

Call-in is a term we, SFD firefighters, use to get time off. I obeyed. I did not feel sick, but I would do as my Father had told me. I had some personal leave days still available for that calendar year, and I knew we could use them on an emergency basis. I was instructed to tell my Chief, "My Father needs me."

Reader, I was not sure what was going on. All I knew was that I was having some beautiful moments on the roofs that I had been shoveling and felt totally loved by God. I was following the instructions that I heard. As long as any message was good and innocent, I had no hesitancy in following.

I went down the ladder and into the warmth of my in-laws' home. When I explained the snow situation on the roof, Veronica, our children and my in-laws reluctantly moved from the kitchen into the dining room. I explained that the snow load could collapse the kitchen roof truss. I checked in the crawl space and checked the truss. They looked intact except over the kitchen area. There was a visible crack in the kitchen ceiling, but I was not sure if that translated into the truss above. I could not see it clearly. My father-in-law was not impressed. I told him that he must never let the snow get that bad again above their kitchen.

I called my Chief at station 9, a nice, caring, different Chief than previously mentioned. I said, "Chief, I need to put in for an emergency PL for both day shifts. My Father needs me." I then said, "Chief, you have always been there for the guys. Thank you." They initially counted my absences as PL or personal leave days but soon changed them to SD/SN (sick day/sick night). (Recounting this brings back some anxiety and, to be honest, is a bit heavy. However, I trust and will follow.)

My wife went out that evening after dinner with some of her girlfriends from our neighborhood; and our children would be spending the night with Yia Yia and Papou, their grandma and grandpa. This sleepover hardly ever happens, and I am so grateful that our children were safe with Yia Yia and Papou that night. The timing could not have been better. I cleared the snow from above the bedroom roof and ensured they were safe. I said good night to our girls around 9 p.m. and continued to work until almost midnight. Veronica would be coming home soon from being out with friends. I got another overwhelming sensation while working on the roof. It was a message to go to my sister Kathy's house and convince her to go to my sister Meghan's house in the morning. I was told that our family could not handle what was about to happen. My sister Kathy would be best to intervene in this situation. This message made no sense.

Reader, at this point, I knew I was either going crazy; or I was truly getting messages from God. As I climbed down the ladder, I saw something in the snow down below. I grabbed it, and I pulled it out from the snowbank. It was a 4" x 9" piece of lattice made from 1"x1" square wood. The lattice had broken off from the flower garden below under the snow and was shaped in the form of a cross with the letter V on it. I grabbed it and brought it home with me. Reader, I call my wife Veronica, "V"; and for me, the shape of this "lattice cross" with the letter V made no rational sense at the time; but it was symbolic of something to come. Reader, at this point, I was having trouble getting out my words; and it was hard to think clearly. Veronica came home at the designated time; and I greeted her with: "Wa, we hhave ta gggo to Kathy's." Veronica was shocked to say the least. "I am not going to your sister's house at this hour. What are you talking about? What's going on with you?" We talked and talked. I finally convinced her — after about 30 minutes — to go to my sister's. (God bless you, V. Through sickness and health, for richer or poorer ..., you were true to your vows. Thank you, honey.) It was about 12:30 a.m. I called Kathy at home and woke her husband. "Kathy, it's for you. It's Danny." I never called at this late hour, and she knew something was wrong. She answered, "Hello? What's wrong?" I replied, "Hi Kath, sssorry to call ssso late. V and I are coming over. I have to talk to you about something." Crickets chirping is an understatement. "You're what, honey? You're coming over?" I replied, "V and I will be over in a half hour. See you soon. Bye."

On the way to Kathy's house, I told Veronica I had to text a friend at fire station 3. I dictated to her this message as I drove, "Hey Tom, hope you're doing well. I'm going to be out sick for a while, but I need you to do something for me. I am not going to be taking calls from anyone. Tom, I need you to get your gut checked out. Stop ignoring the reflux, and go get this checked out. It's imperative."

Reader, Tom is one of the people I was told to contact while on the roof. I had an acquaintance friend die from Barrett's esophagus approximately four years prior. Barrett's esophagus is an abnormal change in the mucosal lining in one's esophagus, and it can lead to cancer. This can sometimes occur through untreated reflux. Tom often would complain of reflux symptoms and would say things like, "If I die from this, I die from this." Tom, at the time, was a young guy at almost 30 years old and had way too much life ahead of him. I like Tom, and I was glad to pass along this message from our Father.

My words were beginning to become harder for me to get out. I had no facial droop and no unilateral weakness. I assessed myself for signs of a stroke and had no other signs and symptoms at this point. As best as I could tell at the time, this feeling was a by-product of communicating with God. I still was going to obey, and I would go to my sister Kathy's. I likened my symptoms to an astronaut getting too close to the sun without the proper shielding and getting radiation burns and poisoning. But in this case, it was not the sun but the Father. The plan to get my sister Kathy to go to our younger sister Meghan's house in the AM began to unravel. My sister Meghan needed help! I was 100% certain Meghan needed help in the morning, I didn't know why, but I knew Kathy would be beneficial in helping her. I had to convince Kathy to go to Meghan's in the morning. Unfortunately, V and Kathy began to "nonverbally talk" through eye signals and head gestures, and they whispered words to each other while I was trying to talk. I felt undermined and hurt. Kathy was a piece of a puzzle, and it needed to fit into place.

Reader, the universal gesture of forefinger to temple in a circular motion comes into play here. No one actually made this "crazy sign," but I would understand if they had. What I was feeling was extreme sadness regarding their inability to understand my fear for my younger sister Meghan. V and my sister Kathy were both well within their right to be concerned. They loved me. I was acting out of character and acting about as odd and out of it as they come. I was physically and mentally stuttering; but outwardly, the stutter was not as apparent. I also was being insistent to Kathy about visiting our sister Meghan and fixing something that was not yet broken. It made no sense! That is, it made no sense to Veronica and Kathy.

As we left Kathy's house, she assured me that she would be there in the morning as promised. *Ahh, mission accomplished,* so I thought. I was exhausted. It was almost 2 a.m. when we got home. I had been shoveling day and night for three days, had not been eating and not sleeping well (two to three hours a night at best). On the way home, all I could think of was my pillow. My body ached all over, and I was physically and mentally exhausted. I hadn't been this thin since early in my college career – 182 pounds. I had lost approximately 12 pounds in less than a week after returning from Florida.

As we got home from Kathy's, V told me she was heading up to bed. I told her I was going to read and pray a little bit at the kitchen table – as was my practice for years. As I was praying and reading the Bible, another very loud, nonaudible message came over me, "Get up there. Veronica needs you. Bring your Bible and your journal." I ran up the stairs to our bedroom. I was commanded, "Kneel down, and do not move; close your eyes; hold your Bible and journal tight; do not open your eyes; you are not strong enough yet." I obeyed. I knelt down at my wife's bedside and prayed. "Father, what if she wakes up?" The Holy Spirit replied, "She will not wake up till morning. Do not worry."

I prayed. I learned that — when I was speaking and praying to Jesus — my head could remain in an upward, normal posture; but when I was praying to our Father, I was to bend my head down in reverence. These instructions went on for a time.

I was beyond exhausted. As I knelt beside the bed, my legs began to shake. "Father, help me. My legs are giving way." I was beginning to uncontrollably sink down, but then I felt two presences come from behind me. They lifted me up to the kneeling position. As I settled myself to the kneeling position, I heard a noise from behind me. It was an audible gasp, "Ahh" – an involuntary utterance from someone else in the room. I knew someone else, I knew multiple people were in the room. The gasp sounded familiar. I knew that sound, have heard it before and believed it was my mother. I so wanted to say hi to my mom. I missed her, wanted to hug her and hadn't seen her in seven years since her death in February of 2008. Then I heard "them" say, "he is coming." I will not capitalize his name for he does not deserve the respect. The circle of people around me opened up, and I felt a large presence walk into the room. I heard four sets of footsteps. I could feel the weight of the floor shift as he walked. I could feel his breath as he huffed through his nostrils into my face. Around and around, he circled me – like a great white shark about to attack its victim. I was so scared that I physically shook. As I knelt there shaking, eyes closed tight, I was being circled by something very large. My Bible and journal kept being pulled from beneath my arms, but I held onto both of them for dear life as instructed.

At one point, as the beast was in my face intimidating me by breathing his breath on me, I was so scared that I uttered the Name "Jesus." His Name just came out of my lips automatically. I felt the beast lurch backward as I said, "Jesus." I said it again, "Jesus." Again, the beast lurched back afraid. The second time was no coincidence. The beast was intimidated by the Name of Jesus. I now realized I had a weapon at my disposal. I said the Name Jesus over and over; and at times I literally blew the Name Jesus at the beast, and it backed up further. I had created an impenetrable wall around my wife and I by using the Name of my Lord and Savior Jesus Christ. This went on for hours, and I followed my Father's command. I knelt; I did not move; I held my Bible and journal tight; and I did not open my eyes.

After that ordeal, I heard a car come down our road and slowly go by our house. *Who would be out at this hour?* was my thought. The car kept stopping in front of our house, and I desperately wanted to go to the window and see who it was. I obeyed God's command. I did not move nor open my eyes.

My body twitched and muscles screamed as sweat poured down over my body. I could feel the sunlight on my face through the cracks of our window blinds. It was morning. *Veronica will be up soon,* I thought to myself. V woke up and yelled, "What are you doing? Why are you kneeling?" I said to my wife, "Push me over! Push me over!" My legs had locked up, and they were spasming from kneeling for the last six hours. Tears rolled down from my eyes as Veronica massaged my legs and wiped the sweat from my forehead. My shirt was soaked through from perspiration, and it looked like I had run a marathon. My body had been through the wringer. I told V that I had been up all night praying, but I did not get into all the details yet. After my legs returned to normal, I went into the bathroom.

I sat down, and I cried. For about 10 to 20 seconds of what we are terming my "2015 experience," I thought I was going crazy; but 10 to 20 seconds are all the time I had to worry about my mental capacity. At every other point during this two-month ordeal, I felt held by my Father. I felt protected, and I knew in my heart that all would be okay.

I started to take a shower when V popped into the bathroom and said, "Where are you going?" I told her that my sister Kathy was supposed to go to Meghan's, but she would not be going. I told Veronica I would now have to go. I now understood — through my Father — that my sister Kathy would not go to Meghan's house as we agreed upon the previous night. It was now up to me and my Lord to intervene in whatever was happening.

I kept getting the feeling that I needed to bring my daughter's baby doll with me to their house. When I asked my wife, "Where are our children's baby dolls?", she almost lost it. "What do you need a baby doll for?" For the life of me, I had no idea. I just knew I needed to bring one to my sister's house.

It's about a 25-minute drive to Meghan's house. As I pulled into her driveway, I could see that there was indeed something amiss. The bunk bed ladder from the girls' room was in the driveway — smashed to pieces; and debris littered the path to the front door. It looked like there was a fight, and someone had thrown these items outside. I rang the doorbell. My sister Meghan answered, "Hey, Dan." She was visibly upset, and I asked if I could come in. I asked, "Wwwhat's going on? Wwhy is all that stuff in the driveway?" Meghan said, "The girls and I have been fighting, but we're okay."

We went in and sat down. Meghan asked, "How are you doing?" She knows me very well. I tried to play it off, but my personal affect and my normal way of operating were off kilter. In other words, I was not quite being myself. My sister made us breakfast and told me that the divorce was still not going great. The kids were upset, and their entire family life had been negatively impacted.

The children came into the kitchen and, in unison, said, "Hi, Uncle Danny." They both wore frowns and appeared to have been crying. The baby doll came to mind, but I left it in the car. "Hey, dddo you girls know how to braid those bracelet things?" They looked up from the table, "Do you mean friendship bracelets?" I replied, "Yyep, tthhat's it – friendship bracelets. Could you make one for your ccousin's doll?" A smile crossed over their faces for the first time since I was there. "Yes, sure we would be glad to." The doll actually had come in handy. It was meant as a distraction for the children and as a conversation piece. The girls and I sat and reminisced about their younger years; and I joked with them about their mom, my sister and about our childhood. I let them know that I understood the pain of divorce — and that it's awful. Children are unfortunate victims of horrendous circumstances. Meghan and I knew from our childhood — all too well — the chaos that stems from divorcing parents.

(See www.familylife.com. What does Jesus say about divorce? What are the lies that destroy marriage?)

I stayed at Meghan's house for about two hours, and I felt comfortable leaving. Mission accomplished. Whatever the reason for going there had passed, and I felt comfortable leaving.

I then decided to drive to my brother Jim's house. I was in the area, and I wanted to say hi. Unfortunately, there is a saying in our fire department that holds true for families as well: "Telephone, tel-a-friend, tel-a-firefighter." In this case, "Telephone, tel-a-sister, tel-a-brother." My family had all been on the phone talking and discussing my recent issue well before I visited any of them. The grapevine is faster than the speed of light – or so it seems.

I walked into my brother's house; and he said, "How youuuu doing??" It's sort of hard to describe the air of curiosity and concern in that question, and he was most definitely concerned. We sat down, and I tried to best describe to him what was happening to me. I saw a buddist statue on his living room floor and felt immediately repulsed. It was as though I had just seen a horrific car accident. Jim said, "What's wrong?" I said, "That statue. When did you get it?" He said, "I like it! Don't look at it if you don't like it." I told him, "It is not I that does not like idols."

> "You shall not make for yourself an image in the form of anything in heaven above or on the earth beneath or in the waters below. You shall not bow down to them or worship them …" (Exodus 20:4-5 and Deuteronomy 5:8-9, NIV).

I tried to explain to Jim that I was okay. However, I also told him that if we were playing pool and someone moved a pool ball, the outcome would be changed. I attempted to tell him not to talk with the family about my recent condition. Unfortunately, this was like asking him not to care about me. My family all talked and raised many concerns.

I took a detour home and drove to the firehouse. I was told the previous night in prayer at my wife's bedside, "Hand in your badge." I called the fire station and requested the Truck officer on duty. I said, "Hey there, this is Dan. I'm not feeling well. I need a couple more days off." I was trying to delay the inevitable, and this phone call was not our normal procedure. We need a doctor's note if we are sick, but we can be granted one day/night shift off by the acting Deputy Chief on duty on an as-needed basis. I was later advised by the Truck officer on duty that I could have a sick night per the Duty Deputy, but I had to go to my doctor if any further absences were needed. At this point in my then 15-year career, I could count on one hand how many sick days I had taken. I was not the guy who called in sick, and I disliked malingerers. I believed that malingers gave our job a bad name. I loved my job. I loved the work. I loved the comradery. However, I was frustrated with certain Chiefs at the time, and some guys annoyed me – but such is any job and any career. Firefighters are, by and large, great guys who have a tough job. There is a firefighter culture that I often sidestepped; but honestly, quitting was not in my mindset. I sidestepped our firefighter culture outside of work because of the drama that sometimes ensues with comradery. The firefighter culture is much like the college lacrosse culture in which I thrived at Canisius College years before. Unfortunately, the firefighter culture can sometimes take a toll on family life; and I wanted to safeguard the gift that I had been given.

God instructed me to hand in my badge while I knelt in prayer. Hand in my badge? Yes, I was frustrated with the transfer to Truck-4; but hand in my badge? No job? How would we pay our bills? I had five years to go! Five more quick years, and I would be able to retire at half pay for the rest of my life. If I died, I could give my pension to my wife, and she could then collect the pension as well. I would be turning my back on my family, on my career and everything I had been working toward. Hand in my badge? Did God really mean hand in my badge?

I called my wife but couldn't speak. "Dan, where are you? Hello?" Tears were streaming down my face as I sat outside the firehouse in my car. I had not gone into the firehouse but called from outside. I gathered myself and said to my wife, "I, I, I just 'called in' for tonight's shift. I am on mmmy wway home."

I was told by many who heard me that my stutter was not that noticeable. However, inside my head, it was excruciating and very difficult to communicate. On the way home, I took the usual route that I had been taking for the last 15 years of my career, a city I lived in most of my life; and I got lost. The highway that I usually drove down seemed unrecognizable, but I managed through muscle memory to get home.

I arrived home and told Veronica about my morning with Meghan and her girls. I told her about the baby doll and what that was meant for. But V did not have ears to hear anything further about the baby doll or any other of my crazy thinking. She was concerned for me and had no idea what was going on. Thanks be to God that she did not call an ambulance. I would have been brought to a psychiatric center, labeled and medicated. This is not what I needed.

A little aside here

Reader, as I write down my experience from 2015 — now in rational thought and mind on 10/30/20, I want to let you know there is truth and legitimacy in what I am writing about in my "2015 experience." You will not read or hear me say, "Boy, oh boy, that was all just crazy thinking!" Yes, I was legitimately out of it — not myself; but I believe the following scripture: "And we know that in all things God works for the good of those who love him, who have been called according to his purpose" (Romans 8:28, NIV). All things, Reader…

Just like I told my friend back in my freshman year of college about seeing a vision in the Buffalo night sky, he thought I was crazy. Reader, you're in good company. However, I am not afraid. I was told to write this book, and this is what I am doing. I will say it again, Jesus is coming soon. When? I do not know. But in this lifetime or the next, Reader, you will meet Him face to face.

And back to the 2015 experience:

I told my wife about everything that happened the night before and while I was kneeling beside the bed. I also told her that God told me to hand in my badge. We were both very concerned about this. Veronica was so very patient with me, and she had never seen me act this way before. We are people and a family of faith. We believe God does speak to us, but it is not usually in this fashion. Veronica had every right to be concerned; but we, together as a couple, had faith.

Later that evening, I drove down to the firehouse that I was recently assigned to. The guys on duty were surprised to see me because I was out on sick time. "Hey fellas, the Chief here?" They replied, "Hey Dan. Yah, he's in his office." I knocked and walked into my Chief's office. He was not my immediate supervisor, but he was the acting Chief on duty for that night shift. I have worked with him over the years, and he is a very solid firefighter and a good guy. He said, "Hey Lieutenan, how you doing?" I replied, "Hey Chief. I'm doing pretty good, but I'm here to turn in my badge." He was shocked to say the least. "You're what!? Have you talked to anyone about this, Dan?" I said, "Yes, I am sure; and I have talked to the right Person. Chief, I am not upset. I am just done. Thanks for everything." I handed him my badge, walked out and shut his office door.

The guys were sitting around in the apparatus area where we have some chairs. It is a place where we gather, have training, recreate and solve world problems. I came out of the Chief's office; and they said, "Hey Dan, everything okay?" I replied, "They are better now. Take care, guys."

I then drove to my old fire station, station #3, to clear out my locker and give away my firefighting and paramedic books. I had a decent collection of books that I was studying for promotional exams.

Telephone, tel-a-friend, tel-a-fighter... The news had reached station #3 before I had even arrived. I was met at the station door by a friend, the driver of the apparatus, who asked, "Is it true?" I replied, "Yes, it's true. I'm out of here." He hugged me and walked away, shaking his head. The guys knew I was upset about being transferred out of the station, and they were concerned I was being rash. What they did not know was that I was acting on a directive from my ultimate Chief, my God.

I had 15 years on the job, and I was throwing away my pension – 15 tough years, grueling at times but 15 good years. Five years would go by in a heartbeat. Five years till retirement. The Captain, who was on duty, is another friend; and we had come on the job together. As I walked into our office, he said, "Dan, what in the world are you doing?" I cleaned out my locker, gave him my books to give to the firefighters and left the station.

I was struggling to follow what I was directed by God to do. I went home in disbelief and extreme sadness, but I trusted my Father. At that time, I was praying 24/7. I was in continuous prayer, and I felt held by my Lord.

Unfortunately, my words became harder to come out, and my memory was now being affected. I was having conversations with various people and forgot I had conversations with them. For example, while I was out on sick leave, I called our pediatrician to schedule doctor appointments for our daughters. My wife gave me a list of to-do items, and I tried the best I could to complete them. I called the doctor's office; and the nurse said, "Dan, we just talked; and we already scheduled those appointments." That was one of many experiences of having a conversation with someone and forgetting we had just spoken about a certain subject. This experience left me humbled and required me to start keeping notes. I made lists of items that I completed and people who I talked to. This definitely helped, but it was not a cure.

In addition to memory impairment, I realized I could not be around any negative talk, including the nightly news. Whenever the news was on or I heard of any negative news whatsoever, it hurt. The pain shot through my body like a shock wave. When I heard the nightly news, I involuntarily would put my hands over my ears to stop the pain. Even basic conversation about troubles throughout the world sent pain through my body. I couldn't hear about anything negative. It was like eating the worst food you can imagine and vomiting from the taste.

I did not know what was happening to me, but I trusted my Father. I knew that I would be alright. I intuitively did what I needed to do. I began reading books. I read like my life depended on it. In a two-month period, I read approximately 15 novels. I read the following books: *The Color of Water, Touching Spirit Bear,* the trilogy of *The Hunger Games* and *The Left Behind* series. My mind could absorb this information, and I had no problem remembering the storyline or characters. I read for hours at a time. It was like my mind was rebooting itself.

I also began taking piano lessons. I advised my piano instructor that I was suffering from symptoms similar to PTSD. My instructor told me that he understood, also suffered from anxiety and that he would be willing to work with me.

I was continuing to exercise, eat right and attempting to take good care of myself. In addition to the physical healing my body was craving, I also continued to journal and pray.

My wife got us into couples' therapy. My wife was so very concerned that her husband of 14 years was losing his mind. We went in for couples' therapy, and Veronica met with the therapist first for about 30 minutes. I then was asked to come in for the last couple of minutes of the session. The therapist immediately diagnosed me with acute manic signs and symptoms. I was not impressed, and I became upset. I told her she could not diagnose me in five minutes, and I did not appreciate her taking at face value my wife's interpretation of what was happening to me. I felt like I was fighting for my life; I felt like I had to defend my actions. The therapist and I would later talk – approximately two months later, and we both apologized. She apologized for making a quick diagnosis, and I apologized for being upset. She had every right to confront me, but I did not want this diagnosis on my permanent record. I knew it was a passing event, and I was assured by my Father that I would be okay.

The Captain, my friend, would later say to me regarding the night I came down to the station to gather my belongings, "Dan, you looked like the poster boy for PTSD (post-traumatic stress disorder)." He told me I was unkempt, my hair was all over the place and I looked about as depressed as can be.

Reader, I was depressed. I did not want to quit! I did not want to lose my job that I had dreamt of for years. I did not want to throw away my pension. How would I support my family? I reluctantly did as I was instructed from my Father.

I was crunching numbers in my mind. I thought about our bills and liquidating my deferred comp to pay off loans. My decision made no rational sense, but I followed.

The next day after when I reluctantly handed in my badge, the EAP (Employee Assistance Program) officer called me. Joe said, "Dan, what in the world are you doing? Come on, man. You have to think about your family. Don't do anything rash. Let's get you in to get some help." I said to Joe, "I was expecting your call. Thank you for calling. Yes, I would like to talk to someone." I told Joe that I did act a bit quick, and I would like to talk to someone.

I think of the passage in the Bible related to Isaac and Abraham. I was asked to hand in my badge, and I followed. However, God wanted to see how much I trusted Him. I trusted Him with my future and everything I had dreamed and hoped for the past 20 years. I placed everything we own and any and all firefighting aspirations at my Lord's feet. I trusted my Father, and I obeyed.

Joe assigned me to talk with the EAP office and asked me if I knew where it was. He gave me the address, and I called and made an appointment. Driving there was challenging. At this point, I was getting lost driving to places where I had been driving all my life. Everything looked unfamiliar. That's when The Holy Spirit came and gave me left/right directions. We did not have a GPS in my 2012 Passat, and I did not yet know how to use my cell phone in that capacity.

Literally while driving to the EAP office, I was told, "Turn right here. Turn left there" and so on. I was told, "That is the building there." I was then told, "Go into the office." I went in and into the first office I came to. There was no one in the office, and I started to walk around. I heard a group of people in a conference room with the door shut and heard their muffled words. I then saw a framed picture on the wall, and the words stirred my soul. It read, "Life is not waiting for the storm to pass. It's about dancing in the rain." I took a quick picture of this sign and then overheard someone in the conference room swear. They had dropped an f-bomb, and it hurt my soul. I had to leave that office immediately. I went into another office and again found an empty office and saw yet another sign on a wall. The sign read, "The future is something we create." I felt like God was giving me pep talks through these framed pictures. I again took a picture of the sign and went out into the hallway. I walked in the hallway; and I was told, "Go upstairs" and I went. I went into the next office, and it was the EAP office. This experience was like walking with a blindfold on and a good, kind friend telling you where and when to turn. Ordinarily, I would be frightened and concerned that I was out of my mind; but that was not how I was feeling at all. I felt assured and comforted. I knew that God was holding me in His arms. I prayed to God, "Father, help me. The EAP counselor will hear my voice and know that I am not doing well. Please help me with my speech." I was concerned that my stutter would be a flag of sorts.

I talked with the counselor and kept everything very "on the surface." I did not stutter at all, and I did not report my hallucinations or directives from God. I simply stated that I was having PTSD signs and symptoms and had been overwhelmed at work. I told her about a fire in the previous November, "the State Street fire." I told her how we had a multiple fatal fire on a very cold winter night. Unfortunately, many people died in their home due to cooking; but we saved a couple of them, including a five-year-old boy. I told her that, after the fire, my wife and I decided to buy clothes for the child because everything he owned was lost in the fire. A week after the fire – as I was picking out the clothes for this child, I stood in Herb Philipson's department store by myself and began to cry. I held the clothes and imagined the horror that this young boy must have gone through.

I told the counselor that feelings from previous calls – fire events and EMS incidents for the past 18 years – were all coming to the surface. The wall that firefighters build to protect us from feeling the secondary trauma was crashing down on me. I got hit with a wave of emotions that I had not been dealing with for many, many years.

The EAP counselor sat and listened. She finally said, "Okay, maybe you need a day off?" I said, "A day?" exasperated. I then said, "How about a month?"

My family of origin also was worried, and they recommended a therapist who specializes in PTSD. Brian, my therapist, was great. He met with Veronica and me. Although I had been to therapy on and off for more than 15 years of my adult life, I had never been to therapy like this before. We met several times a week for two months; and then once the signs and symptoms were calming down, we went back to an as-needed basis.

The other medical piece of the puzzle that I did was go to my allergist. They put me back on a steroid inhaler. The allergist said, "We're not going to do any scratch testing because your bloodwork is already very indicative of extreme allergens and you will have a very bad day if we did this."

Again, I thank you, Veronica, my wife, for helping me research the effects of steroids on the body and the negative impact from stopping steroids abruptly. Low-dose steroids, such as cortico-steroids, impact the adrenal gland that regulates the cortisol levels in your body. Cortisol helps regulate your emotional health. Essentially, I set myself up for a perfect storm. Doctors who read this will question whether a low-dose steroid can do such a thing. Ask yourself this question, doctors, "Have you ever known an asthmatic to abruptly stop their medication like this?" I have known two – myself and a good firefighter friend who also did what I did. He stopped his Symbicort-inhaled steroid abruptly. Harrison later committed suicide. There were many other factors concerning Harrison's suicide, but the similarity in our signs and symptoms were startling. (I will add again that Symbicort is an awesome medication for asthmatics. However, don't stop taking it abruptly.)

So the question remains of whether or not I believe the events that transpired were, in fact, real? I come back to Scripture, "And we know that in all things God works for the good of those who love him, who have been called according to his purpose" (Romans 8:28, NIV).

210

God can and does use various things in our lives to speak to us. Have you ever heard a well-timed song? How about the correct words from a friend at just the right moment? God can and does use people, places and events in our lives and weaves His Holy Spirit into our midst. I pray that we all may have eyes to see and ears to hear God at work in our lives.

Now if you, Reader, ask me, "Do you think you were having medical withdrawal from lack of corticosteroid in your system?" I will — without a doubt — respond, "Yes, of course." Or if you ask me if I thought I was having a PTSD crisis, I also would report, "Yes." The facts that I had not been sleeping well, not eating well but exercised well beyond my capacity all lent to my body reacting the way in which it did. However, for me, this does not minimize the events that took place in my life in 2015. God was indeed working in my life. I have no doubt. No doubt.

After my EAP appointment, I was returning home. I had kept a shovel in the back seat of my car in case I saw someone in need; and I had been using it for the past week, assisting many people. I called this "ministry with a shovel." While driving, I received another "heart" message from The Holy Spirit saying, "Turn here and into the driveway." I took my next right and began to pull into the next driveway on the right. "Not that driveway but up there on the left." I drove up, pulled in and got out with shovel in hand, expecting someone needed help shoveling. I was not sure what I would find.

I walked up and saw a guy on his roof – or so I thought. I walked over and yelled up to him, "Do you need some help?" A woman answered me from around the corner of her house. "Hello, I'm over here!" I walked over and was shocked by what I saw (no pun intended). I introduced myself, "Hi, I'm Dan. Lady, I'm a Syracuse firefighter. Please get off your ladder. The weight of your ladder is on the glass meter of your house. If it breaks, it can electrocute you." She was the homeowner, who had placed her metal step ladder against her electric meter. She placed the ladder and all her weight directly on the glass globe of the meter. She followed my directions. She said, "I placed it there, so I could talk with my handyman up on the roof." I walked through the snow and moved the ladder out of the snowbank. I then repositioned it so that it was not resting on the glass globe but against her house and away from danger.

She thanked me and said, "Do you know Dennis Cody?" I said, "Yes, he is a great guy! He retired just after I came on in 2000. He was a District Chief in the firehouse, where I was assigned initially." She then said, "I went to school with him. If you see him, tell him I said "Hi." I replied, "I sure will, ma'm." I left and returned home.

It is a small world. Firefighters all know someone, and everyone seems to know of a firefighter. We live in a relatively small community, and someone is always asking about this or that person.

I hold onto that experience with the woman resting her ladder on the electric meter as my reality check. During that "2015 experience" as I call it, I had no idea who that lady was. I had no idea what I would find when I was told, "Turn right and then pull into the driveway on the left." For me, I hold onto this event as a reminder. That was my reminder that God can, does and will use us at various times if we listen. At that time period in my life, I happened to be "ultra-tuned" into the right frequency.

"For it is by grace you have been saved, through faith - and this is not from yourselves, it is the gift of God- not by works, so that no one can boast. For we are God's handiwork, created in Christ Jesus to do good works, which God prepared in advance for us to do" (Ephesians 2:8-10, NIV).

I do not boast, but I merely state the incidents and facts of my 2015 experience. I imagine what I have been writing to some has been wrought with skepticism and cynicism. What I can say is this – I once was lost, but now I am found. I was blind, but now I see.

CHAPTER 12

CASAC

"They promise them freedom, while they themselves are slaves of depravity—for 'people are slaves to whatever has mastered them'" (2 Peter 2:19, NIV).

I am currently in the process of receiving my credentials as an alcohol and a substance abuse counselor or CASAC. First of all, I will say that if you, Reader, or someone you know are currently experiencing drug and/or alcohol-related issues, know that you are not alone.

There are several people who I love and who have been affected by the disabling disease of addiction. It was and is hard to watch my friends succumb to their binges. I felt at a loss about how to help those I love; so I decided to do something about the feeling I was having and went back to school to get credentialed as a drug and alcohol rehab counselor. This training has been empowering, and I now feel more equipped to help those in need. However, what I really did by going back to school was empower myself so that I didn't feel overwhelmed by my loved ones' decision-making.

I used to believe that tough love was a good thing. It was once a popular notion among psychologists. If a family member or a friend behaved recklessly in regard to alcohol or drug use, then it was a "good idea" to practice tough love. A tough love practice would be a statement of this sort: "If you don't get your act together, then you're out of my life." What I've learned is that the person who is out of control and in an addictive crisis needs us and our love more than ever.

"… love covers over a multitude of sins" (1 Peter 4:8, NIV).

When we love others with a pure heart, we are loving the Way God wants us to love. As my good friend Don Maldari SJ once said, "If in doubt, follow love." Practicing this statement in my day-to-day life has never let me down.

The following is a true story. I am humbled, amazed and so very grateful for God interacting in our lives.

Karl is a very good friend. He and his wife Alie are close friends of ours, and they have two young children. Unfortunately, my friend Karl struggles with the debilitating disease of alcoholism. I will share this story as an example of the goodness of God permeating my life.

Alie understands the complexity of living with an alcoholic. On one hand, Karl is a loving, caring husband and dad. On the other hand, when he drinks, he will lie about his drinking and have a different persona around friends and family. Our friends are people of faith and active members in their Methodist Church. They are good neighbors, friends and both professionals within the community.

Karl's need for alcohol snuck up on him, and it became increasingly prevalent as he struggled with the complexities of family-of-origin dynamics. Initially, Karl's alcohol consumption began like most with a recreational cocktail with friends and loved ones. Karl was a beer snob or beer aficionado. He knew the challenges of making craft beer and practiced with home brew kits in his basement. It was a hobby initially, but it became a nightmare.

At one point in my life, I had told my wife Veronica, "If a guy doesn't like a good beer, I don't think I could be friends with him." Personally, I enjoy a cold beer after mowing the lawn, after work or while watching a football game. Beer, for me, was and even today is refreshing and tasty. This commonality of beer was one of the reasons I knew that Karl and I could become good friends. Sounds strange, but it was a basis for the initial formation of our friendship.

Our families get along well. Our wives are very good friends, and our children are approximately the same ages. We live a very similar life and lifestyle. Therefore, it is easy to be around each other; and it is natural for us to casually hang out as loving friends. In fact, friends can be another form of God's Way of loving us. Alie and Karl gave my wife and I the following plaque, "Our friends become our chosen family," which is adorned in our home.

It was extremely difficult to watch as our friends' marriage began to spiral out of control and plummet into a cavernous abyss. The effects of alcoholism began to invade their lives. Karl began to drink alone and hide his drinking from family, friends and coworkers. What began as a beer interest became a hard alcohol endurance contest. Karl was consuming vast quantities of alcohol, was confronted by his boss and demoted at his place of employment. His wife Alie was considering leaving their marriage. Their children had begun to be affected as well from the ravages of this awful disease and the tortuous arguments between their parents.

Veronica and I offered our prayers, our ears and our hearts to them. Alie was receptive and grateful, but Karl was more difficult to open up. He attempted to hide his drinking on several occasions, and his wife succumbed to getting a home breathalyzer to check each time she suspected his drinking. Karl was in denial big time!

One morning, while Karl and I were eating breakfast at one of our local restaurants, I confronted him. "Karl, I know you've been drinking this morning. You're slurring your words, and your facial expressions are indicative of someone who has been drinking." Initially, Karl was angry and vehemently denied it. I said, "Okay. Let's do the breathalyzer." I drove him to his house where he had the breathalyzer. Karl blew way over the intoxicated limit. He finally admitted to me, "Okay. I had a couple of drinks before breakfast."

This type of cat-and-mouse relationship went on for several months. It was an awkward place to be; but I felt called to be there for my brother, my friend. However, for Alie, it was a constant battle in which she had been involved for many years. Alie was beginning to become increasingly wary of their future. She expressed deep sadness at the thought of leaving Karl, but the health of their children was her first concern. She loved Karl, and they fit well together. However, we could understand her thought process and the challenging decision that awaited her.

Our neighborhood is a close-knit and unique development. I thank God for placing us here. I have learned many valuable life lessons through friends and neighbors in whom I know God had His hand in.

"But blessed is the one who trusts in the LORD, whose confidence is in him. They will be like a tree planted by the water that sends out its roots by the stream. It does not fear when heat comes; its leaves are always green. It has no worries in a year of drought and never fails to bear fruit" (Jeremiah 17:7-8, NIV).

In the fall of 2018, several members of our neighborhood friend group had planned a wine-and-beer tour, and my wife and I were one of eight couples planning on attending the event. Alie also would be going, but Karl would be staying home. There was and is today a part of me that is concerned about group dynamics in relationship to drinking. Excessive drinking lowers our inhibitions, and we tend to do things we might not do otherwise.

Karl chose not to go on the excursion for obvious reasons. He was professing to be sober for several months, and he did not want to be tempted. He and Alie had begun to mend their relationship, but Alie was tentative at best. We all held our collective breath as Karl attended AA and attempted to live a sober life. They previously had walked down this path back and forth a couple of times, and Alie's patience was beginning to wane.

One morning before the wine-and-beer tour, I sat at our dining room table in prayer. I heard in my being — in the innermost recess of my heart — a whisper of: "Whose do you say you are? Who do you follow?" A thought then entered my mind not to attend the bus wine-and-beer tour. I had an "ah-ha" type of moment that woke me up. If I profess to be changed from inside out, how can I go on a bus wine-and-beer tour, where people will be drinking in excess? Yes, Jesus made friends with prostitutes, tax collectors and sinners. But Jesus did not partake in destructive behaviors. Jesus calls us out of our destructive ways. I knew in my heart that, if I attended the wine-and-beer tour, I potentially would drink excessively. That is the nature of the beast. I have lived that excessive drinking lifestyle for many years, and it is NOT something I wish to continue. In fact, in order for my wife and I to go, we would have our children stay with their grandparents, and our youngest daughter would have to miss her soccer game. We were being selfish, and God was calling me out. Literally, in prayer at our table, I was convinced not to go. It was plain and clear as it was daytime.

I told Veronica that I couldn't go. She understood but asked if I would mind if she kept Alie company on the trip. This was something the entire neighborhood (group) was looking forward to. I told Veronica that I did not mind and that I would take our kiddos to the soccer game. Logistically, this made better sense, and we didn't need a babysitter for the day. I trust my wife with all my heart. She has a better "track record" of drinking than I do. She tends to be more socially practical when it comes to drinking, and she would keep Alie company. She would be a good friend with an open ear for the duration of the trip.

I took our daughters to the soccer game. Our oldest daughter, who was 10 at the time, and I would watch from the sideline. Our youngest was 6 years old, and soccer at that age is interesting to watch. It is like a flock of birds that huddle together and sway in the breeze. The soccer ball goes here and there, and a mass of children run around it. It is cute and a good family memory.

After the game, I took our daughters out for ice cream as a celebratory win or loss (I don't remember who won)? Ice cream is always something we look forward to! As I sat there with our children eating ice cream, I thanked God I did not go on the trip. Our kids were having fun, and they didn't have to miss the game. I had made the right decision for me and my family. However, God had additional plans for me.

As we sat in the restaurant enjoying our ice cream, I received a text from my buddy Karl. "I'm done with it." Texting is one of those things where I have learned there can be multiple meanings to a text and ideas can be misunderstood easily. I gave Karl two thumbs up emoji. I thought he was texting about giving up alcohol. I wanted to keep texting to a minimum, seeing as though I was with our daughters. Karl texted me back, "I can't take it anymore. I am so done. Goodbye." I paraphrased, but the text went something to that effect. The prior text, which I thought was a positive statement regarding his being through with alcohol which many of our conversations had been about, was not accurate. Karl was expressing that he was done with life! He was threatening suicide via text! And I had given him two thumbs up!

I calmly told our kiddos it was time to go and to gather their belongings. They followed my instructions and did not overly question. I called their Yia Yia (grandmother) and asked what she was doing. My mother-in-law began to tell me and started down a conversation path I was not ready to follow. I stopped her and interrupted. "Mom, it's an emergency. I need you to take the girls for a few hours." She readily agreed, and I told her we would see her in two minutes. I politely and calmly did all the previous so as not to heighten the situation and not panic our children. They love Karl and Alie and their children; we are family. We went on vacation with them as families in the spring of that year. We love them, and we wanted to dote on them. We have a timeshare, and we had extra points we could spare for an additional condo. The two families got along well, and we grew together as we created family memories. Our children and their children think of us as extended aunts and uncles.

I gathered our kiddos and brought our children to their Yia Yia's house. I briefly told my mother-in-law, "Karl is not doing well." Mom knew what I meant — for she too once struggled with this addiction — and said, "The girls will be all set for as long as you need." Veronica was on the bus tour,

218

and both she and Alie were hours away. Alie and Karl's children were safe and were staying with their grandparents.

As I got back in my car, Alie called me. "Dan, where are you? Karl texted me that he is going to kill himself." I told her, "Alie, I am on the Way to your house." She replied, while choking back tears, "Please let me know! We are two hours away, and I am stuck on the bus!" I told her I would let her know ASAP.

From the time of Karl's initial text to the time I showed up at his house was under 10 minutes, but a lot can happen in 10 minutes. This was not the first time I had been at his house for this type of situation, but it was the first time he threatened suicide.

At that time in my life, I was a volunteer crisis hotline operator, and I knew not to take the threat of suicide lightly. Unfortunately, a good (firefighter) friend of mine had taken his life the year prior. Suicide had attempted to rear its head in my family growing up. My mother attempted suicide when I was a young boy. I also have seen numerous suicide attempts and, unfortunately, the aftermath of death by suicide while working as a firefighter. Suicidal threat is a serious and possibly dangerous situation for all involved. Unfortunately, it plagues our society.

A little aside, Reader, if you suspect someone is thinking about suicide, do not hesitate to ask. My training has taught me that if you suspect something, say something. It is a myth that we will plant an idea in someone's thinking if we ask them this question. It is better to make an error by asking them bluntly and compassionately than to do nothing but worry about the situation.

I had no idea what I would be walking into. Did Karl do it already? Was he going to blow himself up – as I have witnessed before on calls as a firefighter? Was he violent? Was he armed? Did he have a plan already? All these thoughts bombarded my mind as I opened his front door. "Karl, it's Dan!" Their house was disheveled, and I became increasingly apprehensive. They have a beautiful home, and it was not usually like this! However, I was overcome with a sense of peace and calmness flooded through me. I knew God, The Holy Spirit, was with me.

I walked further into their home and called his name, "Karl, where are you?" No response. The house was dark with blinds drawn, and I walked cautiously. "Karl, it's Dan." Then I found him in their family room. There was a large bottle of vodka on the table in front of him that was almost empty, and pills were scattered in front of him. As a trained paramedic, I learned to gather the medicine and placed the pills back into the container to take with us. Later at the hospital, they would count the pills to establish how many were potentially ingested, and they also would know the type of medicine taken.

Karl awakened with an unintelligible grunt. Karl is much bigger than me, and I would not want to get into a wrestling match. I instinctively told him, "We are out of here! Get up, Karl!" He miraculously got up, and we stumbled arm in arm to my car. Karl weighs nearly 350 pounds, and he came to a thud in our front seat. I thought to myself, "I don't want to be cleaning puke from inside this car." This was our family car, and my wife drove it to work. It's the car we drive on family trips. However, Karl was worth it, and a throw-up is a small price to pay for having a dear friend.

I drove without knowing where to go. I had to clear my mind and gather my thoughts. I parked in our local supermarket parking lot and called his wife. "Alie, I've got him. Karl is okay, but I'm going to bring him to the hospital. I don't know how many pills he's taken, and he drank a lot of alcohol." I drove him to our local hospital, which also had within it a detox center. I parked in the garage, and we "walked" (stumbled) across the street to the hospital. I add this detail regarding walking with Karl because at the hospital they checked his blood alcohol level, and it turned out to be .3%. That high of a BAC could kill most people; but because of Karl's increased alcohol usage and size, he was able to withstand the poisonous alcohol effects. Karl walked approximately two blocks and was still talking! That, in and of itself, is miraculous. Just an fyi – the legal intoxication level in New York State is .08%, and Karl's BAC was four times that.

Alie and I sent texts back and forth while I was at the hospital with Karl. The wine-and-beer tour was over, but they were still hours away. She would be coming to the hospital as soon as possible. Alie called Karl's sister, and Karl's estranged sister came to be with him immediately. Kate is a RN, a wonderful person and a caring and devoted sister and aunt. God, through His infinite grace, was able to reunite their relationship.

"And we know that in all things God works for the good of those who love him, who have been called according to his purpose." (Romans 8:28, NIV).

Karl was safe. I did my part. I knew that if I had gone on the tour with the neighborhood, Karl, more than likely, would not be here today. The nurse at the E.R. said, "The pills that you gathered from the table were blood pressure pills. If Karl had taken the medicine as he was intending, we would not be able to reverse the effect. He would have died." Thank You, Father, for challenging me not to go on that tour with friends. Thank You for speaking into my life so that I could do Your will.

It was a long emotional day, and I was tired. I left Karl at the hospital with his sister and E.R. staff. I then drove to my in-laws' house and got our children. As I pulled into our driveway with the kiddos, Veronica and Alie were just getting home. Unfortunately, Alie was on the fence about seeing her husband. The ravages of alcoholism were taking its toll. Her heart was breaking; and Alie said to me, "I don't think I can see him right now." Something within me spoke up. Usually, I would identify the feelings she was having and try to actively listen. In other words, I would say something like: "You sound tired and hurt. It's been a long journey." I would pause and wait for her response, attempt to identify further feelings and help where I could.

However, on that day – much to my surprise, I said something completely out of character. I said, "Alie, Karl needs you now more than ever! You need to get up there. Whatever you plan on doing in the future with your marriage is up to you, but you have a vow to fulfill today!" Again, I paraphrase; but it was much like that, and I do believe it was Spirit-filled.

221

God used me – this I was certain; and now I would rest in the comfort of our home with my wife and children. We settled in as a family into our nightly routine. We had dinner and watched a show on TV. We put the kids to bed, said prayers at their bedside; and Veronica and I went back downstairs. It was about 10:30 at night, and the phone rang. Alie was on the phone. "Dan, we are still at the hospital. Karl just sat up in bed and told us that he left the stove on with food cooking. Then he passed out again. Could you go up to our house and make sure the stove is off? My mother went to our house earlier. She locked it all up but didn't check the stove."

Ugh!! I was in my pajamas, and I was tired. "Yes, no problem, Alie. Is Karl okay?" Alie replied, "He's been sleeping for hours, but it's been good talking with his sister." Alie and Kate were hashing out family dynamics. God was indeed working.

Reader, make no doubt about it, God has a plan; and He can use all things for the good, for His purpose. Yes, God can use all things for His good. Not just good things that happen in our life – things we are proud of – but ALL things … (idea referenced from Romans 8:28 NIV). The Creator of the universe can weave intricate patterns of our life into the beautiful fabric that makes up our life story – if, that is, we open our minds and hearts to Him.

When I got off the phone with Alie, I told Veronica, "I have to go up to Karl and Alie's house to check the stove." Being an 18-year veteran of the fire department at the time, I knew that most house fires in the U.S. are caused by careless cooking. I knew that if there was food cooking for 10 hours unattended, it would be incinerated, and the house would be in flames. In the 10-hour process, the pan would continue to heat. The smoke and heat would begin to build. The smoke would rise to the ceiling, and the heat eventually would cause the gases within the smoke to ignite. The radiant heat would begin to catch combustible items around the stove on fire. The carbon dioxide within the smoke begins to burn at approximately 1200 degrees Fahrenheit. The kitchen would catch fire; and within minutes, the adjoining rooms also would catch fire until the entire house was engulfed in flame. I had seen this situation before countless times as a firefighter both in a simulator and the aftermath of careless cooking.

Here's my plug for fire safety: Kitchen fires are the number-one reason for house fires in the United States. Make sure your home has working smoke detectors in every bedroom, outside the bedrooms, just outside the kitchen and in every room of your home/residence: living room, family room, den, attic and basement. I recommend interconnected smoke detectors, with 10-year battery backup. If one goes off, they all go off. I also recommend having working carbon monoxide detectors on every level of your home. I recommend getting a digital display carbon monoxide detector. If it goes off, you can digitally visualize how much CO is in your residence. There should be zero! If there is any number other than zero, then call 911!! (If your area does not have that emergency exchange number, call the fire department!)

I also recommend talking about fire safety with your family. What is your family safety plan in the event of a house fire? What is the fastest, quickest way out of your residence? What if that exit is blocked? Can you go out a window onto a roof as a second means of egress? Do you have a meeting place? Have you practiced a fire drill at home? It's not too late for families to do this. Practice tonight.

Back to Karl:

I told my wife that I would have to break into Karl and Alie's house and check their kitchen stove. Veronica knows me through and through. She knew that, although I was exhausted and did not want to get dressed and go over and check their home, I would do it for our friends.

"The King will reply 'Truly I tell you, whatever you did for one of the least of these brothers and sisters of mine, you did for me'" (Matthew 25:40, NIV).

Alie told me that her mom had locked up their house. I went to their home at 10:30 at night, and I knew I would have to break in. I brought the tools I needed to make entry. Firefighters are trained at this, and I knew I could make fast work of it. I envisioned police showing up because we have police circling our neighborhood regularly. What would I say? I really didn't want to have this type of interaction and conversation at night with the police. Ugh!

We are trained as firefighters to "try before we pry" to do as little damage to the residence as possible. I went to their garage and slid up the door. *Hmm, that's weird,* I thought to myself as I walked into their garage. I tried to open the door to their house, knowing it had been locked by Alie's mother. However, I turned the knob and opened the door. *That's odd,* I thought. I turned on the lights and walked into the kitchen. I walked over to the stove. "Stove on. Ha, I knew it would be off!" But it wasn't ...

The stove was on, and there was food cooking on the burner! It was on low, but it was cooking. Karl had cut up peppers and onions and filled the pan with water. The vegetables were cooked perfectly. I turned off the stove and placed the pan and vegetables in the sink.

I was dumbfounded. Karl, who had a BAC of over .30, woke from his intoxicated state, sat up in his hospital bed, and said, "The stove is

I am so glad I was eating ice cream with our daughters than on the beer tour beer with friends.

CHAPTER 12 | CASAC

on" and fell back to sleep. Their house supposedly was locked up tight by Karl's mother-in-law but was open? Karl's mother-in-law was and is very responsible. And this veteran firefighter, who thinks he's seen it all and done it all, was again humbled by God.

Thanks be to God, I am happy to report that Karl, Alie and their children continue to do well. Karl and I remain good friends to this day, talk regularly; and he admits when and if he feels weak. But Karl is a changed man. He has begun work on issues in his life and work on his family-of-origin issues that contributed to him making poor life choices.

About six months before this incident, I led Karl to receive Christ as his Savior. My evangelical friends will know exactly what I mean, but let me explain to those who may not be as familiar with that type of "Christianese."

One night I went to Karl and Alie's house when Karl was having one of his drinking binges. We talked and prayed together in the quiet of their living room. Alie was putting the children to bed. I asked God to bless their family. Karl spilled out his heart and soul and said, "I am screwing up. I'm going to lose them, Dan. I need help." We talked and prayed; and I asked Karl, "Are you ready to take a step toward health?" He said, "I am. I will do anything!" I said, "Karl, then I recommend that you invite Jesus into your heart and make Him the Lord and the leader of your life." Karl said, "I don't know how?" I said, "Karl, if this is what you want, repeat after me, 'Lord, I mess up. I am making poor choices in my life. I am afraid. I love my family, and I don't want to lose them. Father, please send Your Son Jesus into my life, to be the Lord and leader. I can't do it on my own. I believe. I pray this prayer in Your Son Jesus' Name. Amen.'"

Karl, repeated those words out loud in the quiet of his home about six months before his near-tragic suicide. God intervened in Karl's life. Karl opened the door. God didn't make Karl perfectly clean and sober overnight. Karl, like most of us, is a work in progress.

"Here I am! I stand at the door and knock. If anyone hears my voice and opens the door, I will come in and eat with that person, and they with me" (Revelation 3:20, NIV).

225

Recently, I had the pleasure of talking with my friend Karl about his sobriety. Karl has faith, and he is growing in his walk with the Lord. In addition to his faith, he also attributes his healing and sobriety to going to a treatment facility. Karl immersed himself into a sober state of mind. He dove in. God empowers us. In our weakness, strength. This statement is an oxymoron. How can we have strength in weakness? Paul says it better than I can ever articulate.

"But he said to me, 'My grace is sufficient for you, for my power is made perfect in weakness.' Therefore I will boast all the more gladly about my weaknesses, so that Christ's power may rest on me" (2 Corinthians 12:9, NIV).

Karl understands that, in his weakness, God intervened and that His healing was made available through his (Karl's) faith. Both our "yes" and God's interaction in our life allow the Holy Spirit to flow and healing to begin.

Please, Reader, know this: If you struggle with addiction, there is help for you! You're not alone. In our sin and during desperation, we feel alone; but we are never alone. God knows you so intimately that He knows the number of hairs on your head.

"Indeed, the very hairs of your head are all numbered. Don't be afraid; you are worth more than many sparrows" (Luke 12:7, NIV).

He knows you personally, wants the best for you, stands at your door and knocks. He waits for you and does not impose His will.

He knows you, Reader, through and through. God wants the best for you. I know this for two reasons:

1) I have a relationship with my Father God, and I know He wants the best for me.

2) I am a good dad, and every good dad wants the best for his children! And because God is a very good Father, He wants the best for you, Reader, His child.

Amen.

CHAPTER 13

Chuck, Harrison and Two Angels

B oth Chuck and Harrison motivated me to volunteer at Contact Crisis Hotline, a 24-hour, 7 day-a-week telephone crisis counseling, suicide prevention, information and referral call center. However, both Chuck and Harrison motivated me to volunteer there for different reasons – decades apart.

Chuck is a very good friend of mine. Unfortunately, Chuck passed away in the year 2000, one year before Veronica and I were married. I was going to ask him to be one of my groomsmen at our wedding. Chuck, William Durand, was 84 years old when he went home to be with God, his wife and his daughter.

One day while I was shaving Chuck at St. Joseph's Hospital, where he was being treated for pancreatic cancer, I asked him, "Chuck, are you afraid to die?" Chuck's condition was terminal, and he had days to live. Chuck replied, "Danny, why would I be afraid? I am going to see my wife and daughter in heaven." Chuck's faith inspired me and allowed me to witness the sincerity of one's faith in action and in dying.

I first met Chuck in the summer of 1986 before I went to Canisius College. My mother, Betsy, used to go to Chuck's farm and buy flowers. Later on in our relationship, Chuck would tell me that he referred to my mom as the "poppy lady" because she loved her flowers. They would talk and laugh and had a nice relationship. However, it never became a romantic involvement. Chuck was much older than my mom at that time, and she unfortunately felt no physical attraction for him.

I used to seal driveways as a summer job with my best friend Herb. The business was called College Bound Sealers, and we made a modest income to be college kids. However, through my endeavors as a young business entrepreneur, I became friends with Chuck, a farmer. Chuck also was the owner of CreekSide Farm in Manlius, New York. Through word of mouth, Herb and I learned that a farmer was buying used five-gallon driveway sealer containers for his business.

Herb and I drove to Chuck's farm one summer afternoon and introduced ourselves. I said, "Hello sir, my name is Dan, and this is Herb. We understand that you buy five-gallon containers?" Chuck replied, "That's correct. I use them to plant my plants in. They come in handy. And call me Chuck." I went on to say, "We go through hundreds of pails a summer. Would you be interested?" Chuck replied, "I will take all you got." We agreed upon a price and created a win-win situation. We no longer had to go to the dump to discard our pails and now would receive 10 cents per container. Our new business associate, Chuck, would be getting containers for a very reasonable price.

Chuck had a great piece of land. He told me that he once dabbled in

Chuck Durand, my dear friend.

livestock, but that didn't work out too well. In time, he founded a lucrative business, selling plants, flowers, trees and bushes. Chuck had a very large stream that ran through his property and was ideal for his crop. It was the same stream that has a 40-foot waterfall that my friends and I used to jump off in high school. Unfortunately, people have died and/or been severely injured at this site. Now as a daddy of two children and nicknamed "Safety Dan," I would advise against doing this type of risky behavior. The risk is not worth the reward.

Our business relationship lasted for approximately three summers while Herb and I sealed driveways. Chuck was always polite – a man of his word and always paid us in cash. We had a good business relationship, but Chuck made the first step in our friendship. One day Chuck pulled me aside and said, "Danny, have you ever been to counseling?" I was floored! I replied, "No! Why?" Chuck went on to say, "Danny, I can tell that there's stuff bothering you. You may want to look into it."

I knew that this old farmer spoke the truth, and I was not as offended as I pretended. Chuck intuitively could sense that I was struggling with family dynamics; and at times, I would wear a wet blanket of depression around me. He genuinely was concerned for me. We shook hands, and our business for that summer season was ending. However, our friendship was just beginning.

Herb and I returned to Buffalo to our respective schools. Upon my return the following summer, I looked up Chuck – not as a business relationship but as a friend. I told Chuck that Herb had found a new business partner, and I was sealing driveways on my own. I told him that I was supposed to intern at my dad's company, but I was changing my major from Business to Psychology. I also told him that I was volunteering at a place called L'Arche. And, partially through Chuck's prompting but mainly through my desire to become healthy, I began seeing a therapist. Chuck was right; I needed some help.

Our friendship, like any other, developed over time. He was sort of a grandfather, mentor and friend wrapped into one. God knew what I needed. I wasn't in search of some old man as a friend, but that was not how I looked at Chuck. Chuck was just Chuck. Age seemed irrelevant. We had about 50 years in between us, and it was incredible getting to know this man. I look back on our relationship as one of God's greatest gifts to me.

I asked Chuck one day as we sat outside at his farm, "Chuck, did you serve in World War II?" He replied, "No, Danny, I am a conscientious objector to war." Chuck went on to tell me that, because of his faith in God, he could not and would not take another person's life. Chuck spent WWII in a "program" for people who objected to war for religious reasons. Chuck lived his values not only during the 40's but throughout his entire adult life. A part of the Syracuse Peace Council, he volunteered for a local agency called Contact of Central New York – among many other wonderful accomplishments.

Contact is a hotline for people who need a helpful listening ear. Contact serves people who are lonely or have life-threatening suicidal ideation and everything in between. Chuck had volunteered at Contact for years and truly knew how to listen.

Chuck and I often would get together, watch movies at his house and have pizza. We talked about life, and he would listen intently as I spoke. His Way of listening was very much like my mom's. We were friends. I felt valued by an older man. In his declining health, I would take him to the store and run errands with him. We had a reciprocal healthy and helpful friendship.

One movie that we watched together was "Dead Poets Society[5] with Robin Williams. "Dead Poets Society" is about a prep school that is figuratively turned on its head by a young teacher named Mr. Keating. The teacher taught his students to "seize the day," "Carpe Diem" and live life to its fullest.

Chuck was my Mr. Keating, and he taught me to seize life. Chuck showed me a vastly different worldview than I had been raised in. Coincidentally, my sister Kathy and her husband advised me that I should watch this movie because it involved a difficult dynamic between father and son. One of the characters in the movie struggled with his father. His father wanted him to go into the medical field, but the son wanted to follow his passion for theater. Spoiler alert, in the movie, the son takes his own life because he cannot stand up to his father's demands. The son freed himself by the desperate act of suicide instead of standing his ground against his father.

My family recognized similar patterns of behavior within my relationship with my dad. I believe Chuck recognized my difficult and, at times, tumultuous relationship with my dad. That perhaps was one of the reasons we watched that film together. (I am very grateful that, through counseling and therapy, any and all wounds or difficulties between my dad and I are resolved. My dad and I now have a nice relationship, and I am grateful to God for this healing.)

Reader, I encourage you to listen. Listen intently with ears like Chuck and my mother. Listen to another in their time of need. People know when you're listening and when you're listening to make a point. Just listen …. Listen intently and ask specific, clarifying questions to understand their point of view. This is what Contact of CNY taught me and teaches their volunteers. And, as Mrs. Guarnieri, a good family friend, once told me, "Danny, if we all behaved and listened intently, as good friends, we would not need therapists."

Fast forward to Chuck's funeral a couple of years down the road. I went to the funeral with good friends of mine, Kevin and Emily. They recognized my heartache, and we went together to the funeral. I wept uncontrollably throughout the service, and my friends gently placed their hands on my shoulders as signs of support. I will never forget the tender compassion they possessed at the ends of their fingertips. I felt their love and friendship as I mourned my good friend, Chuck. After the church service, we convened at the cemetery to bury our friend. I placed stones on Chuck's gravesite that I collected from his farm. I had carried these stones around in my pocket for years as symbolic reminders of lessons I had learned while visiting with my friend.

Allow me to explain:

I had read a book, during that season of my life, called *Hinds' Feet on High Places*[6] by Hannah Hurnard. The book is an allegory of one's Christian faith and our journey as Christians. In the story, the main character, "Little Much Afraid," climbs a mountain. As "Little Much Afraid" climbs, she partakes in life lessons; and after each life lesson, she symbolically collects a small stone. When "Little Much Afraid" reaches the top of the mountain, she is transformed, and her name is changed to "Hope and Glory." The stones that she has carried — as reminders of her journey — become the jewels in her crown.

I began collecting rocks shortly after I read that book. The rocks were not something I was looking for – much like my friendship with Chuck, but the rocks "found me" when I had learned a life lesson.

Case in point: in 1993, I stood by myself, waiting for the gun to sound to begin the Marine Corps Marathon. I stood with almost 16,000 runners but felt very lonely. I stood there by myself in Washington, D.C. among thousands but completely alone. Just before the race was to begin, a stone was kicked and hit me in my foot. I picked up the half dollar-sized stone and carried it in my pocket for 26.2 miles. I carried the rock, and I am now reminded of that life lesson.

We are not alone! We are never alone – even in our loneliness, for our Father God is here with us always.

I learned many valuable life lessons with my friend Chuck during that season of my life, and I quietly collected rocks as I learned life lessons. I returned the rocks to Chuck on that fateful day in the cemetery. I thanked him for his friendship and for depositing his wisdom into my life. Today, some 20-plus years later, the warmth of our friendship makes me smile; and the heartache of his loss still makes my eyes water.

Like Chuck, I too began to volunteer at Contact in 1994 and again in 2017 after a good firefighter friend committed suicide. My friend Harrison's suicide rocked me to my core. Harrison and I had a lot in common. We were the same age. He went to J-D, my rival high school; and we knew a lot of the same people. We exercised at the firehouse together and worked at the same firehouse for years.

During our changeover from one shift to another, I saw Harrison looking at family photos that he kept in his locker. There was a stack of pictures, and each day he would change the top picture to the one below. We all had memorabilia in our lockers, but Harrison's locker memorabilia was all about family.

In 2015, I had what I term as my "2015 experience," which I have written about in this book. When I returned to the firehouse after a two-month absence, my firefighter friends "came out of the woodwork" to see how I was doing. Harrison was one of them. I told each of them that I was feeling better. I passed it along that my absence was due to PTSD. I believe PTSD was part of it but not the entire picture.

In 2015, I abruptly discontinued my steroid inhaler, Symbicort, without doctor approval. This medicine is tremendous, and I felt great taking it. It worked so well that I believed I didn't need it any longer.

Ironically, my friend Harrison did the exact same thing. He too was asthmatic. He too felt great taking this medicine! And he too didn't want to take medicine if it was not needed. When I asked Harrison how he was doing, he said, "I feel like I'm in a fog."

Harrison was a very competent firefighter, an apparatus driver and an excellent senior man on the job. I have fought fire with Harrison, and I personally knew him to be a great firefighter. He was also, pound for pound, the strongest man on the job.

As Harrison and I were talking, he said, "I look at the pump panel, and I can't remember which lever to pull. It takes me a lot longer these days to figure stuff out." As firefighters, we know that the apparatus driver is the key component to a successful fire operation. He/she has to get us there safely — in a timely fashion — and then deliver water to the firefighters on the inside, with a pump operator procedure that can be complicated. However, good drivers are masters of their craft. Harrison was a master of his craft; and hearing of him struggling with basic, routine things left me concerned.

After several minutes of questioning, I found out that Harrison also had stopped taking his Symbicort. I told Harrison to tell his doctor. I said, "Harrison, tell your doctor that I went through something similar. I too had brain fog. I got lost on 690 (a local highway that I know like the back of my hand!) And I had a speech impediment. Harrison, it sounds similar." He said, "How long did it take to get back to normal?" I told him, "It took me a good couple of months." (A little aside, please, Reader, take medication as directed from a physician; and do not rely on your own understanding.)

That was the last conversation I had with Harrison. I felt horrible that I did not listen better. What did I miss? I felt horrible that I had a piece of the puzzle to his health issue. Was it the same? Did abruptly stopping a medicine cause his suicidal ideation? I am not 100% certain. But what I did know was that I needed to rechannel these feelings into something positive and productive.

I reached out to Contact of CNY. I called and talked with the volunteer coordinator Kristine, who welcomed me into the next volunteer class. I told her of my friend and his recent act of suicide.

By volunteering and helping others in their time of distress, it helped heal my broken heart. I was given the Guardian Angel Award that year (2018) by Contact of CNY for going above and beyond the call of a volunteer. As I spoke at the award dinner, I paid tribute to my friend Harrison, whom I miss very much. I know that Harrison is now with our Father God. Harrison was my motivation to begin volunteering at Contact of CNY once again.

Through volunteering and listening to callers on the phone, I healed deep wounds within me. I had a profound realization that there are a vast multitude of *hurting* people "out there," and this realization allowed me to understand I am not alone! Whether it was the loss of my good friend Harrison or being ostracized from my family of origin, I had experienced a veil being lifted from my eyes. When we struggle, we can fall into a dark hole — sometimes an abyss; but when we realize we are not alone in our grief and suffering, it gives us strength.

Reader, good friends of ours were in a tragic and horrific car accident on September 3, 2020. This accident left Melanie/Mom paralyzed from the waist down; Tim/Dad suffered an extreme concussion; and their two precious daughters were killed. Our small town has been devastated by this tragedy. We have hung teal and purple ribbons, the girl's favorite colors, on our trees, mailboxes and tent posts in remembrance of Emily and Marybeth.

Veronica and I listened intently at the funeral as Tim and Melanie addressed family and friends regarding their dear children. They spoke of beautiful memories and the wonderful gifts of cherished writings and videos of the girls. Tim spoke engagingly and expressed gratitude for the large turnout from the community as he directed his words to the priest. Melanie, with strength from her heavenly Father, said, "I now get out of bed, get dressed and live my life for my girls." As my wife and I wiped our eyes and held each other's hands tight while seated in the pew, we marveled at our friends' strength, faith and courage.

At the funeral, Tim and Melanie shared that Emily and Marybeth loved to entertain their family and friends. They often would dance and sing theme songs from various Disney movies. Melanie and Tim mentioned that the lyrics from the song, *The Next Right Thing*,[7] in Frozen II speaks to their heart and said, "We would do anything to be with our kids a little longer." (Tim and Melanie Arnett)

The following song has become their mantra:

"The Next Right Thing"
"I've seen dark before
But not like this
This is cold
This is empty

This is numb
The life I knew is over
The lights are out
Hello, darkness
I'm ready to succumb

I follow you around
I always have
But you've gone to a place I cannot find
This grief has a gravity
It pulls me down

But a tiny voice whispers in my mind
You are lost, hope is gone
But you must go on
And do the next right thing

Can there be a day beyond this night?
I don't know anymore what is true
I can't find my direction, I'm all alone
The only star that guided me was you
How to rise from the floor
When it's not you I'm rising for?
Just do the next right thing
Take a step, step again
It is all that I can to do
The next right thing

I won't look too far ahead
It's too much for me to take
But break it down to this next breath
This next step
This next choice is one that I can make

So I'll walk through this night
Stumbling blindly toward the light
And do the next right thing
And with the dawn, what comes then?

When it's clear that everything will never be the same again
Then I'll make the choice
To hear that voice
And do the next right thing."

(Song performed by Kristen Bell (Anna), "Frozen II" lyrics, songwriters Kristen Ander-

son-Lopez and Robert Lopez, label Walt Disney Records)

Tim and Melanie live their lives each day to their fullest to honor the memory of their adorable little girls, and they have established a nonprofit organization called Arnett's Angels. They are turning tragedy — through the power of their faith — into hope and love as a remembrance of their children; and they are doing "the next right thing."

Reader, walk in faith – like our dear friends Chuck, Tim and Melanie, knowing they will one day see their loved ones in heaven. Harrison, my friend and brother firefighter, is now at peace. However, I believe there was a lot more goodness in this life in which he could have partaken, and he could have helped many more people in his lifetime as well. It was too early to go, my friend; and I miss you. Amen.

"'He will wipe every tear from their eyes. There will be no more death or mourning or crying or pain, for the old order of things has passed away'" (Revelation 21:4, NIV).

Reader, my Contact training has taught me that if you suspect someone to be thinking about suicide, say something. Ask them if they are thinking of killing themselves. For example, "John, you seem depressed. Are you thinking of killing yourself?" This question is not taboo, and it will not place thoughts of suicide in their brain. It is better to make someone mildly uncomfortable than to have never asked the question.

Also, if you, Reader, feel depressed and are at this crisis point, know that You are loved! Our Father God loves you. He is your good, good Father; and He is ready to hear your prayers! Please know that this too shall pass; this feeling you're having will pass. There are people who will listen. There are people who are there ready to help and give you helpful direction.

There are people who are the arms and ears of God your Father.

Life is good. This took me many years to find out, but I did find this out! I have had many valley experiences in my life that could have changed the course of my life forever. However, my Father God has been here with me; and He is here with you, too, Reader. Trust, believe and walk in faith.

Our minds, our intellect always can rival our step of faith; but once you, Reader, step out in faith — trusting that God hears you — your life will begin to change. Please stop; regroup; talk to a trusted friend, loved one and/or therapist; and put out of your mind any suicidal ideation.

"Finally, brother and sisters, whatever is true, whatever is noble, whatever is right, whatever is pure, whatever is lovely, whatever is admirable - if anything is excellent or praiseworthy - think about such things" (Philippians 4:8, NIV).

You, Reader, are meant to be here; and like the stars in the heavens, you are a gift from God our Father. Live life for a purpose. There are many more productive, loving, helpful, life-giving things you can do with the time you have been given – thanks be to God.

Father, please bless the Readers who are struggling and fill their hears with Your peace beyond all understanding. I pray, dear Lord, that You bring people into the Readers' lives that will minister to them and care for them as they deal with the challenges placed before them. God, I know that You love us, Your children; and I pray that the Readers are now filled with this understanding. Father, grant them peace of mind so that they can do Your will. I pray this prayer in Your Son Jesus' Name. Amen.

National Suicide Prevention Lifeline: 800-273-8255

CHAPTER 14

Conclusion

"If we claim to be without sin, we deceive ourselves and the truth is not in us. If we confess our sins, he is faithful and just and will forgive us our sins and purify us from all unrighteousness" (1 John 1:8-9, NIV).

This Thanksgiving season marks 35 years since my encounter at the Canisius College quad with my Father God, the Lamb of God and the Holy Spirit. God, in His miraculous Way, told me, "It's Not Too Late…." I echo these sentiments and write them here for you.

Reader, who in your life do you need to forgive? Is it a family member, friend, neighbor, coworker, someone from your past or perhaps yourself?

My education, both formally and informally, has taught me that forgiveness is healthy; and it will add years to your life. That's right — forgiveness is good for you. The hatred you hold in your heart for another affects you. I am more than certain you have heard this concept before. However, I also am certain that many who are reading this book still hold grudges, anger and/or resentment toward someone (or toward yourself).

"He said to them, "When you pray, say: 'Father, hallowed be your name, your kingdom come. Give us each day our daily bread. Forgive us our sins, for we also forgive everyone who sins against us. And lead us not into temptation'" (Luke 11:2-4, NIV).

Some 2,000+ years ago, Jesus called us to forgive our enemies and love them. He knew that forgiveness is healthy for us, and it is good for what ails us. I do wish I could have fast-forwarded through some of the difficult learning experiences, but God has a very interesting Way of utilizing both the good and bad in our lives to weave His beautiful tapestry.

Reader, this book originally had an additional chapter contained within it titled "Ostracized." It was a very large chapter, containing over 17,889 words. I worked many months and explained in detail the hurt and pain experienced in my life regarding my family-of-origin dynamics – some of which were a direct result from my mishandling and my miscommunication regarding various family incidents. The chapter was written sincerely in love as I believe we are called to live by the Way of our Father. The chapter spoke of the forgiveness I feel for my family and the hope in reunification I place in my Father God's hands. It is my Father's timeline, my Father's Way; and I am following to the best of my abilities.

I will include a section from this chapter and place it here in the conclusion; for I had lost perspective, and it is a good example of the pitfalls of misplaced thoughts....

(The section below is from the chapter "Ostracized" that I decided not to include in its entirety.)

'Ostracized'

"I have been ostracized from my family of origin for the past five years. Being an outcast hurts very much. I will include this chapter in the book because I know that God can use all things for the good for those who love Him (Romans 8:28) with both the good parts and bad parts of our life. I believe that God is the only answer to my family-of-origin problems.

Heavenly Father, it is my prayer that the Readers knows they are not alone in their pain. I, too, am suffering daily. However, I know that this hour and that these days, You, Lord, are with me. I trust in You.

"'Your word is a lamp for my feet, a light on my path. I have taken an oath and confirmed it, that I will follow your righteous laws. I have suffered much; preserve my life, LORD, according to your word'" (Psalm 119:105-107, NIV).

Growing up the way my brother, sisters and I did left some emotional fractures that never healed well. With any physical fracture that has not been set correctly, it will yield deformity, limping, pain, arthritis or degenerative joint disease. Likewise, emotional baggage or "fractures" from childhood – if not dealt with properly – will have consequences into one's adult life.

I have always felt a strong bond with my younger sister Meghan. When she hurts, I hurt and vice versa. And to a slightly lesser degree, a very strong connection to my older sister Kathy and brother Jim. Kathy was, for me, a "motherlike" figure while growing up. In my adolescence, she was the one to whom I turned to talk about my life. I needed direction, and Kathy helped me navigate the following questions: What was I going to do with my life? What career should I pursue? What education pathway? What girl to date? Kathy was my go-to "parent." My mom was still alive at that point — a tremendous listener and very loving. However, Kathy was wise and strong. I felt comforted after I talked with her.

My brother and I are very different, but we have a strong bond. We were each other's best man at our weddings. Jim did an amazing job at our ceremony. His personality shone through when he toasted Veronica and me at our reception. My toast at his wedding was awful by comparison, but I did my job well as I held him close throughout his subsequent divorce. My brother and I sat together at the hospital, holding vigil at my mother's bedside as she took her last breath. Our bond is strong, and I pray that we continue to grow in our friendship. My sisters, brother and I always have been close. But cumulative stress has had its toll on our relationships. I believe that because we didn't "deal with our stuff" collectively as a family unit, it has resulted in our current state. Our family, my family of origin, is short-circuited. And as we know when things are short-circuited, energy does not flow well. We are meant as a family of believers to flow with God's love and not be "short-circuited."

My friend Bob, my ""born-again" Christian friend, invited me to read the following biblical passage:

> "Finally, be strong in the Lord and in his mighty power. Put on the full armor of God, so that you can take your stand against the

devil's schemes. For our struggle is not against flesh and blood, but against the rulers, against the authorities, against the powers of this dark world and against the spiritual forces of evil in the heavenly realms. Therefore put on the full armor of God, so that when the day of evil comes, you may be able to stand your ground, and after you have done everything, to stand. Stand firm then, with the belt of truth buckled around your waist, with the breastplate of righteousness in place, and with your feet fitted with the readiness that comes from the gospel of peace. In addition to all this, take up the shield of faith, with which you can extinguish all the flaming arrows of the evil one. Take the helmet of salvation and the sword of the Spirit, which is the word of God" (Ephesians 6:10-17, NIV).

"Amen," I say, regarding that Scripture. Reader, there is a battle raging. The people we love can hurt our hearts. Loved ones unfortunately can become enemies as evidenced by divorce or something much more trivial.... However, we need to protect our hearts, minds and spirits with prayer.

"Above all else, guard your heart, for everything you do flows from it" (Proverbs 4:23, NIV).

I do believe: "...our struggle is not against flesh and blood, but against the rulers, against the authorities, against the powers of this dark world and against the spiritual forces of evil in the heavenly realms" (Ephesians 6:12, NIV).

People are influenced by unresolved baggage, and I believe the devil relishes in this fact. How I interpret the dynamic within my family of origin is much akin to "The Screwtape Letters" by C. S. Lewis. Screwtape is a fictional character in the book that depicts a demon figure who interacts with and harms society by infiltrating one's thoughts, feelings and emotions. Essentially, Screwtape and his demon friends are "the devil on one's shoulder." The demons are fed by the raw human emotions of anger, violence, hatred, lust, jealousy, etc. In "The Screwtape Letters," the demons thrive on family misunderstanding. The demons thrive when people get angry at each other, hold grudges and hold hatred in their hearts.

> "Be kind and compassionate to one another, forgiving each other, just as in Christ God forgave you" (Ephesians 4:32, NIV).

Unfortunately, I believe that my family of origin is (metaphorically) living "The Screwtape Letters." After recently writing about the many distressing details of my family dysfunction regarding my family of origin and stepfamily, I had thoughts of suicide. Writing this chapter has brought me low. I realized that these thoughts of suicide were not from my Father God but from the enemy. I decided to focus on the positive in my life and gave praise to my Father in prayer. Although I was not feeling grateful at that time, my praise and thanksgiving turned my clouds of depression to sunshine. I was able to have a productive day; and better yet, I am here to write about it.

Being unable to heal my family-of-origin dynamic is so very hard. Consequently, this was a very difficult chapter to write. Unfortunately, the negative feelings that stirred in me filled my spirit. However, God is good and gave me a Way out.

> "No temptation has overtaken you except what is common to mankind. And God is faithful; he will not let you be tempted beyond what you can bear. But when you are tempted, he will also provide a way out so that you can endure it" (1 Corinthians 10:13, NIV).

Joyce Meyer is a Christian speaker and author, who has written many excellent prayerful books. I recently read her book titled "Battlefield of the Mind".[9] It is a wonderful book, and I highly recommend it to any and all. Throughout her book, she discusses how to train the brain. Our brain is but a muscle, and we can control what we think. Joyce Meyer goes into great detail, and she can explain it much more readily.

I cannot believe that I had that horrific thought, especially after witnessing the emotional aftermath of a dear friend's death by suicide! What helped me tremendously weed out the negative thought was chapter 90, "Meditate on These Things" within "Battlefield of the Mind." Mrs. Meyer states, "If you want to win the battle for the mind, meditation is a powerful weapon for you to use. You must focus on portions of God's Word. You must read them, perhaps read them aloud, and keep them before you." (p. 305, "Battlefield of the Mind").

Reader, if you're ever feeling a low, low, I recommend talking to a good friend, doctor and/or therapist. In addition, I will include the following recipe that helps me:

- Recognition of negative thoughts.

- Deciding to think on good things in my life.

- Prayer and meditation before, during and after any negative thoughts.

Meditating before helps ward off the negative thoughts; but if negative thoughts slip through, prayer and meditation are also excellent tools during the episode. Literally praying in thanksgiving for people in my life, wonderful memories and current blessings help clear away the clouds and let the sunshine of God's love fill my spirit. Having such a regimen will keep you, Reader, in touch with the beauty of life. In my desire to write this chapter, I had not spent enough time in prayer before and had let my guard down. I was writing about some extremely heavy stuff for me, and this allowed the enemy in to try and steal my joy!

Exercise. Good, vigorous exercise for me is helpful. However, just getting fresh air and simply sitting outside in nature can reap huge internal rewards.

Good sleep. Not excessive and not too little. If you can't sleep due to insomnia, focus on your breath in meditation. Do not get overly concerned about not being able to sleep. Focus your attention on breath and on good words, such as *Jesus, peace, love* or perhaps a special prayer that you memorized. But, Reader, train your thoughts. Relax into this meditation, and do not worry. Just repeat these wonderful words over and over and over, and sleep will soon be your friend.

Eat well. We are to do our part, and God will do His part. Saying no to certain food and drink is a good practice. This takes practice and discipline, but it is possible. I always try to eat well, but I eat better when I include prayer in my diet. In other words, try and incorporate not eating sweets for a week for God. Be healthy when trying to be healthy. Don't fast to lose weight but fast for the right reason – to grow in relationship with your Father God.

Music is medicine for your soul. Personally, I most often listen to Christian rock (Zack Williams, Lauren Daigle, Need to Breathe, Mercy Me, Hillsong United, Jesus Culture, Casting Crowns, Crowder, Bethel Music-Jenn Johnson "Goodness of God," Michael W. Smith, Chris Tomlin, Ann Wilson, "Let me tell you about my Jesus," to name a few). When I have Christian music playing, I imagine it as a shield against negative thoughts or attacks by the enemy. The music artists mentioned above will lift your heart and soul, and you will find it is very pleasing.

Do good to others. When we are feeling low, reaching out and helping others are an excellent Way to reap healthy benefits for ourselves. When my friend Harrison committed suicide, I then became a volunteer at Contact, a crisis hotline, as a telephone hotline operator. It was a true blessing to help others in their time of need. "'Now that I, your Lord and Teacher, have washed your feet, you also should wash one another's feet'" (John 13:14, NIV).

And finally, I will include the National Suicide Prevention Hotline (1-800-273-TALK (8255)). The President recently signed the National Suicide Hotline Designation Act into law. **988**, the new three-digit number for the National Suicide Prevention line, is **to be completed by July 2022.** In the meantime, use the 1-800-273-8255 number.

> "Blessed is the one who perseveres under trial because, having stood the test, that person will receive the crown of life that the Lord has promised to those who love him" (James 1:12, NIV).

Amen

This now concludes the section of "OSTRACIZED" that I needed to share. Again, this was a small snippet from the chapter. Reader, what I concluded after writing this chapter was I forgive. I love them all. I love my family of origin and my stepfamily. I "heard" in my heart a "rustling of energy"; and I decided not to include my family dysfunction, baggage and all the family details in this book.

Coincidentally (God-incidentally) the very next day — after I decided not to share family dysfunction details in this book, I was asked to sit with my dad in the hospital as he was recuperating. I spent three amazing hours bonding with him. The time flew, and I am more than grateful to my stepmother, Chris, for this invitation. My dad and I spoke of memories, travel, sporting events, love of family, our faith and his – God willing – soon-to-be discharge. This was sacred time and a gift from my Father God. As I decided not to print the details of my family dysfunction, I laid down "my weapon" – although written in love. God then gave me the desire of my heart — the love of my dad.

From the Preface of this book, throughout this book and into the Conclusion, I have brought forth a message. It's Not Too Late.... Again, I echo these words from my Father; and I speak them to you. It's not too late: to love, to forgive, to walk in His Way. It is my prayer that you have eyes to see and believe, ears to hear the truth within your heart and the courage to begin to walk on the road of forgiveness. It is time...

"Get rid of all bitterness, rage and anger, brawling and slander, along with every form of malice. Be kind and compassionate to one another, forgiving each other, just as in Christ God forgave you" (Ephesians 4:31-32, NIV).

Reader, I am certain you have seen themes running throughout my life. Themes of misplaced hope, themes of forgiveness, themes of love. When I have placed hope in my Father God, He has never let me down. Unfortunately, we, society, humanity are a broken people; and when we misplace our hope, it can break our hearts and lead to despair and

CHAPTER 14 | CONCLUSION

depression. Therefore, place your hope in our Father God as you, Reader, travel on your journey.

"Two roads diverged in a wood, and I ..." (Robert Frost)[10] A small verse from this notable poem points in two different directions. Which road to choose? Reader, you have options. Right or left, believe or not believe, faith or doubt. What I do know is that my life is much better when I give my Father God the reigns and journey with Him in faith.

I feel very blessed. Again, much thanks to guardrails such as Mr. Johnson, Gramma Connors, Fr. Moleski, SJ, Chuck, Mr. and Mrs. Collier, Mrs. Guarneri, Fr. Don Maldari, SJ, Peg and Pastor Paul Saya, Bob and Marsha Chopko who each spoke into my life as a young man. God used these individuals to help me, to guide me and – perhaps unbeknownst to them – to be God's arms, hands and feet, helping me along the Way. Rather than dwell on the negative and succumb to the "poor me" road I was traveling on as an adolescent, I learned that my mom needed love – as passionately expressed by my dear friend Mrs. Guarneri, "You love that woman, Danny. She needs you!"

Yes, my mom was debilitated for years from depression; but she was also a wonderful mom. She did her best, and I am beyond grateful for her. She taught me about compassion, listening with one's heart; and she loved her children through and through without exception. She never intended to harm any of us by way of her collecting habits. I know this now. I'm sorry, Mom, for not being more understanding when I was younger. I'm sorry that you went through what you did in your lifetime. And I thank you, Mom, for trying your best. I always knew that you loved me. You, Mom, role modeled the unconditional love that God has for His children. I do hope that you hear my words now in Heaven. If not, I will tell you again someday when I see you.

Mom's healing and the bottomless pit of collecting were healed and filled in with love – thanks be to God. Ironically, my mom's healing came at the end of her life when she was dying from emphysema. Mom was diagnosed with emphysema seven years before she died from this horrific disease. I began to realize that Mom was sick when she couldn't walk a ¼ mile from the parking lot to the Shania Twain concert to which I had bought her tickets. I carried her that evening in my arms — like a small child — to the concert; and it is today a wonderful memory. In 2001, at my and Veronica's wedding, my mother and I danced the mother-groom dance to Shania Twain's beautiful song, "I Hope You Dance." Today those words, "I Hope You Dance," hang on our wall as a wonderful memory of Mom. I thank God for my mom's emotional healing and for many good memories of love and healing with my mom.

In 2005, I was working at St. Joseph's Hospital part-time as a LPN and was working full-time as a firefighter. I received a phone call while working at the hospital; and they said, "Your mom is on the way to E.R. She is having difficulty breathing." I excused myself from the floor where I was working and ran to the 1st floor Emergency Room.

My wonderful, loving, kind hearted mom and I at my and Veronica's wedding

My brother, sisters and I watched the respiratory therapist struggle to ventilate Mom with the Bag Valve Mask. A BVM is a handheld plastic piece of medical equipment that fits over the mouth and nose of a patient and has a small, heavy-duty plastic bag attached to it. The bag is squeezed, and it forces air into the lungs to ventilate the patient.

As an EMT, I have used this device countless times in emergency medicine. I stepped forward in the E.R. to assist the therapist and reached under my mom's head. I then placed the seal of the mask around her nose and mouth, held the seal tight and told the therapist, "bag" to squeeze the bag. I bent down and whispered in my mom's ear, "We're all here, Mom. I love you." All her children were in the room with her, and we were not sure if she would make it…. I am grateful for my EMS training, but to ventilate my own mother in her time of distress was overwhelming.

Mom lived for approximately five more years after the E.R. incident described above. The Emergency Room became a frequent occurrence as did hospital stays. During this time, my brother, sisters and I decided to clean our mother's house when she was at the hospital rehabilitating.

It was cathartic to clean out her house. We gathered together as siblings at my mom's home. It was emotionally difficult to weed through the mountain of debris, but we got the job done. We filled multiple pickup trucks but also found that Mom had some beautiful treasures hidden among the piles of clutter. My brother and I were the muscle, and my sisters were the decorators. We did a fantastic job, and Mom's home never looked so beautiful.

When we brought Mom home from the hospital, she would be on oxygen for the remainder of her life. As her children, we knew that Mom no longer could live in a hoarding environment. We intuitively knew that her physical health needed a clean environment. For her sake and for all of our well-being, we moved mountains with God's grace.

Initially, the change of living conditions was difficult for her; but she soon got very used to having a clean home. Mom no longer desired to collect. Her last remaining years were focused now on spending time with her children. It was wonderful to visit with Mom again. We were able to sit and have conversations. Years of unsaid words flooded out, and love abounded for many years. Our healing was not physical but emotional as a weight was lifted from our collective hearts. "God does indeed work for the good in our lives in both the heartache and the joy!" (adapted from Romans 8:28)

One lasting, notable gift that my mom gave her children was the juxtaposition of the idea of thunderstorms. My childhood home was a split-level ranch built on a hill. We had a wonderful view; but when storms came, our home was scary. The children's rooms were downstairs, and our parent's bedroom was upstairs. When there were thunderstorms at night, Mom would call her children upstairs to the living room. We would sit and watch the storm. What was once now scary, became beautiful. My mom had changed our fear into something beautiful. She once told us, "Don't worry. The thunder and lightning are God's fireworks." This description has changed forever my feeling for thunderstorms. For where there once was fear, there now is awe and wonder; and the thought of my mother is within each passing thunderstorm.

Unfortunately, Mom passed away on February 2, 2008. The day after Mom's passing, I sat in my home office and wrote her eulogy. As I wrote about the beautiful memories of Mom and retold memories of old, it began to thunder. I thought to myself, "Thunder in February?" However, I took that sound — the sound of thunder — and weaved it into her eulogy. For my mom — even in death — transformed what was scary and overwhelming into something beautiful. I sat and wrote and cried and thanked God for His fireworks.

"*Consider it pure joy,* my brother and sisters, whenever you face trials of many kinds, because you know that the testing of your faith produces perseverance. Let perseverance finish its work so that you may be made mature and complete, not lacking anything" (James 1:2-4, NIV). *emphasis mine*

- Was it pure joy to have parents who fought constantly and subsequently divorced?

- Was it pure joy to have a mother who slept all day, was depressed and attempted suicide?

- Was it pure joy not to have clean clothes as a child?

- Was it pure joy to be reared in a hoarding home?

- Was it pure joy to have been taken advantage of by an older man as a young boy?

- Was it pure joy to have anxiety so great as a young man that I didn't know if I could go outside?

- Was it pure joy to have issues as an adult as a direct correlation to my family upbringing that I had to sort out for decades?

- Was it pure joy to be ostracized by my family of origin?

Reader, the answer to all of these questions is no! It was not pure joy. It was awful! However, God is good and allowed me to learn and grow from each of the above situations. In growing from these unfortunate circumstances, I have found joy. In hindsight, I have felt protected by my Father. God was there with me through The Holy Spirit. God was calling me and guiding me in small Ways. I am so grateful for the people God placed in my life as guardrails to walk alongside me as the arms of Christ, holding my hand. No, I am not grateful for the various situations listed above. Thanks be to God He has healed me in body, mind and spirit. However, I will allow my Father to deal with the people in my life who did not act appropriately.

Reader, I am so grateful to God that I could pray all day and night in thanksgiving. It is my prayer that my life radiates the love and the gratefulness that I feel for God. I believe that God does protect us, and He can move mountains in our life. How come God protects some and not others? How come He moves mountains for some and not others? How come bad things and trials happen to us, to our family members, to friends, to loved ones?

Reader, the short answer is: I don't know? All I can say is that my experience has shown me that — although my childhood and parts of my adult life were chaotic — I have learned many life skills and have developed a deep appreciation and empathy toward others because of my past. The Holy Spirit has guided me despite and through my past to my present life for which I am beyond grateful. I pray that God moves mountains in your life... believe and walk in faith. It has taken me 53 years to become the person God has intended me to be. However, I am not done learning, growing and searching for God. For the past 10 to 15 years, I can say that my journey has been on the right path, and I have been intentional as I walk. I have not always made healthy choices, but I am certain I'm now traveling in the right direction. Reader, when I fall (sin), I get back up and ask God for forgiveness. And, when possible, I ask anyone whom I sinned against for forgiveness also.

I include both my triumphs and failures in this book — in my life story — to illustrate to you, Reader, that I am no one special. Yet our Father uses me as He has used many throughout history. He has used fishermen, prostitutes, tax collectors and sinners of all kinds to humble the learned teachers and the powerful religious. I now — through God's good Grace — follow Him in reverence and awe. For as Pastor John Newton said, "I once was lost, but now am found, was blind but now I see."

I recently was reading a segment on Pastor John Newton who, of course, was not always a pastor. In the earlier part of his life, he worked on a slave ship; but through the transformation of his heart, mind and soul, it inspired the song "Amazing Grace[2]". Pastor Newton had a dark past. By God intervening in his life, Pastor John was saved. He was figuratively blind, but sight was restored through God's good grace. I understand this transformation of heart, mind and soul. I understand the "yes, Lord" and the "Amen." We have to be open to God intervening in our lives for God to do His work in our lives. For when we open our hearts, minds and souls, God truly can act in our lives.

CHAPTER 14 | **CONCLUSION**

My soul sings,
"Amazing Grace
How sweet the sound
That saved a wretch like me
I once was lost
But now I'm found
Was blind but now I see

'Twas grace that taught
My heart to fear
And grace my fears relieved
How precious did
That grace appear
The hour I first believed

Through many dangers,
Toils, and snares
I have already come
'Tis grace hath brought
Me safe thus far
And grace will lead me home

When we've been here
Ten thousand years
Bright, shining as the sun
We've have no less days to sing God's praise
Than when we first begun
Amazing Grace
How sweet the sound
That saved a wretch like me
I once was lost,
But now I'm found
Was blind but now I see."

(Pastor John Newton, 1772)

For when we make poor life choices, our sin is like a ripple in the water when a stone is thrown into a lake. Sometimes our sin is a boulder, and the ripple in the water can become a wave. Therefore, prepare yourselves beforehand so that we may cast only pebbles – if at all. When I find myself in the midst of temptation or feeling tempted, I pray the Lord's Prayer. And I focus my attention and repeat the following verse, "And lead me not into temptation."

Battle on your knees, and ask our Father to lead you and guide your decision-making. For our God is a good God, and He will give you a Way out when you're struggling with temptation.

"No temptation has overtaken you except what is common to mankind. And God is faithful; he will not let you be tempted beyond what you can bear. But when you are tempted, he will also provide a way out so that you can endure it" (1 Corinthians 10:13, NIV).

I am now respectful of people's boundaries, and I know the right Way to behave. I have been deprogrammed, and I now operate under "new programming." However, on my own, I know I can trip or slip up; therefore, I place my strength in God.

"So, if you think you are standing firm, be careful that you don't fall!" (1 Corinthians 10:12, NIV)

As I am writing this book, I also am planning a bicycle trek from Syracuse to Washington, D.C. as a fundraiser for The Brady Faith Center. I am no longer a young athletic man, but I have remained in relatively good shape as a 53-year-old middle-aged man. I have asked my daughters to help me train for this ride, and I look forward to once again listening to the hum of the tires as they move down the road. It is a beautiful sound that stirs a deep part of my heart center. The ride is intended as a fundraiser but also as a public relations event to announce the opening of the new Brady Market and continue to announce the wonderful nonprofit organization in Syracuse, New York, The Brady Faith Center.

The Brady Faith Center was named after a Roman Catholic priest who ministered to the people on the southwest side of Syracuse, New York. Since his passing, The Brady Faith Center, or BFC, still ministers to people on the southwest side of Syracuse; but it has grown tremendously. The executive director, Kevin Frank, is one of my best friends and an instrument of God.

BFC, through The Brady Farm, has a 5.8-acre farm in the inner-city limits and is the third largest contiguous inner-city farm in the country. The produce is sold at local markets, and the proceeds go toward their general fund.

The Brady Center is a small house on South Avenue that has 20+ programs that assist youth, families and individuals educationally, spiritually and in community. Kevin was inspired by the work of Father Greg Boyle from HomeBoy Ministries. Father Boyle established HomeBoy Ministries to assist inner-city gang members in Los Angeles. I recommend reading Father Greg's book "Tattoos on the Heart".[11] Father Greg is a visionary in loving people into health and in his business entrepreneurial skills. His 501(c)(3) nonprofit is extremely successful in rehabilitating former gang members' lives.

Inspired by Father Greg's model, Kevin brought a similar concept forward by helping the individual in need holistically. Not only do they, BFC, minister to their spiritual and emotional needs but also minister by Way of offering employment.

BFC has started a new arm of their ministry and has opened The Brady Market. The Brady Market is a small grocery store that is truly more than a grocery store. BFC hires people in need and teaches them a skill set by working in a supermarket administered by BFC. Not only are they employed, but then they are given a mentor who walks beside them emotionally and mentors them in their day-to-day working environment. For some, it is their first work experience. They also are offered counseling services if they are so inclined. The new employee learns each aspect of the grocery business from cashier to maintenance, to stocking shelves, to customer service and food preparation.

They also have a butcher apprentice program that allows the participant to earn a $25-an-hour job upon graduation. Presently, there is a shortage of butchers in our country; and BFC is finding unique job opportunities for inner-city residents.

In addition to the butcher apprenticeship, the employees also are offered a pathway for various educational opportunities. The new employee is asked, "What would your dream job be?" When we —as individuals — can think only about where our next meal is coming from, it is hard to dream about our future career. Brady Faith Center allows their employees to dream their dream and then assists them to make their dream a reality. For instance, if their employee said, "I want to be a librarian," the staff would educate them regarding the education needed and walk alongside them as they pursued this goal.

I believe in this concept, and I want to help my friend with his organization. My wife and I will be cochairing this fundraiser; but more importantly, we will announce BFC (and Brady Market) to the community and the leaders in Washington D.C., and I believe The Holy Spirit will be guiding us along the Way. To make a donation, please visit their websites: BradyFaithCenter.org or BradyFarm.org or BradyMarket.org.

Our fundraising mission statement is simple: "Come and See." Once people see for themselves the extraordinary work being done in this organization, they will want to become more involved. At least, this is what happened to my wife and me. Kevin invited us to "Come and See"; and we ended up running his fundraising campaign for 2021, "Bike for Brady."

Today is October 8, 2021. My friends and I returned from our bicycle ride to Washington, D.C. We traveled 450 miles in six days. It was an epic journey and, once again, filled with God's awe and wonder. Traveling as a small four-person bicycle unit filled me with joy and deep appreciation. We had support vehicles womaned by two of the wives of the bicyclists. We couldn't have done this without you, ladies! We traveled 46 miles the first day, 110 miles the second day, 108 miles in the pouring rain the third day, 85 miles the fourth day, 88 miles the fifth day and a leisurely 20 miles into the Capitol, Washington, D.C., on our last day.

Bicycling into Washington, D.C. from the C&O river trail (Chesapeake and Ohio) was beauty beyond compare and fed into the Potomac River. With each pedal stroke along our journey, I sensed that The Holy Spirit was there with us — in the beauty all around us, in the friendships within our small community — and sanctioned our mission along the Way to Washington, D.C. The Potomac River was to our right as we bicycled toward our destination. It was a beautiful, sun-filled day that was mixed with the majesty of the Lincoln Memorial, the grace of the Washington Monument and the beauty of the Lincoln Memorial reflecting pool, making for a surreal bicycling finale. We did a victory lap around the reflecting pool and made our way to The Capitol. As we slowly bicycled along the pathway, we saw the Capitol Police on horseback and wished them well. In my mind's eye, I can see the officer and her horse galloping down the Mall lawn, and I am filled with pride to be a citizen of the United States.

However, as we bicycled up toward the Capitol, we saw hundreds of thousands of small white flags placed in the ground, flowing in the breeze. The flags were arranged in an orderly fashion, depicting a flag for each person who has died from COVID-19 in our country. As of October 5, 2021, 702,630 people have died from COVID-19 in our nation.

We exceeded our fundraising goal and met with our local Congressman in Washington, D.C. We took pictures on the Capitol steps. As we stood on the Capitol steps, I was very grateful for our Congressman greeting us. It was a wonderful culmination of five months of planning, physical preparation and hard work. I now think of our Founding Fathers; I believe they would congratulate us on our fundraising and bicycling effort and would endorse our noble cause.

Our bicycling group brought the message of good news from The Brady Faith Center to Washington, D.C. and symbolically brought the

"Good News" that Jesus Christ shared with His followers some 2,000 years ago. Jesus brought a message of hope in His resurrection from the dead, a message of forgiveness of sin; and He taught us to love by Way of His actions. It is my prayer that this journey of ours resonate in you, Reader. Being a follower of Jesus is actually a lot of fun! I have done some truly amazing things in my life that God has been endorsing. I pray that you also find as much joy in your life journey.

When I look back on my life, on my journey, I believe it was when I took the step of faith in confessing my sin as a young boy about to be confirmed in the Roman Catholic Church that placed God's hand of favor on my life. I feel blessed. Unfortunately, I could not always say that.... I did not always stay on the path that leads to God. I went my way and turned from God. And in those seasons of my life, I was scrutinized by coworkers, neighbors and disciplined by my Father God.

When I returned to the path that God lay before me, a banquet feast was waiting for me as I returned to my Lord and Savior, my Father God.

Flags memorial for those who died from COVID-19 Washington D.C.

He turned pain into joy. The pain of broken relationships miraculously healed. I attribute this healing as a direct correlation to my relationship with my Father God.

I never, in my wildest dreams, would believe that my father-in-law would become my friend. I never would have imagined calling my mother-in-law Mom, but now I do! We had our ups and downs; and through it all, we have grown together as a family. Thanks be to God.

I believe when we choose to follow The Way in which God calls us to live, we find favor. This favor is what I seek. The Only One who can provide it is my Lord and Savior Jesus. I justifiably could have written off my in-laws for various infractions and circumstances – or they me. Things said and done could have led to dismissal of the relationship. Instead forgiveness has led to beautiful family dynamics. What was once scorn, angst and anger have been replaced with love.

I pray in thanksgiving that my heart breaks with the passing of my father-in-law. A man, who more than once hurt me deeply, I have grown to love. I mourn his passing. When he died in my arms, a part of me died that day. However, I am grateful to my God that He allowed my heart to grow.

Reader, I was like the Grinch whose heart grew and grew. "What happened in Whoville they say that the Grinch's heart grew three sizes that day. And then the true meaning of Christmas came through. The Grinch found the strength of ten Grinches plus two." ("How the Grinch Stole Christmas" by Theodor "Dr. Seuss" Geisel)[12]

With the growth of one's heart comes the inevitability of heartache. But in this heartache, I thank my Lord and my God for allowing me to love a man I once despised. Only through God's enduring love were Fotis and I able to become friends. I sit here and shake my head in awe of God's miraculous intervention in our relationship. We went from the lowest of lows — him threatening my life — to the immeasurable expression of friendship and love. In his last days, he recounted his life story as I interviewed him for this book. As the hours passed, his wife came home;

and he said, "Cathy, today I give Dan a piece of my heart." Yes, Fotis gave me a piece of his heart that day. I, too, gave him a piece of my heart as I held him in my arms as he passed on to be with God. Together we became family – each desiring peace through the gift of God our Father.

The 15 years of therapy, the experiences of bicycling across the United States on two occasions, running three marathons, commercial salmon fishing in Alaska, firefighting for 20 years and obtaining my BA in Psychology, LPN, Paramedic and CASAC training – all collectively helped and were made manifest through God.

God does His part, but we must do our part. I did my part: I called the therapist. I went to the appointments and paid the co-pays. I pedaled across the United States and faced daily anxiety attacks. I got in the boat and went out to sea in Alaska. I fought fires. I went to school. But none of these achievements or successes would be possible if not for the strength provided to me by my Father God. Through each of these experiences — working in conjunction with each other, God intervened and assisted me in healing my heart, mind and soul. Together God and I have been on a journey. A journey of health and healing.

I ultimately contribute all my healing to God. Therapy fertilized my field, preparing me; but it is God's ground. He is the Harvester, the Good Shepherd and my Lord. God has been there with me through it all. He has placed guardrails in my life, caught me more times than I realize and protected and loved me through various friendships and loved ones.

Now that my healing has been made complete, I have to do His bidding. I will announce what He has asked me to tell you.

Jesus is coming soon. Wake up, sleeper…. The Bible makes it clear not to fall asleep because the hour and the day are not known when He will return.

"'Therefore keep watch, because you do not know on what day your Lord will come. But understand this: If the owner of the house had known at what time of night the thief was coming, he would have kept watch and would not have let his house be broken into. So you also must be ready, because the Son of Man will come at an hour when you do not expect him'" (Matthew 24:42-44, NIV).

God calls us to humble ourselves before Him. I was taught by The Holy Spirit — in a vision experience in 2015 — to bend my knee and bow my head before my Lord God; but my Friend and Lord Jesus, I may "look upon" in respect and awe. In my time at the Canisius quad, I was given an insight and an understanding that our time here on earth was limited. Exact dates and times were not given, but a deep understanding that the end is near has been within me for many years. Now more than ever, the feeling – from that moment in time – overwhelms my thoughts and prayer.

"'Look, I am coming soon! My reward is with me, and I will give to each person according to what they have done. I am the Alpha and the Omega, the First and the Last, the Beginning and the End'" (Revelation 22:12-13, NIV).

Pictured from left to right: Kevin Frank, John Rizzo, Daniel Connors, Charlie Reller

The end is near. I know this to be true. Any way you slice it, we may have a day, a week, a month, a year or years to live. But one day we will be held accountable for all our actions, and we will meet Him face to face. I also believe that — if we collectively humble ourselves before our Lord — we will be spared.

As in the Old Testament in the book of Jonah, I too wanted to run from this message. When Jonah was taken to the city of Nineveh to proclaim God's Word, he told the Ninevites to repent and they did.

If we collectively as a society and individually as people repent, He will graciously listen. Like any good parent, our Father, our Creator, our God loves us and will forgive us our sins – if, that is, we repent with a truly repentant heart, mind and soul. He cares and wants the best for His children. You (good) parents know exactly what I am talking about. For every good parent wants the best for their children – as does our Father God.

Pictured John Rizzo (left) Kevin Frank (right during the Washington, D.C. 2021 victory lap for The Brady Faith Center fundraiser

We bicycled with awe, wonder and gratitude upon reaching Washington, D.C. The Brady Faith Center fundraiser 2021, 450 miles

To write this book and place myself out there will forever change the direction of my life. It is with the "Fear of God" — in humility and with sincere appreciation — that I take this time to devote a message from my Father, **"It's Not Too Late…"** (The Holy Trinity)

(Working definition of "Fear of God": to have profound appreciation of God; to be in awe and reverence of His creation; to fully love God and want to grow in relationship with Him and worship Him because of His amazing grace.)

I place my hope in God; yet there is a very large part of me that *hopes* I am wrong in my assertion that the end of times is near. I would love to grow old with my wife, our children and someday look adoringly at our grandchildren. I would love to live a long life and hold, with deep appreciation, our family and friends at holiday gatherings. It's a wonderful life, but there is something much better waiting for us....

If this message takes root within your mind, heart and soul, do not worry nor fear. The Lord our God mentions more than 365 times in the Bible not to fear and/or a theme of that sort. So do not fear the message that I bring from my Father but rejoice. Live your lives as if these were the last days, but live with a repentant heart. Live a life worthy of the Gospel. The actions you choose going forward will make a large impact on your future in eternity.

This I know to be true – God has forgiven me of my sins; and it was a wet, itchy, smelly, nasty blanket that has been removed from my life. Thanks be to God. For years, God was encouraging me through trusted friends and loved ones, "Take a step in faith. Come on, Danny. You can do it." Unfortunately, it was only when I found the bottom of a deep cavern did I realize I couldn't do this life well on my own. I needed God. In 2012, through the loving guidance of my dear friend Bob Chopko, I renewed Jesus as the Lord and leader of my life. What does that mean? For many of you reading this, the above type of "Christianese" does not make sense or perhaps does not ring true. When I state, "I renewed Jesus as the Lord and leader of my life," what I mean is I no longer have to worry and fret about life. God has got this; God has got me in His hand and in His embrace. In 2015, when I went through a tremendously difficult mental health crisis, God had me. He held me upon His chest; and I felt loved, comforted and had a deep peace beyond understanding. In the midst of the chaos, the PTSD, the overwhelming sensations, I knew in my heart, mind and soul that God had me, held me tight; and I did not worry. This feeling and this knowledge that God has me was not just a passing sensation but has been a part of my understanding for almost a decade now.

> "'Come to me, all you who are weary and burdened, and I will give you rest. Take my yoke upon you and learn from me, for I am gentle and humble in heart, and you will find rest for your souls'" (Matthew 11:28-29, NIV).

Are you weary and burdened from addiction? Are you burdened from past sins and regret (divorce, infidelity, lying, stealing, cheating)? Do you want your integrity back? Do you carry secrets? Or perhaps you carry the

Charlie Reller left, Daniel Connors middle, Kevin Frank right Susquehanna trail in Pennsylvania

pain of deep-seated memories or fresh traumatic events?

God is here for you. He is not some mythical concoction designed to help the masses. He is a friend, a loved one as real as you or I; and He wants to help you. He is calling you, encouraging you to take a step of faith – like a baby learning to walk. Trust and believe and call out to your Father God. He is waiting and He is listening. He wants the best for you. As a good dad wants the best for his children, our Good Daddy, Abba, Father, God wants the best for us, His children.

Reader, if after reading this book, you wish to receive Jesus Christ as your Lord and Savior, then repeat these words:

"Father God, I ask You to come into my heart and make Your Son Jesus the Lord and leader of my life. I have not walked a perfect life, and I am sorry for my sins. Father, please free me from the sin that binds me, and help me along my journey daily. I take this step of faith in Your Son Jesus' Holy Name. Amen"

If you repeated that prayer desiring to know God, then you have been born again…. Now go live your life in both works of mercy and faith in God.

Father, I pray that the words written in this book be interpreted and read by family, friends and all readers as intended – in love.

Thank you for taking time to read this book. Please place your hope in God alone and learn from my failures and triumphs. May the peace given by Jesus the Christ rest upon you, your family and loved ones.

Amen

February 2022. My family has been brought back together. Not by any works of mine or theirs... but our Father God. Healing is a journey. I know we just begun, but there is love. And Love conquers all. Pictured left to right- Jimmy, Kathy, Meghan, Danny. I know my Mom is smiling down, and my Dad recently told me how happy he is we are all, once again, acting in love — as family.

Good morning Dad.

In prayer this morning a fond memory came to mind, and I would like to share it with you.

When I was a young boy I was lost in a crowd of people, and got very scared. I cried out to you, and said, "Daddy, I am lost." You in turn replied, "I can see you, Danny. I will come get you." You could see me in a large crowd of people. I am grateful for this memory.

The same holds true for my Father in Heaven. I once was lost, but now have been found.

Today I read:

"The LORD your God is with you, The Mighty Warrior who saves. He will take great delight in you; in His love He will no longer rebuke you, but will rejoice over you with singing."
Zephaniah 3:17, NIV

A great memory, and a wonderful application of scripture on my heart this morning.

I hope you're doing well. Dad, you are a great dad. I consider you to be a great mentor, a model of ethical behavior, and I respect you more than you know.

I have many, many good memories.

All my love,
Dan

ENDNOTES

1. Vikram Babu, *The Poems of Vikram Babu* (Host Publications, Austin, TX 2009)

2. Pastor John Newton, *Amazing Grace* - Public Domain

3. 60 Minutes *Treating Childhood Trauma* (CBS March 11, 2018, Oprah Winfrey and Dr. Bruce Perry)

4. Anthony DeMello SJ, *The Spiritual Wisdom of Anthony De Mello* (Jazzybee Verlag, Altenmunster, Germany 2012)

5. Tom Schulman, *Dead Poets Society* Touchstone Pictures, Silver Screen Partners IV 1989)

6. Hannah Hurnard, *Hinds' Feet on High Places* (Christian Literature Crusade 1955)

7. Kristen Anderson-Lopez and Robert Lopez *The Next Right Thing* (Walt Disney Records 2019)

8. C. S. Lewis, *Screwtape Letters* (Geoffrey Bles 1942)

9. Joyce Meyer, *Battlefield of the Mind* (Warner Books Inc. 1995)

10. Robert Frost, *The Road Not Taken* (first published in The Atlantic Monthly 1915)

11. Fr. Greg Boyle, *Tattoos on the Heart* (FP Free Press A Division of Simon & Schuster, Inc. 2010)

12. Theodor "Dr. Seuss" Geisel, *How the Grinch Stole Christmas* (Random House Children's Books 1957)